The Scarlet Mob of Scribblers

The
Scarlet Mob
of
Scribblers

Rereading Hester Prynne

$\mathcal{J}$amie $\mathcal{B}$arlowe

Southern Illinois University Press
Carbondale and Edwardsville

Grateful acknowledgment is made to Oxford University Press for per-
mission to reprint material from the author's essay, "Rereading Women:
Hester Prynne-ism and the Scarlet Mob of Scribblers," *American Literary History* 9.2 (1997): 197–225.

Library of Congress Cataloging-in-Publication Data
Barlowe, Jamie, 1943–
    The scarlet mob of scribblers : rereading Hester Prynne / Jamie
Barlowe.
        p. cm.
    Includes bibliographical references (p.) and index.
    1. Hawthorne, Nathaniel, 1804–1864. Scarlet letter. 2. Historical
fiction, American—History and criticism—Theory, etc. 3. Women
and literature—United States—History. 4. Criticism—Authorship—
Sex differences. 5. Prynne, Hester (Fictitious character) 6. Women in
literature. I. Title.
PS1868.B37 2000
813'.3—dc21   99-20051
ISBN 0-8093-2273-0 (cloth : alk. paper)   CIP

The paper used in this publication meets the minimum requirements of
American National Standard for Information Sciences—Permanence of
Paper for Printed Library Materials, ANSI Z39.48-1992. ⊗

Dedicated to
Mandy and Jason
and to
Mabel Carter Barlowe
(1915–1998)

Contents

Preface

*I*n this book, my primary context of analysis "takes gender ... to be the most radical division of human experience, and a relatively unchanging one" (Sedgwick 11), despite all claims of progress. This concept of gender, as I use it, is informed by other divisions of constructed human experience (race, class, and sexuality) and by history, as well as by other theoretical frameworks, political exigencies, and professional or institutional criticisms. On similar contextual ground, I began in graduate school to ask what seemed a simple question: Why is there an absence or token representation of women's scholarship on Nathaniel Hawthorne's *Scarlet Letter?* This absence or tokenism, I noted, occurred not only in critical arguments but also in the bibliographies and works cited sections of almost all the mainstream scholarship, as well as in reading lists for graduate examinations and bibliographies for theses and dissertations. In the 1980s none of my professors assumed that I or any other graduate student *should* include women on such lists—nor, later, did hiring committees, editors, or publishers—but all determined the falsifiability of my claims and arguments by my inclusion of and engagement with a long list of this mainstream scholarship, what Amy Ling and other feminists would later call the "malestream" (152). When I asked about the absence of women, I was told what generations of Americanists have been told: that few women had published good scholarship on this text; otherwise, mainstream scholarship would have known it. Their absence thus functioned as evidence for their absence. Moreover, I was often encouraged in graduate school, when I did engage with women's scholarship, to place it on the contextual ground of the "malestream" and to attempt to falsify the women's arguments (see Barlowe, "Reading Against the Grain").

After continuing to notice the absence of women's scholarship in the new work published by men on *The Scarlet Letter,* I began to search for women's (not just feminist) scholarship and am still discovering its remarkable extent. My problem, however, was demonstrating its absence; that is, what would count as evidence if I were to read the body of scholarship on *The Scarlet Letter* as a text? My solution was an empirical examination of all of the scholarship because I knew the resistance to my argument would be dismissive or defensive or, worse, would attempt falsification (see, for example, the responses by Herbert and Budick to my essay in *ALH*). As I began such work, I was fully aware of how delegitimized such empirical scholarship is in literary studies. I hope, however, that my readers can see it as part of the textual evidence for my claim that actual academic conditions for women lag far behind the proclamations of progress and change, rather than as mere "numbers games" or an attack on the "malestream" whose constituents, because of their own social and academic conditioning—their own habitus—participate in the continuing exclusionary traditions (see chapter 3). Discovering reasons for the exclusion was more difficult, so I have theorized some answers, and more questions, from my contextual ground (see chapter 1), particularly that of the construct I call Hester-Prynne-ism (see chapter 2) and demonstrated its pervasiveness and consequences (see chapter 3), as well as the resistances to it (see chapters 4 and 5).

The implications of this case-specific study on *The Scarlet Letter* are potentially wide-ranging and far-reaching. Literary criticism generally has made claims that exclusionary traditions in scholarship have ceased and that progress and change have occurred. The institution-within-an-institution (literary studies within *academe*) has made similar claims about hiring, tenuring, promoting—even of supporting and mentoring women and other Others—yet superficial, easily reversible alterations in procedures have substituted for examinations of the assumptions and principles that generated and perpetuate our institutions and their primary policies and goals. This book, then, although specifically focused on Hawthorne's *Scarlet Letter* and its scholarship, urges all of us in literary studies to acknowledge our inadequacies, even failures, in accomplishing real changes, in recognizing and honoring difference and diversity, or in exposing the myths and received beliefs that have allowed us all to deny the actual, continuing (though now often more subtle and disguised) climate of hostility, discrimination, and exclusion. In fact, defensive posturing and attacks on the "messenger" of the news that we have not reached stated goals or achieved claimed progress is more evidence of literary studies' problems. Facing the challenges of those problems is work that we *can* do—more significantly, it is work that we *must* do.

Acknowledgments

*M*any colleagues and friends have supported and challenged the message of this book, and for that I am deeply grateful. Those who generously read and responded to all or part of the manuscript include Harriet Adams, Dale Bauer, Jane Bradley, Walter Herbert, Ruth Hottell, Gordon Hutner (who suggested the apt title for chapter 3), Debra Moddelmog, Joan Mullin, Peter Rabinowitz, Russell Reising, Linda Wagner-Martin, and Priscilla Walton. Cheryl Glenn, Alan Nadel, and Lee Person read the full manuscript several times, offering astute commentary and making provocative suggestions that were fully devoted to the purposes and methods of my work. I stand in awe of them as readers, colleagues, and friends.

Although I did not know it at the time, the seed for this book was planted in a seminar in graduate school taught by James Phelan at Ohio State University. This two-term seminar on the novel created the space for my first sustained examination of *The Scarlet Letter* and Hester Prynne. The second concentrated exploration of this novel and its body of scholarship came during my dissertation, also directed by James Phelan. Although my current position on the text, its various contexts, and its Hester Prynne are very different from those earlier forays, without them—and without Jim's serious challenges of various kinds—this book would not have been shaped as it is. Also as a graduate student at Ohio State, I worked as an assistant textual editor on two volumes of Nathaniel Hawthorne's letters, as well as on many of Sophia Hawthorne's letters and diaries. Thomas Woodson, general editor of that project, and James Rubino, textual editor, gave me the opportunity for immersion in the biographical, historical, social, and literary contexts of Hawthorne, as well as becoming an "expert" reader of Hawthorne's nearly indecipherable handwriting. My thanks go to them as well.

Other colleagues, friends, and graduate students have offered supporting shoulders and open, ready ears for ideas, new insights, and the general crankiness that accompanies the research for and writing of a book manuscript. In that regard, I want particularly to thank Akua Duku Anokye, Sara Lundquist, James Saunders, Renae Saunders, Elspeth

Kydd, Christine Child, Matthew Wikander, Molly Abel Travis, Susan Calovini, Elizabeth Patnoe, Suzanne Jones, Theresa Reid, Scott McNall, Sally McNall, David Hoch, Don Bialostosky, Sharon Barnes, Blythe Howard, Karla Murphy, Danielle Demuth, Jennifer Kohout, Traci Knapper, and special thanks to Theresa Stowell, who did most of the index, as well as helped me search for books and obscure sources. I also want to thank Roger Ray of the University of Toledo Humanities Institute for the research fellowship for 1993–94. Further funding came from the University of Toledo in the form of a summer research grant in 1994.

Although last on this list, though certainly not least in deserving of thanks for their sustained support and encouragement are members of my family: my mother, Mabel Carter Barlowe; my children, Amanda and Jason Kayes; and my brother and sister-in-law, Philip and Carol Barlowe. You are an awesome family. Thank you.

The Scarlet Mob of Scribblers

1

Introduction: Self-Defining Narratives and the Racial and Gendered Other

*F*or some time now, feminists have examined literary works in terms of the absent/objectified presence of the Other, in whatever form Other might be recognized (for example, anyone not white, male, or educationally and economically privileged). We have also critiqued culture and history in these terms, articulating at least some of the consequences of such constructed oppositions and exclusions. For example, Toni Morrison, in her critical text *Playing in the Dark,* has argued that everything that constitutes whiteness as a racial identity—from the national literature of the United States to its Constitution to the daily practices of its citizens—is a response to the absent/objectified presence of the black Other or, in her words, "to a dark, abiding, signing Africanist presence" (5). She goes on to say:

> Just as the formation of the nation necessitated coded language and purposeful restrictions . . . so too did the literature, whose founding characteristics extend into the twentieth century. . . . Through significant and underscored omissions, startling contradictions, heavily nuanced conflicts, through the way writers peopled their work with the signs and bodies of this presence—one can see that a real or fabricated Africanist presence was crucial to their sense of Americanness. And it shows. (6)

Thus, racial opposition—though misrecognized by whites—has allowed for the creation of a self-narrative of the (so-called) white race in the United States. Extending Morrison's claims about race to gender, I would say that gender opposition—though, again, misrecognized—has allowed for a self-narrative of men. In other words, the space for the creation of self-narrative of whites in the United States has been in the opposition between their freedom and the enslavement of Africans, and the space for the creation of the self-narrative of white men has been in the opposition between their public power and women's domesticity and reproductive capacity. As Deborah McDowell and others, following

Simone de Beauvoir, have put it, "Man is *self*, and woman, other" (151). To take this analysis one more step, without the opposition of the Other, which is always tautologically defined as the absence of the privileged defined, the privileged cannot be defined. Put slightly less abstractly, men are not definable without the absent/objectified presence of women, whites are not definable without the absent/objectified presence of blacks, and Americanness is not definable without the absent/objectified presence of bondage and exclusion. The consequences of self-definitions and self-narratives based on an opposition to a repressed Other are sexism and racism, which are also repressed. These practices of self-defining and narrativizing, as well as their consequences, operate in and constantly reproduce an exclusionary system of social relations, symbolic positionings, and cultural products.

In this book I will argue that, despite insistent claims to the contrary, this same tautological method of self-defining repeats itself in literary studies in terms of its scholarship, positions, and practices—a field-specific set of social relations and symbolic positionings that "closes in upon itself, and affirms itself capable of organizing its production by reference to its own internal norms of perfection" (Bourdieu 140). Moreover, repressing the racist and sexist consequences of such academic practices and definitions obfuscates the homologous connections among literary scholarship, the academy, and the culture, and hides the academy's racism and sexism from its (defined/privileged) self, allowing for their continuation. To demonstrate the validity of these claims, I will critique and theorize the absent/presence of women's scholarship and criticism in the mainstream body of scholarly and critical work on *The Scarlet Letter*, the most often taught literary text in American classrooms (see also Peterson). This mainstream body of scholarship has argued that Hawthorne's text focuses on the cultural oppression of women through the representation of Hester Prynne, and has therefore claimed itself and the text as radical, progressive, even woman-centered. Ironically, then, mainstream scholarship on *The Scarlet Letter* has self-defined by focusing on a fictional representation of a woman while excluding women scholars and critics from its focus and engagement—that is, Hester Prynne as presence in the absence of women scholars and critics.

My examination will expose the fact that the mainstream body of scholarship on *The Scarlet Letter*—which generation after generation of students, teachers, scholars, and critics have studied as models—remains entirely male-dominated, both in terms of its comprising population and its attitudes and assumptions, which function as the source of its truth-claims. In other words, I am putting a slightly different spin on

Jane Tompkins's description that "criticism creates American literature in its own image" (see also Baym, "Melodramas"). Seen in that light, the consequences of Hawthorne criticism's self-image—the male face it continues to wear in mainstream scholarship on *The Scarlet Letter*—have been not only to create and recreate Hawthorne's text as part of the literary canon (which was constructed in terms of the absent/presence of literary works by women, who are viewed as the literary Other), but also to create and recreate itself as a body of scholarship (which, whatever its intentions, has been constructed in terms of the absent/presence of scholarship by women, who are viewed as the academic Other). My examination of the scholarship on Hester Prynne and *The Scarlet Letter*, then, can function as an example of the more generally implied beliefs and standards of the field of literary scholarship and its continuing exclusionary and Othering practices.

Academic Other(s)

The academy has traditionally defined itself as an elite institution, separate not only from the cultural masses but often from other institutions such as church and state. As Mariam Chamberlain notes in *Women in Academe,*

> [C]ertain currently existing universities are the oldest continuously existing institutions on earth, with the sole exception of the Roman Catholic Church. The earliest universities were not created by either church or state; they created themselves. For both historical and policy reasons, institutions of higher education have guarded this independent status assiduously and subtly ever since. (16–67)

I would add that even those universities formed by church and state have guarded their so-called independent status assiduously and subtly, even obscuring their genesis in church and/or state. Also, the academy, from its inception, was male. As Chamberlain explains,

> Women were never considered as students and were not accepted as faculty. . . . This tradition, long observed and deeply embedded, seemed to become a myth with a life of its own. Even the advent of scientific rationalism in the nineteenth century failed to dispel it. At that time it was decided that women should not be allowed into higher education because the mental energy necessary . . . would be drained directly from the uterus and would therefore weaken women's reproductive capacity and destroy *the race*. (167, emphasis mine)

Many in the American academy today argue that conditions for black and white women have altered radically; they also argue that the attitudes that supported those conditions have changed. For example, Henry Louis Gates has claimed in *Loose Canons* that

> [f]or a woman or person of color, there has never been a more ex-
> citing and rewarding time to be in the academy than today. More
> women and black people are tenured than ever before, and more
> occupy tenure-track positions. We are in the midst of a renais-
> sance of black scholarship. (121)

His enthusiasm, however, disregards the professional and personal narratives of lived experience of black and white academic women, neglects
the available statistical information on publishing, hiring, tenuring, promotion, and sexual/power harassment, and ignores the significant math-
ematical fact that a little added to nothing is still a little. Rita Carroll-
Segun and James Geschwender argue even more vehemently in *Signs:*
the "popular myth that asserts African-Americans have made a great deal
of progress . . . is both dangerous and false" (285). Moreover, in "1920,
when women won the right to vote, 26 percent of the full-time faculty
in American higher education were women. In 1995, 31 percent of full-
time faculty in American higher education are women—an increase of 5
percent over seventy-five years!" (West 26).

Destabilizing rereadings. Therefore, rather than celebrate the minimal handouts of the academy to women and minorities—and of the
culture that nurtures and supports the academy's continuing repression
and oppression of the Other, this book will perform a series of destabilizing rereadings of the rather pitiful state of affairs at the close of the
twentieth century. To that end, in addition to my examination of the
excluded scholarship and criticism of white and African American academic women and feminists on *The Scarlet Letter*—and the contextual-
ization provided by their experiential circumstances, including their
"habitus,"[1] as well as by the continuing representations of women,
based on a model I call Hester-Prynne-ism—I will turn, then, in the
space provided by that context, to reread Hawthorne's text as well as the
various film translations of *The Scarlet Letter,* resituating them in their
cultural moments and critical reception.

The method of examination I am using is one I call "ReReading
Women." Its destabilizing rereadings depend on contextualizations—
akin to Pierre Bourdieu's "radical contextualizations,"[2] although I am
focusing specifically on raced and gendered aspects of habitus and of
symbolic positionings as constructed and perpetuated within the field of

literary studies, as well as its relation to other fields of artistic production and analysis (such as film and film studies) and the positionings and functionings of these fields "within the broader field of power," which is inevitably classed, gendered, and raced (9). My destabilizing rereadings depend as well on juxtapositions that recognize and expose difference, which allow us to see what we have not previously seen and to begin to know what we do not know we do not know. To adapt Barbara Johnson's description:

> Far from being a negative or nonexistent factor, what is not known is often the unseen motivating force behind the very deployment of meaning. The power of ignorance, blindness, uncertainty, or misreading is often all the more redoubtable for not being perceived as such. Literature, it seems to me, is the discourse most preoccupied with the unknown, but not in the sense in which such a statement is usually understood. The "unknown" is not what lies beyond the limits of knowledge, some unreachable, sacred, ineffable point toward which we vainly yearn. It lies, rather, in the oversights and slip-ups that structure our lives in the same way that an x makes it possible to articulate an algebraic equation. . . . It is not, in the final analysis, what you don't know that can or cannot hurt you. It is what you don't know you don't know that spins out and entangles "that perpetual error we call life." (xii)

I have been led to do such contextualizations and rereadings because, although "our socially gendered identity is constructed and fixed as we are 'put into our place' within the conceptual order," various texts, cultural economies and codes, and academic procedures and practices also contain "the excess of meaning that constantly threatens to disrupt the boundaries of these defined identities and expose the fiction of any imposed 'truth'" (Morris 138). Or as Toni Morrison puts it, "certain absences are so stressed, so ornate, so planned, they call attention to themselves; arrest us with intentionality and purpose, like neighborhoods that are defined by the population held away from them" ("Unspeakable" 15). That is, traditional academic ways of knowing, of self-defining through Othering, of doing the work of literary analysis and scholarship, and of connecting academic relationships to the culture can be called into question when differently contextualized. Otherwise, as Lorraine Code, a feminist philosopher, argues, "mainstream epistemology, in its very neutrality, masks the facts of its derivation from and embeddedness in a specific set of interests: the interests of a privileged group of white men" (x).

Such contextualizations shift from the traditional focus on the *intentions* of the culture, the academy, history, texts, laws, politics, writers, scholars, critics, and colleagues to contexts that are continuously experienced by the Other and that focus on the *consequences* for the Other. In fact, the traditional academic ways of knowing, of self-defining, of obscuring its relationships to the culture, and of Othering are examined and analyzed in this book *inside* the context of the Other—a shift that privileges the Othered side of the binary opposition only to expose the unacknowledged ("unknown") means by which the traditional ways signify.

More significantly for this study, I am exposing the means by which the traditional field of literary studies *continues* to signify in terms of the self/other, man/woman, white/black binary oppositions (among others), no matter how much previous exposure and analysis has been done. Thus, the method of ReReading Women recognizes that the idea of a text shifts as the context shifts; in other words, a text or context in this study may be anything from a literary text or film to Hester Prynne to academic practices to literary scholarship and its symbolic capital to cultural beliefs, constructs, and myths. Such traducive rereading is done to demonstrate that Othering is not only practiced, but is also the genesis of the academic system and its literary scholarship. Othering is thus built into the culturally constructed beliefs that determine our literary scholarship. ReReading Women, then, assumes that, as academics, we have not recognized the extent to which literary scholarship has functioned in terms of constructed identities (like Hester-Prynne-ism, which I will discuss in the next chapter), while we simultaneously claim to be resisting such identities and changing literary scholarship. Nor have we recognized the extent to which our conscious awareness of some of the problematic practices and constructions (often as the consequence of recontextualizations and rereadings by the Other) have resulted in the construction of new epistemologies rather than in our continuing to reread our cultural and academic economies, policies, traditions, and practices.

Significantly, then—because recontextualizations have been done for decades by white and African American feminists in order to expose problems and problematic relationships—ReReading Women as a method also rereads academic claims of radical changes in attitudes, opportunities, and conditions for women. It rereads as well the fear-based perceptions that black and white women are taking over the academy and its scholarship and that if some women have power because they have prominence, then other women can have both power and prominence—when, in fact, little has changed and when, in fact, the prominence of a few women has substituted for the possibility of our hearing many women's voices, or of enhancing women's positions in the academy. In other words, the myth of change and the myth of takeover function to avoid facing the deeply embedded, unacknowledged racism and sexism in the academy and in the culture, as well as function to escape from acknowledging that women (black and white) have been systemically and systematically excluded.

Thus, ReReading Women as a method always begins with the recognition that pathologically defensive myths beget more myths to obfuscate and support the existence of the original myths and practices, and also recognizing that, like Paul D in Toni Morrison's *Beloved,* the repressor will do almost anything—even commit acts of atrocious self-sacrifice and humiliation of others—to avoid coming to what bell hooks has called a "critical consciousness." As Morrison's narrator claims, even Sethe "worked hard to remember as close to nothing as was safe" (6). Take one step further these literary examples of victims like Paul D and Sethe who repress in order to survive, and imagine bringing the character of Mr. Gardner, who views himself as a liberal humanist working *within* the conditions of slavery, to critical consciousness and you can imagine the task that the Other faces daily in academe.

ReReading Women also challenges the myth that we are now in a postfeminist time. Like Tania Modleski, I believe, instead, that those who are "proclaiming or assuming the advent of postfeminism, are actually engaged in negating the critiques and undermining the goals of feminism—in effect, delivering us back into a prefeminist world" (3). Such a challenge also always takes into account the distinction between feminism and feminization, as Modleski discusses:

> [Peter] Brooks, whose previous book on narrative theory contains only a single sentence about feminist criticism, [has] remark[ed], "Anyone worth his [!] salt in literary criticism today has to become something of a feminist." . . . And he goes on to assert, "The profession is becoming feminized." . . . Yet the male critic's confusion here, of feminism with feminization, may belie the authors' major claim— that feminist criticism in becoming absorbed into the academy has lost its ability to threaten the male literary establishment. (3)

ReReading Women could also be described as radical dialogizing: as Bakhtin says, "[D]ialogizing opens up fresh aspects" of utterances/texts, which then "become more immediate to perception" (789). I am using "radical" in the sense of taking dialogizing to an extreme level of recontextualization and rereading to demonstrate that even the radical discourse of mainstream scholarship functions in terms of an authorized discourse; for example, Peggy Kamuf has called the body of scholarship on *The Scarlet Letter* the text's "order of authority" (74). I am not using "radical" in the scientific sense of an atom that is replaceable or unchanged when it faces the reactive process—perhaps an apt metaphor for the kind of self-proclaimed academic radicalism that continues to Other women, often practiced in literary scholarship). ReReading Women can thus be seen as using a "bricolage" of methodologies (see Grossberg et al. 2) "in order to offer a self-consciously 'positioned' analysis of cultural [and academic] practices" (Walton and Jones)—those methodologies include feminist rereadings of psychoanalysis, deconstruction and other discourse analyses, and cultural studies.

Descriptions of Chapters

The chapter that follows, "What's Black and White and Red/Read All Over?: Hester-Prynne-ism," exposes and explains one kind of cultural and academic Othering, which can be recognized in the almost constantly duplicated figuration of Hester Prynne. As I will show, the context provided by the cultural economy I have named "Hester-Prynne-ism" repeats itself in the academy not only in the content and conclusions of its mainstream body of scholarship on *The Scarlet Letter,* but also in its practices and methods, which are not different from the practices and methods of mainstream literary scholarship in general. My claim is that Hester-Prynne-ism provides a particular kind of answer to the question of why women's scholarship has been so completely disregarded by mainstream scholarship on *The Scarlet Letter.* Further, it challenges the myth of change and the myth of takeover by women in departments of English, as well as other myths about women that continue to circulate.

Chapter 3—"The Scarlet Snub"—rereads the mainstream body of scholarship of *The Scarlet Letter* as a text, demonstrating the ways in which it has functioned (and continues to function) in relationship to women's scholarship. I begin my rereading in the mid-1950s, although such a beginning does not signify that earlier decades functioned differently. It is merely an arbitrary but necessary limitation on the numbers of texts and periods of time that can be effectively examined and discussed in one book.

Chapter 4—"The Scarlet Woman and the Mob of Scribbling Scholars"—is my rereading of the textual Hester Prynne, informed by the more than 230 articles and books by women on *The Scarlet Letter* that I have found. By revealing that there is a century-long, alternative history of women's literary scholarship on this text, despite its subterranean status, I also continue my refutation of various academic myths about women and their scholarship. So, despite the academic reality that women's scholarly work on *The Scarlet Letter* has received almost no attention or engagement from mainstream critics and scholars, and despite the gendered, often unsafe, potentially victimizing territory where they have had to work, women have continued to write about the text, producing a stream flowing beneath the mainstream in chasms and crannies, unnoticed or viewed as inconsequential.

Chapter 5—"Demi's Hester and Hester's Demi(se): *The* (New) *Scarlet Letter* and Its Spectators"—examines the latest film version of *The Scarlet Letter* (1995), directed by Roland Joffé and starring Demi Moore as Hester Prynne. This film, I argue, rewrites Hawthorne's text and re-envisions Prynne rather than sexualizing her, as the criticism of the film suggests. Instead, it is the critics who re-inscribe Prynne as the sexualized object of their gaze, this time in the person of Demi Moore. The film and Demi's Hester will also be examined in the context of the earlier cinematic translations of *The Scarlet Letter* and the other actors who have played Hester Prynne, with a specific focus on Colleen Moore and Lillian Gish.

Chapter 6—"Conclusion: Implications of Hester-Prynne-ism and ReReading Woman"—examines the implications of my recontextualization and rereadings, not only for Hawthorne studies and American literary studies, but for literary scholarship in general as an institution within an institution.

2

What's Black and White and Red/Read All Over?: Hester-Prynne-ism

... they wanted to drive you
back to namelessness,
were jealous at the thought of you ...
you, miracle
. . . .
At night i curled over you
guarding my rage ...
i lay without husband
and drank at the stream of light
. . . .
now you are with me ...
hold, i say, hold ...

—Toi Derricotte, "Hester's Song"

Just think: we live in a culture in which Scarlett O'Hara and *The Scarlet Letter* compete with the *Bible* and *The Exorcist* for popularity ... Where the Lady in the Red Dress ... is all danger and unresolvable mystery ... Where Hester Prynne [Anita Hill] has the uppity self-promoting audacity to try to recast herself as "the Rosa Parks of sexual harassment."

—Patricia J. Williams, "A Rare Case of Muleheadedness and Men"

Your silence will not protect you.

—Audre Lorde, *Zami: Sister Outsider, Undersong*

I could not keep silent.

—Anita Hill, Senate Hearings for Clarence Thomas

ReReading Women: Radicalism in Literary Scholarship on *The Scarlet Letter*

For almost 150 years, readers and critics have examined the nature and extent of Nathaniel Hawthorne's radicalism. Those who find him most radical point to his irony and his romancer's love of "deception and concealment" (Bell, "Arts" 41), even to his proto-deconstructive tendencies (Thickstun 132–33)—or they claim as evidence Hester Prynne's stoic dignity, antinomian rebelliousness, nonconformity, or her "powerfully transgressive free-*thinking*" and "powers of moral reimagination" (Brodhead, *School* 43).[1]

Hawthorne's subversive side, as described by Michael Davitt Bell, is part of the romancer's identity as one who is "in opposition to the most basic norms of society: reason, fact, and 'real' business" ("Arts" 37). In fact, Bell argues that Hawthorne goes further than this kind of societal opposition, rejecting even Jeffersonian "'reason and fact, plain and unadorned'" ("Arts" 39). Bell thus agrees with Nina Baym's claim that "the romance originated as an expression of [Hawthorne's] own feelings of societal defiance and discontent" (*Shape* 146). Baym even names Hawthorne a feminist ("Thwarted Nature").[2]

Many of these critics who argue for Hawthorne's radicalism implicate themselves as cultural resisters as well—as those who do not go with the flow, perpetuate the status quo, or depend on received beliefs (the "acquired knowledge" that Melville too rejected); some call themselves the "New Americanists" (see Pease, "New"; see also Shumway, *Creating*).[3] For one of these New Americanists, Jonathan Arac, Hawthorne's radicalism is apparent and relevant because of the radical interpreter: "Only to the extent that the ideal Hester exists can Hawthorne be considered a fundamentally subversive writer; otherwise, we must value the hope he offers in his openness to our interpretive energies but must recognize his own limitations within a 'framework'" (259).

Despite their professed radicalism, these critics of *The Scarlet Letter* have remained traditional and conservative in their relationship to women—both to Hester Prynne as a metaphoric representation of a white American woman and to women scholars and critics who have written about this text, and whose work has been almost entirely disregarded. Whatever their intentions, these male scholars and critics have continued the limiting, sexist cultural practice of Othering anyone whose difference calls tradition into question, or even into the light. In the tradition of Hawthorne scholarship, the Other is "woman" (yes, despite the very prominent presence of a few female scholars), and in Hawthorne's work, the Other is also "woman" (yes, despite Hester Prynne's presence). As T. Walter Herbert argues, for Hawthorne "male and female serve as defining opposites; and the axis of gender, so established, crosses an axis of power" (*Dearest* 9). And, more than a decade ago, Joyce Warren argued about nineteenth-century writers in general that

> [i]n a nation that stresses the development of the individual, there has been little room for the "other." . . . Nineteenth-century individualism . . . encouraged an insular self-assertion that prevented the individual from recognizing . . . others. Persons regarded as outside the American experience . . . Women, blacks, Indians, and "others" had no place in the drama of American individualism. Like the legendary Narcissus, the American individualist focused on his own image to such an extent that he could grant little reality to others. (4)[4]

Pam Morris's more recent theorizing supports Warren's insight:

> [B]y seeing women as other to themselves, as not-men, men can read into "femininity" whatever qualities are needed to construct their sense of the masculine. So, a mythicized "Woman" becomes the imaginary location of male dreams, idealizations, and fears: throughout different cultures "femininity" is found to represent nature, beauty, purity and goodness, but also evil, enchantment, corruption and death. Because men persistently see women as other, [Simone] de Beauvoir argues, "Woman" as represented by men "has a double and deceptive image . . . incarnat[ing] all moral virtues from good to evil, and their opposites. . . . He projects upon her what he desires and what he fears, what he loves and what he hates." (14–15)

The male self-legitimizing, yet un(self)conscious, cultural tendency toward Othering, I argue, has also determined the scholarship on *The Scarlet Letter,* including the critical relationships to Hester Prynne and the (conscious or unconscious) exclusion of women's scholarship. One of the ways such Othering has been manifested (has been projected onto women) is in what I call "Hester-Prynne-ism," the continuously and relentlessly functioning cultural dichotomy of the good-woman vs. the bad-(but desirable)-woman-who-needs-instruction-or-punishment. In this chapter, I will explain the decidedly nonradical, but deeply mythicized, Othering cultural economy of Hester-Prynne-ism; this explanation will then contextualize my rereading of some of the practices and conclusions of mainstream scholarship on *The Scarlet Letter,* which has replicated rather than (radically) resisted the culture's relationships to women—and continues to do so, despite claims to the contrary (see Barlowe, "Rereading"; see also Schwab).

Hester-Prynne-ism is a profoundly negative construction of female sexuality and subjectivity, one that becomes available to our perception through various feminist, theoretical, and cultural recontextualizations of the familiar figuration of Hester Prynne. Hester-Prynne-ism, I will argue, has been imposed on academic women, whether individual women have sought to be judged according to that construction or not. And, further, as a consequence of literary scholarship's continuing connections to Hester-Prynne-ism and other Othering traditions and practices, women's/feminist scholarship has been generally disregarded in the academy, and specifically disregarded in the case of the body of scholarship on *The Scarlet Letter*.[5]

The self-proclaimed radical scholarship on *The Scarlet Letter*, like Hawthorne's kind of radicalism, has had consequences as negative as those of blindly following the "norms of society," not only because that notion of a radical individualism is at best fraught and at worst naive and deeply oppressive, as it has had been constructed on the back of the Other—and not only because, as Sacvan Bercovitch has argued, American ideology can co-opt its dissidents (*Office* 159)—and not only because, in both Hawthorne's and the critics' cases, the primary focus has been on men's lives, their creations, their abilities, their analyses, their struggles, their results, and their rights—and not only because, as Jane Tompkins helped us to see, "The social and economic processes that govern the dissemination of a literary work are not more accidental to its reputation, and indeed to its very nature . . . than are the cultural conceptions . . . within which the work is read" (23) and created—and not only because, as Joseph Silver, Vice Chancellor for Academic Affairs, Board of Regents, University System of Georgia, claims: "The academy is but a microcosm of the larger society. . . . The character of a given society shapes . . . every institution which is part of that society" (84)— but also because, as Pam Morris argues about the specific academic institution of literature:

> Once we recognize that our perception of reality is shaped largely by our representational systems, the predominant one being language, it becomes clear that the distinction between literature as a body of texts and life is more complex than it seemed, and that the boundaries between the two may well be permeable, allowing interaction and influence. . . . [F]eminists are interested in literature as an influential cultural practice embodied in powerful institutions. They are

concerned to discover how literature as a cultural practice may be involved in producing the meanings and values that lock women into inequality rather than simply reflecting . . . women's lives in literary texts.(8)

I am arguing further that unless our institutions and their practices—especially those like literary scholarship's claims of male radicalism and of women's radical subjectivity or immorality as they relate to Hawthorne, *The Scarlet Letter,* and Hester Prynne—are reread in the light of various contexts that question rather than blindly support them, then whatever progress or change occurs will be as conditional and easily erasable as the scholarship of generations of women has been. In other words, we can never stop rereading.

ReReading Women: Hester-Prynne-ism

The Scarlet Letter has often been taught as a moral text in high school and university classrooms in the United States, with Hester Prynne as the scarlet (white) woman/adulteress who serves as a cultural warning to girls and women and, therefore, as part of the social conditioning they internalize. Darrel Abel, in *The Moral Picturesque,* articulates the warning as he moralizes about Hester's "moral inadequacy" and "moral dereliction," saying that she "unwomaned herself and deluded herself with mistaken notions" (181, 187). Wendy Martin recontextualized this kind of warning more than twenty years ago:

> As daughters of Eve, American heroines [including Hester Prynne] are destined to lives of dependency and servitude as well as to painful and sorrowful childbirth because, like their predecessor, they have dared to disregard authority or tradition in search of wisdom and happiness; like Eve, heroines of American fiction are fallen women. (258)

Yet despite Wendy Martin's prominence in feminist studies, her challenging critique has had almost no effect on mainstream scholarship on *The Scarlet Letter.* Similarly, such critiques by other women have had little measurable or lasting impact on the culture's or the academy's attitudes about women.

In fact, Hester-Prynne-ism has taken all kinds of bizarre and moralizing cultural twists and turns—for example, in 1991, in Iowa: "Pointing to Hester Prynne's badge of shame as a model for their recommendation, some officials . . . hoped to curb drunken driving by requiring offenders to display car tags labelling themselves as having been guilty of

DUI charges" (*NHR* 26; see also Schell, "Three-Time Loser DUIs get a Scarlet Letter 'Z'"). In an article entitled "Handing Out Scarlet Letters," *Time* magazine reports that partners seeking divorces are relying on outdated anti-adultery laws that primarily privilege men (see A. Sachs). There is even a chapter by Peter French in a book on business ethics, called "The Hester-Prynne Sanction." In *Computerworld* Thornton May describes how electronic commerce approaches the Internet through four literary categories, one of which is the scarlet letter, and in *Broadcasting and Cable* Joe Flint argues that a ratings system for violent television shows "could be an economic scarlet letter" (33; see also Gordon, *The Scarlet Woman of Wall Street*, and McCormack on the 1990 elections). The scarlet A shows up as well in an article by Harry Hadd in *Steroids:* "The Scarlet Letter: Reichstein's Substance S"; in a *Policy Review* essay, "A Farmer's Scarlet Letter: Four Generations of Middle-Class Welfare Is Enough," by Blake Hurst; and in an essay in the book *Misdiagnosis: Woman as a Disease,* published by the People's Medical Society, entitled "Norplant: The 'Scarlet Letter' of Birth Control" by June Adinah. Hester's A has also been modernized to symbolize AIDS—for example, in *Computer/Law Journal* as "The Scarlet Letter 'A': AIDS in a Computer Society" (van Dam)—or, to designate modern women who, "as Hester Prynne before them, are 'challenging the mores set down for them by contemporary society . . . [and have been] similarly stigmatized, branded with the scarlet A, for Autocratic, Aggressive, Authoritarian, Arrogant'" (S. Easton 740). In *Time,* the A is designated as "Today's Scarlet Letter: Herpes" (see also Osborne), and Brenda Daly uses the scarlet letter to discuss incest survival and incest narratives (155–88).

   Newsweek describes Reggie Jackson as "the Hester Prynne of sluggers . . . with a scarlet dollar sign on his chest" (*NHSN* 8), and the scarlet letter is used in *Sports Illustrated* as a reference to Ohio State and Penn State football rankings (see Layden). In a 1989 article in the *Houston Post* the scarlet letter refers to an affair between baseballer Wade Boggs and Margo Adams (Robertson). In an interview question on the NBC *Nightly News* the A is mentioned when the registration of sex offenders was likened to an "unfair scarlet letter" (July 3, 1995; see also Earl-Hubbard, "Child Sex Offender Registration Laws"; Suffolk University Law School, "Ex Post Facto Analysis of Sex Offender Registration Statutes: Branding Criminals with a Scarlet Letter"; Kabat, "Scarlet Letter Sex Offender Databases and Community Notification"; Kimball, "A Modern Day Arthur Dimmesdale: Public Notification When Sex Offenders Are Released into the Community").

Recently, a newspaper article reported that "Nathaniel Hawthorne's Hester Prynne had to wear a single scarlet letter to identify herself as an adulteress. A judge in Illinois went much further . . . ordering 48 letters, each 8 inches high, on a sign on a felon's property . . . WARNING A VIOLENT FELON LIVES HERE. TRAVEL AT YOUR OWN RISK. The Illinois Supreme Court, however, decided that such "humiliation is unnecessary and unfair . . . and ordered the sign taken down" ("Scarlet letters in Illinois"; see also Feldman, "The 'Scarlet Letter Laws' of the 1990s" and Reske, "Scarlet Letter Sentences"). This judgment exceeds even that of Hawthorne, who read about such punishments in Joseph B. Felt's 1827 *The Annals of Salem*, which explained: "[I]n 1694, a law was passed requiring adulterers to wear a two-inch-high capital A, colored to stand out against the background of the wearer's clothes" (*TSL: Case Studies* 12; see also Hawthorne, "The Custom-House" 41). By 1782, the use of the scarlet letter for adulterers was discontinued in New England (Davidson and Wagner-Martin 950).

Hester-Prynne-ism shows up even in the military. The first woman bomber pilot, Lt. Kelly Flinn, was generally (not honorably) discharged in 1997 by the Air Force for the admitted charges of adultery and lying. Wire services reported as follows: "Lieutenant Flinn, 26, who is single, was charged with committing adultery with a married man. Her allies assailed the military for branding her with a scarlet letter for allegedly committing an act that many male officers have done with impunity" ("Embattled Female Pilot"). The *New Yorker* also picks up on the connection between the treatment of Flinn and Hawthorne's romance:

> There is nothing funny about the contretemps for Lieutenant Flinn; she is no longer in danger of doing time in a military prison, but her pioneering military career has been ruined, and her less than honorable discharge is a stigma. The rest of us, though, can be forgiven for having found entertainment in this unexpected Pentagon production of "The Scarlet Letter" and in the enduring ridiculousness of our antiquated and unenforceable sex laws. (Angell 4)

Another instance of a reference to the scarlet A and Lt. Flinn occurs in a May 29, 1997 newspaper cartoon in which a line of formidable-looking Air Force officers are headed by one who holds a branding iron with a red-hot A; he says, "Lieut. Flinn, Step Forward." In the corner of the cartoon, a little bird says, "They want you to take it like a man" (see also Barto, "The Scarlet Letter and the Military Justice System"; S. Chase, "The Woman Who Fell to Earth"). Even more recently, William Ginsberg, the former attorney for Monica Lewinsky, stated on CNN on January 25, 1998 that Lewinsky may have to wear "the scarlet letter of indictment for the rest of her life."

Literarily, John Updike's book *S* "turns to Sarah Worth, a modern version of Hester Prynne. . . . Instead of having a way with a needle Sarah has a way with a pen or tape recorder—after all she is a woman of the 1980's," (*NHR* 26; see also Updike's *Roger's Version*). Grace Jones argues convincingly that another Sarah, John Fowles's Sarah Woodruff in the *French Lieutenant's Woman*, "is a Victorian Hester . . . Hester's true child . . . [and] proof of how slow is the evolutionary process Hester envisioned" (78, 71). Christopher Bigsby's novel, *Hester: A Romance* (1994), is a prequel to *The Scarlet Letter*, narrating the time from Hester's birth, as herself a "bastard" child, to her death; Bigsby claims to have written the novel because, "repeating Dimmesdale's sin," he "fell in love with" Prynne (188). Charles Larson's novel, *Arthur Dimmesdale* (1983), opens after Hester Prynne's admission to Dimmesdale that she is pregnant and ends as Pearl kisses him and he dies. The protagonist of Bharati Mukherjee's novel, *The Holder of the World* (1993), Beigh Masters, discovers her ancestor Hannah Easton, who was Hester Prynne. Born in Salem, and later marrying an Englishman, Hannah moves to India, where she becomes the mistress of a Raja. Then, pregnant by him, she returns to Salem. (See also Kathy Acker's *Blood and Guts in High School*.)

From the 1870s on, dramatic productions have refocused attention on Prynne's scarlet A; for example, Joseph Hatton's *The Scarlet Letter, or Hester Prynne* (1870), Emile de Najac's five-act tragedy *The Scarlet Letter* (1876), James Edgar Smith's *The Scarlet Stigma* (1899), Phyllis Nagy's adaptation of *The Scarlet Letter* for the *American Theatre* (1995), and the opera based on *The Scarlet Letter* (Lathrop and Damrosch 1896). Mysteries, both dramatic and literary, have also made use of Prynne's symbolic A, as it designates evil and adultery or threatens disruption—for example, in *The Perfect Crime*, now in its eighth year of off-Broadway production, in Ellery Queen's *Scarlet Letters*, and in a recent detective novel by Julie Smith, *The Axeman's Jazz* (see also Maron, Steinberg). In *Primal Fear*, a film released in 1996, the killing of a Catholic bishop is underscored with references to *The Scarlet Letter*. The killer, in fact, leaves an underlined section of the text as a clue to his motivation for the slaying (see also Diehl).

Paradoxically, the mainstream body of scholarship on *The Scarlet Letter* has functioned as both a moralizing warning and radical model to women who choose not to act fully in terms of their social conditioning—for example, women in an academy where male critics and scholars admire the duplicitous radical subversion of men like Nathaniel Hawthorne and hold up as a model his male fantasy of a radical, subversive woman, Hester Prynne, who can be reread as profoundly (hetero)sexualized and objectified, as one who "stands by her man," and as one who finally self-punishes.[6] As Sacvan Bercovitch has claimed, Hester finds "conversion to the letter" at the end of the text (*Office* 3). Or, as Millicent Bell put it more than thirty years ago, Hester, like other of Hawthorne's "most memorable female characters" (Beatrice, Zenobia, Miriam, and Drowne's mysterious model), "suggests experience . . . knowledge . . . [and] sin, the moral cost of experience and knowledge, which is the artist's [and the critic's] peril" (*Hawthorne's View* 133).

Hester-Prynne-ism has also functioned as a model/warning for feminists who practice what is viewed by the academy as problematic (even abhorrent) "noisy" politics. With her quiet dignity (and, of course, her beauty), Hester Prynne is offered as a real American heroine, suffering as she does in silence and maintaining the separation of the private from the public. Her few "noisy" moments—in the prison after her hours on the scaffold and her impassioned plea for Pearl at the governor's—are met, in the first case, with drugs (sinisterly administered by Chillingworth) and, in the second case, with admonishments about her moral responsibilities to Pearl. Her final "noise" in the forest is appropriated by Dimmesdale and used as energy for his last two performances (his sermon and confession)—what Leland Person calls an "almost vampirish transfer of energy" (134). Her "noisy" plan of escape is thwarted at the fictional level by Dimmesdale's guiltiness and death and Chillingworth's intrusion, and, more significantly, thwarted by Hawthorne's writing agenda.[7]

In fact, fiction, criticism, and culture, no woman has been viewed as more continuously desirable to white men than one who, like Hester Prynne, is beautiful, strong, silent, and (hetero)sexualized; who is subversive enough to break the sexual codes with men who (like Dimmesdale) will also break the codes (as long as these men are not held publicly accountable); and who, ultimately, will regulate, control, and even punish herself. This American relationship to and representation of the "scarlet woman"—as good/bad, as desirable because she is physically beautiful and sexually transgressive, but also in need of warning/punishment—has been translated into other versions of Hester Prynne. Even in "The Sadder but Wiser Girl" from Meredith Willson's *The Music Man*, a so-called wholesome musical, a woman of slightly questionable virtue is referred to as Hester, whom the singer hopes will get another A.

Playboy articulates such male desire in a famous cartoon that foregrounds Hester's sinful but desirable nature. It "depicts [Hester] at the head of a bevy of Puritan lasses. Beaming smugly and proudly, Hester sports an A+ on her bosom while all her companions have just simple A's" (*NHSN* 8). These references to Hester Prynne appeared in a publication of the Nathaniel Hawthorne Society in a section entitled "Some Recent Allusion to Hawthorne," as if to show that Hawthorne's influence is still alive and well. I am arguing here that while Hawthorne's influence may be celebrated, it also needs to be reread and critiqued in terms of its continuing implications and consequences.

Following at least seven earlier film versions of *The Scarlet Letter*,[8] a 1995 release, starring Demi Moore, attempts to rewrite Hester Prynne by exposing the sexual objectification and violence that are at the heart of Hawthorne's text through its representation of the Puritan's community's fear of (and desire for) Hester, and of rape and sexual abuse, including the process by which women were accused of witchcraft and brutally interrogated and indicted. Not only does the film represent the sexual violence directed at Hester Prynne, but also at Mistress Hibbins and other women in the community—for example, a prostitute and a former captive of Native Americans. In this case, then, it is not so much the film that functions to reinscribe male desire, but all of the reviews and critiques. For example, *Newsweek,* in an article entitled "Hester Pryncess," reports that "[t]he producers, presumably, had chosen Moore knowing that the audience would spend 90 percent of the movie staring right at the big red 'A' on her chest" (Adler 58). Other critics also note Moore's chest and body, derisively dismissing actor(ess), director (Roland Joffé), and film, oblivious to its attempts (albeit Disneyized at times) to expose rather than participate in the ongoing American pastime of objectifying Hester Prynne. This time the critics had two targets, Prynne and Demi Moore, but they missed the revelations of their own nostalgia as they cried out for the *real* Hester Prynne of Hawthorne's text—the beautiful, silent one, a gendered example of what anthropologist Renato Rosaldo calls "imperialist nostalgia" (quoted in Montgomery-Fate). In this film, Hester Prynne is never silent and refuses to self-punish, thus consistently bringing down Puritan punishments and hatred on herself (Adler 58; Marion 90–156; Oates, Welsh, Bona, Waxner, Lane, Scharnhorst 233–53 for earlier film versions; see my chapter 5).

Other representations of the good/bad, fearful/desirable "scarlet woman" do not even attempt such self-reflexivity, however. The "scarlet woman" in many contemporary bestseller, film, and television narratives appears without direct reference to Hester Prynne, translating instead into characters who (in a post-Freudian world) do not self-punish, but instead become "noisy," "hysterical," and dangerous, even murderous. These "hysterical" female characters are represented in opposition to, and sometimes are punished by, "good," "civilized" (in Freud's sense) women/wives, for example, in *Fatal Attraction* (see also Michie), *Presumed Innocent, The Hand That Rocks the Cradle,* and various Amy Fisher stories (see also Schwab, Turow). As Susan Faludi puts it, "In typical themes [in 1980s Hollywood films], women were set against women . . . women's lives were framed as morality tales in which the 'good mother' wins and the independent woman gets punished" (113). In fact, Faludi calls 1987 a

> scarlet letter year for the backlash against woman's independence. In all four of the top-grossing films released that year, women are divided into two groups—for reward or punishment. The good women are all subservient and bland housewives (*Fatal Attraction* and *The Untouchables*), babies or voiceless babes (*Three Men and a Baby* and *Beverly Hills Cop*). The female villains are all women who fail to give up their independence. (116)

In some of these films, the male lead is not punished, nor held accountable, but instead is the "prize" won by the "good" wife after destroying the "bad" but obsessive (and obsessed-about) scarlet woman. These male characters hide behind the claim that they were indefensibly tempted by these women. In some films with similar constructions of desire, punishment may be meted out by law-enforcement types or professional men bonded together—successfully, as, for example, in *Final Analysis* (a "remake" of Hitchcock's *Vertigo*), *Shattered, Body of Evidence, Malice,* or *Consenting Adults,* or not so successfully, as in *Basic Instinct* (in which the "hysterical" woman is also bisexual). These films play into the good vs. bad woman binary opposition, preying on culturally constructed fears of hysterical or bad women—particularly as those fears work out in competitive relationships between women for men's attention—yet furthering the kind of paradoxical desire in men that such fear has been constructed to elicit. Punishment for the "bad" woman and promise of a man as a reward for the "good" woman are equally clear.

Punishment in nonfictional cases has taken forms different from outright torture and murder. For instance, perhaps remembering the consequences faced by Gary Hart, Bill Clinton's steadfast refusal to admit publicly his involvement with Gennifer Flowers, like Dimmesdale's with Hester Prynne, was generally more acceptable and admired than Flowers's "hysterical" public admissions of her long-term relationship with him. As a man who was shortly thereafter elected president, Clinton was not finally held publicly accountable (though he was no doubt held privately accountable). Public accountability came as a consequence of the accusation of sexual harassment by Paula Jones and the admitted affair with Monica Lewinsky. Yet the House impeachment hearings, the Senate trial, and the media frenzy were, in the spirit of Puritan trials, replete with details rendered sexually titillating by secretive surveillances and by socialized constructions of male desire. They also exposed the hypocrisies and logical inconsistencies necessitated by white male self-narratives and self-definitions. Thus, exposing Clinton also exposed several of the congressmen and senators, and exposed, momentarily at least, the kinds of cultural and legal assumptions on which sexual desire, power, and positioning rest in the United States. Clinton's public self-chastisement (like Dimmesdale's on the scaffold), the public interpretations of Hillary Clinton's silence, the relentless congressional moralizings, and the acquittal of the president also revealed the desperate attempts at recontainment of the narratives (see chapter 5). Yet, Monica Lewinksy, Paula Jones, and Gennifer Flowers have been turned into American dirty jokes—likewise Marilyn Monroe, Marla Maples, Amy Fisher ("the Long Island Lolita"), and Lorena Bobbitt; the list could continue endlessly. Similarly, "the characters in *The Scarlet Letter* continually exist at the anxious edge between private knowledge and public revelation" (Burbick 212). Sylvie Mathe implicates Hawthorne in these issues when she says that even his

> art . . . is one of indirection, running through the novel both as motif and technique and culminating in the final moral exhortation inspired by the tale: 'Be true! Be true! Be true! Show freely to the world, if not your worst, yet some trait whereby the worst may be inferred!' This dubious admonition to lift the veil only enough for the worst to be glimpsed ultimately speaks of Hawthorne's unrelenting defensive strategy. Secret sin, subversive impulses should be 'freely' released, but through a slanting process of diversion and displacement, thus evading the threat of private disclosure and its unsettling public consequences. (609)

Unlike Hawthorne's Hester Prynne, but like Demi Moore's portrayal, these 1980s and 1990s women did not suffer in silence. In fact, some of them have been faulted for selling their stories to feed the insatiable hunger of the American public for such private "dirty jokes." But the very public quests for money, prestige, and power by the sometimes already powerful men with whom these women "coupled" remain significantly unquestioned and generally sanctioned, as is Dimmesdale in his fictional community, even after his confession:

Without disputing a truth so momentous, we must be allowed to consider this version of Mr. Dimmesdale's story as only an instance of that stubborn fidelity with which a man's friends—and especially a clergyman's—will sometimes uphold his character; when proofs, clear as the mid-day sunshine on the scarlet letter, establish him a false . . . creature. (SL [1962] 259)

Competition with and punishment of women considered iconoclastic by other women continues in the culture and in the films, as well as in *The Scarlet Letter*. Women like Phyllis Schlafly and Beverly LaHaye have assigned themselves the tasks of maintaining traditional values and expectations of women's roles and rights. LaHaye, in fact, is now considered

the most powerful woman in the new religious right. . . . Like some soldier plucked mid-battle to lead . . . [she] now claims command of the nation's largest women's group. Counting 600,000 Christian soldiers, Concerned Women for America daily wages a spiritual war for what it calls the country's soul. (A. Wilson J1; see also Ferraiuolo)

Although Hawthorne appears to denigrate the women who seek Hester's death as punishment for her crime of adultery, he does so more clearly in terms of their physical appearance (as opposed to Hester's physical appearance) than in terms of their harsh judgments:

The women, who were now standing about the prison-door, stood within less than half a century of the period when the man-like Elizabeth had been the not altogether unsuitable representative of the sex. They were her countrywomen; and the beef and ale of their native land, with a moral diet not a whit more refined, entered largely into their composition. The bright morning sun, therefore, shone on broad shoulders and well-developed busts, and on round and ruddy cheeks, that had ripened in the far-off island, and had hardly yet grown paler or thinner in the atmosphere of New England. (50–51)

These women discuss Hester Prynne as a "hussy" and a "naughty baggage"; one mentions Hester's shame (51). And, by the end of *The Scarlet Letter*, Hawthorne's narrator comes to agree with the assessments of these women in terms of Hester's sin: "Here had been her sin; here, her sorrow; and here was yet to be her penitence" (263). All of the community's ostracizing and punishment of Hester Prynne does not serve as full penitence. Hawthorne insists on her self-denigration ("Never afterward did [the A] quit her bosom" [263]) and her self-imposed isolation (she continues to live in "Hester's cottage" [263]). Likewise, Hawthorne portrays Prynne's recognition of her inappropriateness as a model for social change:

> Earlier in life, Hester had vainly imagined that she herself might be the destined prophetess, but had long since recognized the impossibility that any mission of divine and mysterious truth should be confided to a woman stained with sin, bowed down with shame, or even burdened with a life-long sorrow. The angel and apostle of the coming revelation must be a woman, indeed, but lofty, pure, and beautiful; and wise, moreover, not through dusky grief, but the ethereal medium of joy. . . . *So said Hester Prynne.* (263–64, emphasis mine; see also my chapter 4)

A contemporary of Hawthorne's, Margaret Fuller, felt the sting of being considered an inappropriate model and spokeswoman, to name only one whose life was affected by such cultural judgments about her sexuality and subjectivity—judgments with which Hawthorne concurred (see DeSalvo 11). Mary Wollstonecraft, in the previous century, suffered similarly.

The black scarlet woman/adulteress is an even more complex and disguised (therefore often unacknowledged) construction. It is complicated by slavery's legalized demand that black women, as property, could be used in whatever sexual ways the master desired. "[T]he sexual abuse of slaves has been widely documented. One indication of the extent of sexual abuse is the number of children with white ancestry born to black women" (Milburn and Conrad 147). The bad/good binary opposition was used to construct the black woman as both the secretly desired, mystified, (hetero)sexualized Other and the all-nurturing Earth Mother, the "mammy" whose allegiance to the white family and its children was to supersede her allegiances with her own family—and whose silence was assumed about the painfulness of the demands, the allegiances, and use of her body as the site of sexual desire and motherhood. This construction was also complicated by white women's responses to black slave women as competition for white men's sexual attentions and by (continuing) assumptions that white women have suffered similarly oppressive conditions when we have not. The consequences of such constructions of sexualized subjectivities for black women have been doubly negative, doubly oppressive, and doubly Othering—through racism and sexism: "Like no other group, African-American women stand at the intersection of race and gender, two of the most powerful characteristics of humankind" (Etter-Lewis 154).

Perhaps on no site has this sexualized, Othered, silenced, good/bad construction of black women been more apparent recently than during the Senate hearings for Clarence Thomas. When the Senate committee had heard enough of Anita Hill's accusations—when their collective repressed guilt had blanketed that room with sweat—first, they resexualized her, making her the one who desired the good man (who resisted her); then, they simply stopped listening. And the senators silenced the remaining corroborating witnesses (see Barlowe/Travis). The dictum of *The Scarlet Letter,* "Hush, Hester, Hush," echoed through that Senate room, restated and racialized in "Hush, Anita, Hush." As Patricia J. Williams, an African American feminist legal scholar says, when she connects Hester Prynne and Anita Hill:

> Just think: we live in a culture in which Scarlett O'Hara and *The Scarlet Letter* compete with the *Bible* and *The Exorcist* for popularity . . . Where the Lady in the Red Dress . . . is all danger and unresolvable mystery . . . Where Hester Prynne has the uppity self-promoting audacity to try to recast herself as "the Rosa Parks of sexual harassment," and where Reverend Dimmesdale breaks with his faith and martyrs himself, giving birth to the world's first case of "reverse sexual harassment." Where "witch-hunt" is used to mean not a posse for, but by; where "high-tech lynching" means a Broad with a Bullhorn. (170)

The Othering of black women that occurred during and after slavery—and that was publicly replicated in the treatment of Hill, Lani Guinier, and Joycelyn Elders—also occurs in the academy's disregard for their scholarship. Because this treatment is manifested somewhat differently in the academy, the connections are either not recognized—because of the extent of the self-mystification—or are recognized, then defensively denied.[9] But either way, because the academy's self-narrative, like the culture's, is based on Othering, it cannot really seriously consider African-American women or their scholarship without calling that self-narrative into question and undermining it irrevocably.[10]

My examination of Hester-Prynne-ism neither negates nor erases all differences between Hawthorne's representation and those that have followed, nor between various, possible interpretations of the fictional characters of Hester Prynne and Arthur Dimmesdale and historical persons. Instead, in order to expose and examine a context in which to answer my question about why women's scholarship on *The Scarlet Letter* has been so disregarded by male mainstream scholarship on that text, my rereading records similarities in presentations and representations in order to hear the echoes and traces and patterns of Hester-Prynne-ism as a version of Othering that continues.

ReReading Women: Academic Hester-Prynne-ism

Although I have not included a discussion of the constructions of sexuality and subjectivity of women of other races, ethnicities, and sexual orientations as part of the context of Hester-Prynne-ism, such rereadings can be done, further confirming my claim that Hester-Prynne-ism can be reread as part of the cultural heritage of Hester Prynne—acknowledging that, of course, the assumptions on which Hawthorne's representation rest were culturally shared, not Hawthorne's alone, and certainly pre-existed him. Novelist Nicholas Guild has said "that he thinks of Hester Prynne and her scarlet letter as having a life outside [the] novel, pointing out that they now serve as widely understood symbols of confessions and guilt" (*NHSN* 8). My rereading examines some of the consequences of Hawthorne's specific culturally and academically iconized representation and its particular heritage, as they play out in the culture and in the literary scholarship on his text. It allows us to see how a single fictional character has become an Othering shorthand, a stereotype, embodying (as I would argue she also did for Hawthorne) both white male desire and fear (see Herbert, *Dearest*). Further, we can see how those desires and fears can be traced through the mainstream scholarship on this text, not just in the discussions about Hester Prynne but also as a complex and deeply gendered answer to the question of why women's scholarship on *The Scarlet Letter* has been so consistently disregarded, especially by generations of scholars/critics who have argued that they have a radically subversive relationship to the culture.

Cultural attitudes and beliefs about women—and academic practices, policies, and procedures that Other women—function to support and perpetuate the mythicized economy of Hester-Prynne-ism and thus remain fully unradicalized. They are deeply rooted, fundamentally unacknowledged (even unknown) yet excessively manifested, stabilized by a transcendental signifier, and problematically connected to the bad/good binary opposition about women that functions, explicitly and implicitly, to affect the lives of women.[11] These problems remain inadequately examined; if publicly discussed, they are done so only long enough to justify and perpetuate the mythicized (degrading) stereotypes and exclusion of women by maintaining the focus on the intentions of the men (e.g., authors, critics, filmmakers, directors, literary and film characters, professors, scholars, critics, mentors, and politicians) rather than the women and their theoretical/critical/public/professional/ literary/personal analyses and narratives that often describe those consequences.

The mainstream body of scholarship on *The Scarlet Letter* has consciously and unconsciously participated in and perpetuated the Othering of women through its various unacknowledged relationships to such mythicized cultural economies as Hester-Prynne-ism, which has been used to construct fictional metaphors of women, and which has inevitably been imposed on women in terms of behavioral expectations, constructed (often sexualized) roles, and "deserved" judgments and punishments. In its various forms, Hester-Prynne-ism has been imposed, too, on academic women, though somewhat differently, but in no less limiting and exclusionary ways.

Besides the kind of covert but influential messages sent by cultural Hester-Prynne-ism, the most obvious imposition concerns academic women's attempts to enter the critical conversations about Hester Prynne. Mainstream scholarship has assumed ownership of a territory where radical inquiries made by the Other are shunned—where the Other, represented by Hester Prynne, is the object of the radical inquiry, not a subject doing her own inquiry or (viewed as more dangerously problematic) questioning and resisting the inquiries already in place. The woman doing scholarship has been expected, in other words, to work in terms of authoritative, predetermined definitions of radicalism and cultural subversion and of constructions of women's sexuality and subjectivities. At the same time an academic woman is writing about Hester Prynne, she must always battle the cultural and academic attitudes that are the gendered consequences of such definitions, constructions, and representations, ones that are both external to her and yet may have been, to some extent, also internalized by her. As Cheryl Glenn has argued more generally, "Even though *gender* is merely a concept borrowed from grammar, it, nevertheless, continues to have far-reaching effects on cultural notions of the relation between the sexed body and its behavior. . . . [T]he masculine gender, just like every male experience or display, has come to represent the universal . . . the feminine experience (that of bodies sexed female) has come to represent exceptions, or the particular" (173). Many women, then, have either aligned themselves with Hester Prynne, negatively critiqued her (and Hawthorne), or discussed their ambivalence about both (see chapter 4 and the listing of women's scholarship on *The Scarlet Letter*, a section in the bibliography).

The imposition of Hester-Prynne-ism on academic women has functioned also in the specific ways that women's scholarship on *The Scarlet
Letter* has been appropriated, ignored, or tokenized. This practice of
disregarding women's scholarship is so complexly related to Hester-
Prynne-ism that a full discussion of the connections, manifestations,
and implications is almost impossible. However, one way of rereading
the connections is to examine what some cultural theorists have called
received beliefs—unexamined, familiar, generalized ideas shared by large
segments of the culture (or by groups or institutions within the culture—fields and sub-fields) which influence, even determine, attitudes,
theories, and practices. Some cultural constituencies might even state received beliefs as truth claims. These received beliefs constitute part of
the (tauto)logic of the various homologous fields that operate in the
larger field of cultural power; certainly, they constitute part of the logic
of the field of literary studies and its sub-field of Hawthorne studies.

For example, one of the received beliefs of American culture has been
that women are Othered because they deserve it. The tautological thinking behind such a belief works something like this: women are Other
because they are Other to men, and they deserved to be Othered because they are Other and not men. Another version of this belief is that
women are sexualized and objectified because they have invited it—because of their Othered bodies and sexualized behaviors. Yet another version is that it is women's essential nature, as the phallically impaired,
both to desire men and to elicit desire in men. All three are related to the
cultural territory on which Hawthorne constructed Hester Prynne and
to the ways Hester Prynne has been interpreted and internalized. The
cultural economy of Hester-Prynne-ism can be reread in terms of its
tautological functions as both the cause and effect of some of the received beliefs about women.

For many generations of academics, Othering attitudes, beliefs, and
judgments about women could be articulated unproblematically in literary scholarship, particularly as it was directed at fictional female objects
like Hester Prynne—even to refiguring her sexual transgressiveness as
political radicalism (akin, perhaps, to what happened to women in the
1960s, trapping them inside the same sexual economies they sought to
politicize and escape). Also unproblematically, scholars and critics (consciously and unconsciously) have replicated this practice of Othering in
their relations with women authors—for whom Othering in terms of the
good/bad binary opposition has been translated into claims about their
bad writing, characters, content, sentimentality, focus, simplicity, and

form. They have been viewed as deserving to be ignored, because they are seen as not as good, complex, and objective as male authors, and as incapable of separating themselves from their biological and sexual functions.[12] The female protagonists created by female authors have even been viewed as losing a competition with Hester Prynne; in fact, one of the primary critical claims about Hester Prynne in the body of scholarship on *The Scarlet Letter* is that Hawthorne created the only significant female protagonist of the nineteenth century.[13]

As I indicated in my introduction, such rethinking and rereading puts a slightly different spin on Jane Tompkins's astute (and accurate) description that "criticism creates American literature in its own image" (199). Thus, the consequences of Hawthorne criticism's white male self-definition can be reread as not only creating and recreating Hawthorne's text as part of the literary canon (constructed in opposition to literary works by women and minorities as Other), but also to create and recreate itself as a body of scholarship by circulating (and perpetuating) the mythicized economies and received beliefs about women—in their discussions of Hester Prynne and in their disregard for women authors—and, then, translating them into Othering received beliefs about academic women and their scholarship. These received beliefs are gendered in such a way that women are consistently eliminated, except as fictional objects—such as Hester Prynne.

For example, if the critical conversation of the mainstream body of scholarship on Hester Prynne/Hawthorne and *The Scarlet Letter* continues without benefit of more than a very few women's voices, insights, and analyses, then it appears that only a few women have written about this text, its author, and female character—or, even more damning, that what has been written is not credible or even adequate enough to be considered (two academic received beliefs). If women had written or if they had written well—so patriarchal tautological mythmaking goes—mainstream scholars would be aware of their work, and the women's scholarship would not have been disregarded. This argument replicates the arguments used to justify the academy's disregarding of literary texts by women authors: they have been ignored because they deserve to be ignored. Thus, the familiar, accepted, and acceptable practice of disregarding women's scholarship, however illogical and unsupportable, becomes both self-fulfilling and self-perpetuating, continuing to justify the exclusionary practices of literary scholarship.

Another received belief about women's scholarship on *The Scarlet Letter* is that women's essays have been published primarily in inconsequential journals and their books published by small presses.[14] Such beliefs have circulated in graduate programs that train Americanists, and sometimes justify the editorial policies of academic journals and, often, the institutional policies that decide on hiring, tenure, and promotion within English departments. These beliefs often have the consequences of putting women in competition with each other for attention of male academics who control policies and procedures. On the surface, such competition is viewed as different from the competition generated between women for men's sexual attention (discussed earlier as part of Hester-Prynne-ism), but may merely be another version of the same problem. And, of course, these beliefs and myths engender other myths—for example, that there are no role-modeling foremothers who blazed trails, forged paths, asked questions, balked at traditions, wrote blindingly brilliant analyses, and set the pace for following generations; in other words, what has been seen as the consequential work of forefathers. Therefore, the idea of a history of women's scholarship—the idea of connections between generations of academic women—gets lost. The consequence of such a loss is that women are expected to function as though no ground has ever been gained, as though every generation should begin anew the (erased) work of previous critical generations.

The good/bad binary oppositions about biological and sexual subjectivities have not functioned, then, all that differently from the good/bad binary oppositions used to judge women's work and positions in the academy. In the same ways that men's sexuality and cultural subjectivities have been defined in opposition to women (women as Other), their public and professional subjectivities—including those of professors/ teachers/critics/scholars/mentors passing on the traditions of male self-definitions, such as those by male authors—have been defined in opposition to women authors, women scholars and critics, and women students. Furthermore, the connection between the binary oppositions of bad/good female sexualities and subjectivities and the good/bad professional woman; that is, the public translation of private male fears of and desire for women—continues because its existence, function, and consequences are denied. Therefore, anything more than superficial professional interaction with the Other—after generations and generations of viewing her in terms of the good/bad woman binary opposition, of trying to instruct her in the ways of men, and of then sitting in judgment on her as a way to exclude her—has been impossible so far. Even when (as a consequence of women's insistence that Othering and exclusion be addressed legally) it has become unlawful to view women only as sexual objects in the workplace and to discriminate against them on the basis of their gender, the more disguised, defensive, and subtle such

Othering has become. As I argued earlier, pathologically defensive myths beget new myths and disguises.

Thus, men's (for example, Hawthorne's) imaginary representations of oppressed women's (for example, Hester Prynne's) experiences have consistently and monolithically defined women's experience, substituting almost completely for female expressions of individual women's experiences; likewise, the serious, mainstream criticism on *The Scarlet Letter* has been that of men remarking on the skill of a man to define and articulate a woman's experience, all of it substituting for, speaking for, replacing, disregarding, or appropriating women's scholarship on that text. Hester Prynne's experience, moreover, has been defined in terms of a sexuality and subjectivity grounded in her Otherness and in her embodiment of the bad/good binary opposition.

Whether her radical individualism has been interpreted as evidence of Hawthorne's revisionary picture of women's potential power to change society, or as the elevating of "isolated figures such as Natty Bump[p]o, Ahab, and Hester Prynne," which empower them "beyond the constraints of civilization and the wilderness" (Mizruchi 15), or, as Phyllis Barrett and other women have argued, as male experience transferred to a female character (Barrett calls Hester an "American Adam," not an "American Eve" [40]), Hester Prynne's subjectivity in Hawthorne's text is biologically and sexually constructed, and whatever radical (male?) thinking Hawthorne allowed her is tempered and ultimately neutralized by his insistence on our focus on her sexual transgression (as I discussed earlier) and by his insistence that such radical (male?) thinking has defeminized her:

> [T]here seemed to be no longer any thing in Hester's face for Love to dwell upon; nothing in Hester's form . . . that Passion would ever dream of clasping in its embrace. . . . Some attribute had departed from her, the permanence of which had been essential to keep her a woman. Such is frequently the fate, and such the stern development, of the feminine character and person, when the woman has encountered, and lived through, an experience of peculiar severity. If she be all tenderness, she will die. If she survive, the tenderness will either be crushed out of her, or—and the outward semblance is the same—crushed so deeply into her heart that it can never show itself more. . . . She assumed a freedom of speculation, then common enough on the other side of the Atlantic, but which our forefathers, had they know of it, would have held to be a deadlier crime than that stigmatized by the scarlet letter. . . . A tendency to speculation, though it may keep woman

quiet, as it does man, yet makes her sad. She discerns, it may be, such a hopeless task before her. As a first step, the whole system of society is to be torn down, and built up anew. Then, the very nature of the *opposite sex,* or its long hereditary habit, which has become like nature, is to be essentially modified, before woman can be allowed to assume what seems a fair and suitable position. Finally, all other difficulties being obviated, woman cannot take advantage of these preliminary reforms, until she herself shall have undergone a still mightier change; in which, perhaps, the ethereal essence, wherein she has her truest life, will be found to have evaporated. A woman never overcomes these problems by any exercise of thought. They are not to be solved, or only in one way. If her heart chance to come uppermost, they vanish. (163–66, emphasis mine)

Mainstream scholarship, then, has generally interpreted Prynne as sexually transgressive and thus morally inadequate and/or defeminized, or as sexually transgressive and thus politically radical.

If Hester Prynne had instead been created by a female author, she might have been outspoken, written books, and gone on a speaking tour; then she, like most feminist critics and writers in the academy and like radical women in the culture from Anne Hutchinson to Sojourner Truth to Margaret Fuller to Elizabeth Peabody to Sui Sin Far to Charlotte Perkins Gilman to Anna Julia Cooper to Eleanor Roosevelt to Gloria Steinem to Adrienne Rich to Anita Hill to Hillary Rodham Clinton to Joycelyn Elders to Sandra Cisneros to Winona LaDuke, would have been considered hysterical, noisy, pushy, intrusive, out of place—even bad, and then ignored, devalued, undermined, ridiculed, or vilified. But such a woman would not have been created by a nineteenth-century male writer and never elevated by male academic critics for more than 140 years.

3

The Scarlet Snub

America is now wholly given over to a d——d mob of scribbling women.

—Nathaniel Hawthorne, letter to William D. Ticknor,
January 19, 1855

Condescension, not criticism, is the true mark of chauvinistic male hostility.

—David Van Leer, "Hester's Labyrinth: Transcendental
Rhetoric in Puritan Boston"

*I*n this chapter, I will demonstrate some of the ways and extent to which male mainstream scholarship has Othered women in its response to women's scholarship on *The Scarlet Letter*. What follows is a kind of close reading of the body of mainstream scholarship as itself a text; thus, this chapter functions as evidence for my claims, not mere citation counting.

One kind of Othering has been to assimilate and appropriate the most threatening kind of women's scholarship: feminist arguments. A stunningly revelatory example of this appropriation occurs in a footnote to David Van Leer's essay, "Hester's Labyrinth," in Michael Colacurcio's *New Essays on "The Scarlet Letter"* (1985). Van Leer claims Leslie Fiedler's *Love and Death in the American Novel* (1960) as the "*classic* statement of [*The Scarlet Letter*'s] feminism" (93 n22, my emphasis), although Nina Baym has cogently argued to the contrary that the

> most influential overall view of American female character portrayal has been, *unfortunately*, Leslie Fiedler's. . . . Fiedler is not really interested in women characters. His argument substitutes the portrayal of guilt-free heterosexual males for the portrayal of women, assuming that if the male characters are normal and healthy, then the women characters must be so also. ("Portrayal" 233 n6, my emphasis; see also Baym "Melodramas"; also on Fiedler, see Pease "Leslie Fiedler")

Van Leer notes David Leverenz's "Mrs. Hawthorne's Headache: Reading *The Scarlet Letter*" (1983) as a more recent feminist reading (93 n22). My point is not that these two works are not, or cannot be, profeminist because they were written by men, but that it is astounding that by 1985, Van Leer did not also cite feminist criticism by women or recognize Fiedler's problematic critical relationship to women. As Tania Modleski argues in *Feminism Without Women,*

> [H]owever much male subjectivity may currently be "in crisis," as certain optimistic feminists are now declaring, we need to consider the extent to which male power is actually consolidated through cycles of crisis and resolution, whereby men ultimately deal with the threat of female power by incorporating it. (7)

Moreover, upon examining David Leverenz's essay, I see that he notes five women on *The Scarlet Letter* (including the 1850 reviewer Anne Abbott)—and mentions them to refute their arguments as being "dubious" (Judith Fryer) and "over-stat[ed]" (Nina Baym) (558 n8; 564 n17)—or to oppose them (Sharon Cameron, Jane Tompkins) (561 n15; 555 n6). The work he seems to value is, for example, that of Morton Cronin in "Hawthorne on Romantic Love and the Status of Women" (1954) and Frederic I. Carpenter's "fine essay," "Scarlet A Minus" (1944) (566 n20), as well as the more recent work by Richard Brodhead *Hawthorne, Melville, and the Novel* (567 n21). In the reprinting of this essay in his book, Leverenz adds a woman to his notes, Amy Schrager Lang, whom he says argues "wrongly" about Hester's repentance (353 n19). Again, men's articulations of feminist reading experience are appropriated, rearticulated, and cited by male critics, more often than not ignoring women/feminists critics, who seem not to be part of the critical dialogue (see Doubleday; see also Modleski 3–22, Newfield 66; for a different slant on male feminism, see R. K. Martin 122–39).

As Elizabeth Meese puts it, "They are self-perpetuating in their authority, these generations of powerful men. . . . [T]he only real common denominator underlying today's various interpretive schools is the patriarchal substructure of the discipline of criticism as a whole" (89, 98). The patriarchal substructure has been particularly visible in a genre category of novels about "adulteresses." In fact, Hawthorne's fictional representation of the adulterous Hester Prynne has been argued as deeply influential in subsequent portrayals of "adulterous" women—for example, in Donald Griener's *Adultery in the American Novel* (in which he quotes only one woman, Judith Armstrong). Try to imagine, if you will, a category of novels about adulterous male characters (and authors).

Richard Brodhead attempts, in *The School of Hawthorne* (1986), to account for the changing cultural, literary, and critical/theoretical contexts in which Hawthorne has been examined in the last few decades and "to extend the range of our literary attentions out beyond canonical boundaries" (viii)—but these attempts end, finally, in reauthorizing Hawthorne's status as "American literature's great survivor" (so far) of canonical wars and changing cultural focus (215). As Brodhead says in his preface, he works to "establish the centrality of Hawthorne in a line of writers virtually unbroken from his time into modernity" (vii). Brodhead refers to some women's scholarship (for example, Elaine Showalter's [6], Mary Kelly's [19–20], Ann Douglas's [19, 220 n4], Myra Jehlen's [20], Nancy Cott's [220 n4, 230 n22], and Nina Baym's [12]) in relation to their work on "women's fiction" or Melville, although he does note Bertha Faust and Tompkins on Hawthorne's reputation (223 n7), Rita Gollin on his portraits (229 n11), and Baym on the reception of *The Marble Faun* (230 n15). In his earlier book *Hawthorne, Melville, and the Novel,* Brodhead neither notes nor quotes women scholars on *The Scarlet Letter* (1973).

Another example of Othering has a longer history than the appropriation of feminist scholarship and has had consequences for women's scholarship, whether overtly feminist or not. This version became apparent when I examined mainstream Hawthorne scholarship's marginalization and ignoring of women's scholarship on *The Scarlet Letter.* For example, in its bibliographic supplement listing critical work on Hawthorne from 1955 to 1962, *Eight American Authors* notes only four women who wrote about *The Scarlet Letter:* Virginia Birdsall, M. Hilda Bonham, Barbara Garlitz, and Anne McNamara (Mathews 429–38, 428 n34). In the section covering research and criticism on Hawthorne during the nineteenth and twentieth centuries, only six other women on *The Scarlet Letter* appear among the many male scholars: Elizabeth Lathrop Chandler, Françoise Dony, Marion Kesselring, Jane Lundblad, Q. D. Leavis, Amy Reed (Blair 112–52). Even a 1990 bibliography, compiled by a female bibliographer, Jeanetta Boswell, names and annotates only five women on *The Scarlet Letter.* From 1955 to 1992 *American Literature* published several essays specifically on *The Scarlet Letter* by men (Maclean, 1955; Whelan, 1968; Reynolds, 1985), two by women (McNamara, 1956; Baym, 1982), and another on Hawthorne generally, including *The Scarlet Letter* (Johnson, 1973; see Cady and Budd). In the *Nathaniel Hawthorne Journal,* from 1971 to 1978, there were twelve items by men specifically on *The Scarlet Letter* and four by women. (See also, for example, *Nineteenth-Century Fiction;* see, however,

Nathaniel Hawthorne Journal, 1971–78; *Nathaniel Hawthorne Newsletter,* 1975–85; and *Nathaniel Hawthorne Review,* 1986– , for bibliographies that have consistently included women; see also Melinda Ponder's informative essay on Katharine Bates.)

A chronological sampling of mainstream scholarship from the 1950s to the 1990s shows consistent evidence of the disregard for women's scholarship. R. W. B. Lewis refers to no women scholars or critics on Hawthorne (or any other author) in *The American Adam* (1955). The only scholarship by a woman in Roy Male's chapter, "The Tongue of Flame: *The Scarlet Letter* in *Hawthorne's Tragic Vision*" (1957) is Anne McNamara's "'The Character of Flame': The Function of Pearl in *The Scarlet Letter.*" There are no women included in Roy Harvey Pearce's collection, *Hawthorne Centenary Essays* (1964). In *Sins of the Fathers* (1966) Frederick Crews neither quotes nor notes any women on *The Scarlet Letter,* and when he notes Millicent Bell on art, he says that her final answer to her question about Hawthorne's guilt in his "fictional treatment of art . . . is as meaningless as it is melodramatic" (155n). He footnotes three women critics on other Hawthorne texts (61n, 83n, 155n) while referring to almost sixty male mainstream critics. Women do not appear in Bernard Cohen's *The Recognition of Nathaniel Hawthorne: Selected Criticism since 1828* (1969), except for a possible attribution to George Eliot on *The Blithedale Romance* (63–67). Arlin Turner's 1970 collection of criticism on *The Scarlet Letter* includes ten prominent male scholars but no women. In the chapter "Hawthorne's Boston," in *The Imperial Self* (1971), Quentin Anderson makes no references to women scholars. Eric Sundquist's *Home as Found: Authority and Genealogy in Nineteenth-Century Literature* (1979) includes a section on Hawthorne in which he fails to include any women's scholarship (he does mention Ann Douglas and Annette Kolodny elsewhere in his book). Michael Davitt Bell's influential *Development of the American Romance* (1980) refers indirectly to Douglas (97, 260 n15) and includes only Nina Baym's *Shape of Hawthorne's Career* in two footnotes for his two chapters on Hawthorne (262 n2, 263 n3). (See also Bell's *Hawthorne and the Historical Romance of New England.*) Another influential Americanist text—Larzer Ziff's *Literary Democracy: The Declaration of Cultural Independence in America* (1981)—cites Louisa Hall Tharp's *The Peabody Sisters of Salem* (1950) in his chapters on Hawthorne, but no women's scholarship on Hawthorne. Harold Bloom omits women from his collection of essays on *The Scarlet Letter* (1986), although four women are named in his bibliography. Bloom includes as an entry "Feminism," which directs the reader to "See Women"; the "Women" entry is actually

"Women and antinomianism" and refers the reader to pages discussing "Hawthorne's attitude towards" women. (See, however, Bloom's collection of essays on *Hester Prynne,* 1990.)

Evan Carton fails to engage with or cite any women scholars on *The Scarlet Letter* in his chapter "The Prison Door" in *The Rhetoric of American Romance: Dialectic and Identity in Emerson, Dickinson, Poe and Hawthorne* (1985). Donald Pease, one of the New Americanists, does not include a single reference to a female/feminist scholar in Hawthorne studies in his two chapters on *The Scarlet Letter* in *Visionary Compacts: American Renaissance Writings in Cultural Context* (1987). In fact, the few references in his text to scholarship by women include one gesture to Barbara Johnson's work on Poe and several notes directing readers to texts by female historians. But rather than citing the source for Johnson's discussions of Poe, Derrida, and Lacan, Pease instead cites his own review article on their discussion (289 n2). In *The Office of "The Scarlet Letter"* (1991) Sacvan Bercovitch discusses, quotes, or notes influential male Hawthorne scholars, philosophers, and literary theorists. His index indicates that Nina Baym, Lauren Berlant, Emily Budick, and Louise DeSalvo are mentioned in his notes, but actually they are not. Millicent Bell, Ann Douglas, and Amy Lang do appear in the notes, but not in the index (168, 166, 162). Also mentioned, but only in his notes, is Laura Karobkin's forthcoming essay, "*The Scarlet Letter* of the Law: Hawthorne and the Puritan Criminal Justice" (164).

Readings on Nathaniel Hawthorne (1996) contains four essays on *The Scarlet Letter:* one by Hyatt Waggoner (1955), one by Richard Chase (1957), one by Davitt Bell (1971), and one collaboratively written by Randall Stewart and Dorothy Bethurum (1954). Even the section "For Further Research about Nathaniel Hawthorne," which includes two books by women—Millicent Bell's *Hawthorne's View of the Artist* (1962) and Gloria Erlich's *Family Themes and Hawthorne's Fiction* (1984)—primarily refers readers to critical texts written in the 1940s, 1960s, and 1970s. Erlich's is the only book cited that is published in the 1980s except for Terence Martin's *Nathaniel Hawthorne,* which is a revised edition of earlier work. The single text mentioned from the 1990s is Gary Scharnhorst's collection. By not focusing on work done in the 1980s and 1990s, most of the scholarship by women on *The Scarlet Letter* can be ignored. (See *Readings on The Scarlet Letter,* 1998, which contains four reprints of essays or book chapters by women—McNamara, Baym, Easton, and Johnson—and adds Millicent Bell in its "Further Research Section;" see also Morey.)

Besides generally ignoring women's scholarship on Hawthorne, mainstream Hawthorne scholarship reveals other problematic, adversarial, marginalizing, or Othering relationships to women and women's scholarship. For example, when Paul John Eakin examines Hawthorne's female characters in his 1976 *New England Girl,* he notes his indebtedness to Perry Miller's "lively treatment" of Hawthorne's women characters in Miller's course at Harvard (233 n25); evidently, Eakin considers women's treatment of women characters as insufficiently lively. Or, for another example, Seymour Gross, in his preface to *A "Scarlet Letter" Handbook* (1960)—a text to be used in conjunction with *The Scarlet Letter* in classrooms—explains the rationale for his selections:

> In selecting essays, I have tried to choose the best expressions of as wide a variety of viewpoints as possible. Any approach to the novel which is not included in the anthology (such as the psychoanalytic one) can be found listed in the annotated bibliography of *Scarlet Letter* criticism and scholarship which makes up part Four of this volume. (vii)

Of the thirty-six short essays included (by every major mainstream Hawthorne scholar of the time), he includes only three by women: two on Pearl (Anne McNamara and Barbara Garlitz) and one on symbolism (M. Hilda Bonham). There are no essays by women on Hester Prynne, Dimmesdale, or Chillingworth in Gross's anthology. The bibliographic section adds only two works by women (Lois Adkins and Q. D. Leavis) other than Anne Abbott's 1850 review: "The first reviewer to cast doubt on the morality of the novel . . ." (152). There are seventy-seven male, mainstream critics listed in this bibliography. Thus, not only has this mainstream critical conversation on *The Scarlet Letter* generally excluded or marginalized women scholars, but also such attitudes and practices have been demonstrated unproblematically in classrooms in which this text has been used.

Much the same could be said for the *Norton Critical Edition of "The Scarlet Letter,"* edited by Sculley Bradley, Richard Croom Beatty, and E. Hudson Long in 1961, and used extensively in classrooms. There are no women included in the "Essays in Criticism" section, although Marion Kesselring is named in one note in one essay (220). There are three women named in the "Bibliography of Criticism Relating to *The Scarlet Letter*" (Anne Abbott, Barbara Garlitz, Anne McNamara). (See, however, St. Martin's "casebook" edition of *The Scarlet Letter* 1993.)

Other examples of marginalization and adversarial relationships to women's scholarship include *In Hawthorne's Shadow: American Romance from Melville to Mailer* (1985). In this book Samuel Chase Coale notes some women scholars and critics (for example, Ursula Brumm, Sharon Cameron, Patricia Carlson, and Rita Gollin), and he mentions Brumm, Gollin, Cameron, and Gloria Erlich in his bibliographic essay as having influenced him (233–36), along with thirty-six male scholars. But in light of his dedicatory remarks about his wife in his preface, one wonders about the extent of the influence. He praises his wife Gray as a woman

> who helped insulate me from the rest of the world so that my own obsessions and ideas could both fester and flower. And at day's end, as I staggered out of my study, she would engineer sweet reunions between us, son Sam, Mavro the black lab, and Tanqueray. Such devotion cannot go unrewarded. And when I returned from a jaunt in India . . . Gray presented me with a complete new study . . . there's a vote of confidence! (ix)

A. Robert Lee's *Nathaniel Hawthorne: New Critical Essays* (1982) includes such critics as Mark Kinkead-Weekes, Eric Mottram, and Richard Brodhead. Of these three essays treating *The Scarlet Letter,* Mottram's notes Helen Lynd's *On Shame and the Search for Identity,* then attacks Rosemary Jackson's *Fantasy: The Literature of Subversion* to "expose such simplifications, [and] reiterate [Hawthorne's] complex enquiry." (226). Kinkead-Weekes's essay does not refer to women's scholarship, and Lee's notes refer only to Q. D. Leavis (67 n4). Harold Simonson's *Radical Discontinuities: American Romanticism and Christian Consciousness* (1983), includes in its extensive bibliography Millicent Bell, Ursula Brumm, and Marjorie Elder, though it should be noted that in the chapter, "Hawthorne's Dilemma," Simonson argues, in reference to these three women, that the "lack of profundity that Brumm attributes to Hawthorne's ambiguity . . . is a judgment open to serious challenge" (48), and that "What Elder overlooks . . . Millicent Bell recognizes." (49). Brumm, Elder, and Bell are not mentioned again.

In Philip Young's *Hawthorne's Secret: An Un-told Tale* (1984), one of the two references to female scholarship is a footnote in the "Afterthoughts" recognizing Rita Gollin's 1983 book, which gathered "all known portraits of Nathaniel Hawthorne," as well as her suggestion to him about Hawthorne's sister, Ebe (167). Young's other footnote citing female scholarship acknowledges G. J. Barker-Benfield's *The Horrors of the Half-Known Life* as an "interesting treatment" of "male anxiety" (67n). Of the more than 115 scholars whose work is noted in Edward Wagenknecht's *Nathaniel Hawthorne: The Man, His Tales, and Romances*

(1989), there are ten women writing on *The Scarlet Letter:* Celeste Lough-
man, Mona Scheuermann, Anne McNamara, Dorena Allen Wright, Millicent Bell, Nina Baym, Carlanda Green, Frances Kearns, Rosemary Stephens,
and Grace Pleasant Wellborn. Of these, only Dorena Wright is discussed in
his text, and then only briefly. Moreover, she is named Dorena in his chapter (84) and index and Donna in the endnote (235 n19).

In Milton Stern's *Contexts for Hawthorne: "The Marble Faun" and the
Politics of Openness and Closure in American Literature* (1991), he discusses *The Scarlet Letter* also, noting Alice Letteny's Ph.D. dissertation
(101 n1) and Ellen Moer's *Literary Women* (18 n9). In another note
Stern discusses feminist scholarship specifically:

> I owe a debt of prompting to Nina Baym, Ann Douglas, Ellen
> Moers, Jane Tompkins, and writers of several essays of feminist
> criticism. There are many who provide bright and controversial
> new insights into nineteenth-century American writing generally
> and Hawthorne in particular. Clearly an account of criticism pro-
> vided by feminist scholarship would demand a different book
> from the one I have written. Nevertheless, the one I have written
> owes a debt to some feminist perspectives, and I am happy to ac-
> knowledge it. (183 n2)

Myra Jehlen is also acknowledged as one of Stern's influences (xi). While
such recognition may seem satisfying after the long, dry spell of few references to women scholars, it is also clear that Stern views their insights
as both "new" and "controversial," even though some of their work was
published ten to fifteen years prior to this attribution—hardly new, but
still seen as controversial. Apparently, these women have not made him
rethink his own argument. Their scholarship is circumvented, in other
words.

Other mainstream Hawthorne scholarship conflates all women's and
all feminist scholarship into the position of one woman—Nina Baym,
although one white male scholar would never be the spokesman for all
the others. It has been suggested by various critics that Baym's work invites such tokenism, particularly essays such as "The Madwoman and
Her Languages: Why I Don't Do Feminist Literary Theory"—in which
she argues against "gender-differentiating theory" when it exposes and
articulates victimization, either intentional or as the indirect consequence of patriarchy—and "Thwarted Nature: Nathaniel Hawthorne as
Feminist" (1982)—in which Baym not only argues for Hawthorne's
feminism, but, as in "Why I Don't Do Feminist Literary Theory," has
also been seen as attacking feminist critics. For example, Baym says that

"when you start with a theory of difference, you can't see anything but. And when you start with a misogynist theory of difference, you are likely to force women into shapes that many may unnatural or uncongenial" ("Why" 159). She also says that the kind of feminist analysis that finds Hawthorne "conservative in his view of women's place, patronizing in his estimate of their capacities, while all the while secretly fearful of their sexual power, identifies precisely the sort of patriarchal mind-set that feminists expect to find in writings by men" ("Thwarted" 60). Baym thus echoes the critique of many text-based critics who believe that feminists distort texts, finding only what they want to find, based on their political beliefs. These text-based critics, however, have refused to acknowledge that their own readings have theoretical and political agendas and use particular reading strategies that have inevitable interpretive consequences, as feminist critics have been arguing for decades. These critics also failed to notice that feminist critics are not necessarily interested in recovering an author's intentions or attempting to discover what has been called *the* meaning of the text—but are often engaged in the critical activity of examining the *consequences* of an author's narrative strategies or the *consequences* of historical and cultural contexts, constructs, accounts, and practices that depend upon Othering, even to exist, or the *consequences* of exclusion *for* the Other.

Baym has also steadfastly insisted on Hawthorne's thoughtful relationship to the feminist movement of his time: "It is evident that Hawthorne had [Margaret Fuller's manifesto, "The Great Lawsuit"] and other early manifestations of feminism in mind, and that the question of a specifically female psychology was preoccupying him, as it would have to if he were seriously attempting to work with a female protagonist" (*TSL: A Reading* 81)—as well as on his representations of women as having "desirable and valuable qualities lacking in the male protagonist. They offer him the opportunity to attain these qualities through erotic alliance or marriage. The man's invariable failure to take the opportunity is harshly judged by the narrator in fiction after fiction" ("Thwarted" 60). Baym has been particularly insistent that Hawthorne's representation of Hester Prynne is a positive one; she calls Hester the "first true heroine of American fiction, as well as one of its enduring heroes" (*TSL: A Reading* 80; see "George Sand" and *Shape;* see also DeSalvo on Hawthorne on Fuller).

Despite whatever differences I may have with Baym's work, I find the argument that her scholarship invites its tokenism deeply flawed. Tokenism is neither the responsibility nor the fault of the woman who is proffered as a token; that is, tokenism is the action, and thus the responsibility, of the tokenizer, not the tokenized. To locate the problem of tokenism *in* Baym—or even to focus on her work *as* a problem—shifts the focus, as I have argued in earlier chapters, away from the responsibility for the consequences of patriarchal practices and policies, whatever the intention of the practicer might be, and makes it seem as though the responsibility for one's Othering, as well as one's victimization, tokenization, or exclusion—lies in the victim, the tokenized, the excluded.

Therefore, I will maintain here that mainstream Hawthorne scholarship's tendency to conflate all women's and feminist criticism into Baym as a spokeswoman needs to be exposed, and the responsibility needs to be placed where it belongs: squarely on the shoulders of those who believe in consciously (or have internalized unconsciously) and who participate in and thus perpetuate patriarchal, Othering, exclusionary practices.

The following are *some* of the examples of Hawthorne scholarship's tokenization of Nina Baym's work. In Michael Colacurcio's introduction to his 1985 collection of essays on *The Scarlet Letter,* he describes the feminist position on Hawthorne's text as "committed . . . to the belief that adequate psychological depth does not preclude an appropriate ethical or political circumspection"; Baym, he says, "proposes . . . that *The Scarlet Letter* reveals Hawthorne's complex involvement in what we have come to call 'sexual politics'" (19).[1] Jonathan Arac refers only to Baym's "Hawthorne and His Mother" in his "The Politics of *The Scarlet Letter* (1986) (264 n14); the few other critical works by women he cites are not on Hawthorne or *The Scarlet Letter.* David Kesterton says, in *Critical Essays on Hawthorne's "The Scarlet Letter"* (1988), that Baym "has become the leading feminist critic of Hawthorne and *The Scarlet Letter,* having advanced some of the most provocative and cogent analyses in Hawthorne criticism over the last ten years" (14). Kenneth Marc Harris, in his chapter on *The Scarlet Letter* in *Hypocrisy and Self-Deception in Hawthorne's Fiction* (1988), refers only to Baym's work (51, 60), as does Gordon Hutner in *Secrets and Sympathy: Forms of Disclosure in Hawthorne's Novels* (1988) (224 n16, 225 nn25, 39). Jonathan Auerbach, in the short section on *The Scarlet Letter* in his *The Romance of Failure: First-Person Fictions of Poe, Hawthorne, and James* (1989), does not quote any female scholars, although he does note Baym in relation to Hawthorne's first-person tales (186 n2). Charles Swann argues, in his chapter on *The Scarlet Letter* in *Nathaniel Hawthorne: Tradition and Revolution* (1991), that "Nina Baym writes about Hester's return in a particularly disappointing, even surprising, way" (93). He does not refer to any other criticism by women on *The Scarlet Letter,* but notes Alice Felt Tyler on the Shakers (266 n6) and Jane Tompkins on the Stowes (266 n7).

In his annotated bibliography of biographical and critical studies of Hawthorne (1975), Donald Crowley claims that Baym's "Hawthorne's Women: The Tyranny of Social Myths" is the "most complete and reliable treatment of feminist themes in Hawthorne's fiction" (147), as though other feminist analyses are not complete or reliable and as though one feminist should bear the responsibility of speaking for all. Other than a citation of Millicent Bell (147), the remaining twenty-eight entries in the bibliography annotate the work of "classic" male Hawthorne scholars. (See also Fogle.)

Hyatt Waggoner critiques Baym's *Shape of Hawthorne's Career*, arguing that it is the "least 'trendy'" of works on Hawthorne he examines (119), yet Waggoner "suspect[s] Hawthorne would repudiate, if he understood, many if not most of the meanings Baym finds in his works" (121); Waggoner's accusation is not inconsequential as Baym argues that she is articulating Hawthorne's intentions. A 1981 collection, *Ruined Eden of the Present: Hawthorne, Melville, and Poe,* includes only Nina Baym (Thompson and Lakke). Of those essays that consider *The Scarlet Letter* (Baym's plus Male's, Donald A. Ringe's, and William H. Shurr's), none refers to work by female scholars. Terence Martin's revised edition of *Nathaniel Hawthorne* (1983) notes only Baym in his chapter on *The Scarlet Letter* (119), although he includes ten women in his bibliography of 113 scholars; six of the women refer to *The Scarlet Letter.* (For male scholars who do engage with or cite women's scholarship, see, for example, Girgus, Herbert, R. K. Martin, Millington, Person, Pfister, Reising, Scharnhorst, Shaw.)

Implications of this Rereading

As I recontextualized and reread the mainstream scholarship on *The Scarlet Letter,* it became increasingly clear that the Othering of women in texts and women on texts has become so familiar, so accepted and acceptable, that generation after generation of critics and scholars have been lulled into complicity. In that somnambulant space of epistemological familiarity, assumptions are not acknowledged or discussed, critical paradigms are not deeply challenged, questions are not asked, the unconscious does not exist, consequences for the Other are not considered, and changes (other than superficial, easily reversible ones) are not made. When challenges come from outside the mainstream body of scholarship, they can be easily ignored: mainstream scholarship can close its ranks, while claiming not to do so and while attacking anyone who draws attention to the absences. Consistently perpetuated, then, is a body of scholarship steeped in the work of men on a man about a fictional woman who has come to represent real women. The fantasy of Hester Prynne includes her self-imposed silence and self-recrimination; the fantasy of the academy, despite its claims to the contrary, is that its female constituents follow Hester's model and heed Hawthorne's warnings rather than engage with male scholarship. And, certainly, mainstream (or what Amy Ling has called the "malestream" [152]) scholarship has not known about or engaged with women's scholarship.

This is not to say that other contexts for rereading the academy, the culture, literary scholarship, radicalism, Nathaniel Hawthorne, and Hester Prynne could not be effective for reaching a different kind of recognition; I am not claiming that my recontextualization is the only possible one. I am claiming instead that this method of destabilizing recontextualizations of the familiar, the accepted, and the acceptable can result in new insights into the oppression, exclusion, and Othering of women, which *continues,* whatever anyone's intentions might be and whatever claims the culture and the academy make about progress and change.[2] Neither am I claiming that the consequences of academic or cultural practices or the lived experiences of all academic women are identical or even essentially alike. Rather, I am claiming that there are cultural and academic constructions of female identity and experience, like the one I called Hester-Prynne-ism, that continue to have negative consequences for academic women's scholarship in general—and specifically for the many women whose writings on *The Scarlet Letter* have been considered erasable. These constructions also continue tautologically to justify and legitimize both the constructions and the consequent practices.

4

The Scarlet Woman and the Mob of Scribbling Scholars

Red in religious parlance has through the centuries had a two-fold function: to represent sin and evil, or to symbolize atonement.
—Grace Pleasant Wellborn, "The Golden Thread in *The Scarlet Letter*"

When the celebrated lawgiver Solon was elected to govern Athens around 594 B.C., he established legal houses of prostitution, called *dicteria.* There girls and women were confined and forbidden to enter the better parts of the city. They were policed by being assigned other disabilities such as the obligation to wear a certain costume by which they could be quickly recognized and avoided. . . . The world's most famous prostitute [courtesan] worked in Athens some two hundred years after the death of Solon. Her name was . . . Phryne, meaning toad. . . . Phryne is still recognized as having been sexually and illicitly associated with . . . men of the highest political power in the state or courts . . . [and] lived under the ban of social and religious ostracism.
—Norma Lorre Goodrich, *Heroines: Demigoddess, Prima Donna, Movie Star*

*I*n this chapter, I will continue my rereadings, focusing specifically on the textual Hester Prynne, in order to demonstrate the extent and nature of the tradition of women's scholarship. These rereadings will inevitably destabilize some of the familiar, accepted mainstream critical positions on her. I will not be arguing how Nathaniel Hawthorne might have intended his representation of Hester Prynne, but rather discussing a particular set of consequences of that representation—ones that emerge when it is examined in the context of the socially, politically, and religiously constructed male gaze that has captured Hester Prynne, as well as shaped and directed the gaze of women at women. Neither will I argue how Hawthorne might or might not have been more personally sympathetic to Prynne than to the Puritans or Roger Chillingworth, nor demonstrate the endless ambiguous multiplicity of the sign of the A, as many critics do, nor engage in a "close stylistic analysis . . . in order to demonstrate Hawthorne's techniques for gaining the reader's confidence, good will, and involvement" as Mary Gosselink De Jong does so well (359).

I will instead reread Hester Prynne inside the contexts I have set in the first three chapters, particularly that of Hester-Prynne-ism (chapter 2)—itself one of the consequences of various historical, cultural, and academically constructed versions of the male gaze—and that of the missing scholarship of women on *The Scarlet Letter* (chapters 1 and 3). These consequences are informed not only by the re-representations of Prynne in the century and a half since the publication of *The Scarlet Letter* (see chapter 2), but also by feminist theories, which, in turn, are informed and inflected by history, culture, psychoanalysis, and poststructuralism. This chapter, then, rereads Hester Prynne as spectacle, the consequence of the patriarchal gaze. The chapter also examines how such objectification of the female is inevitably attached to the continuous canonical status of *The Scarlet Letter*—the consequences of what Mara Dukats calls the "enabling and formative conditions of canonized texts" (338)—and the academy's (sometimes obfuscated) insistence on reading Hester Prynne in terms of either Hawthorne's or the mainstream critical community's intentions about how she *should* be read and understood. These *shoulds* I see as related to James Sosnoski's argument about falsification in "A Mindless Man-Driven Theory Machine":

> The distinction between an unsound and a sound argument is the only condition upon which literary study as a discipline can be said to "accumulate knowledge." Hence, "falsification," "falsifiability," "verification," and "verifiability" are crucial theoretical terms. . . . [F]alsification is a judgment that takes the general form of the utterance: "Professor X is 'mistaken/incorrect/wrong' when he . . . " Correlatively, the falsifiability of critical discourse is the condition of possibility for grades, ranks, publications. These uses . . . depend upon a belief which, in turn, the institution of criticism depends: that a claim about a text can be proven wrong. . . . [F]ar from being an impersonal, detached, logical judgment, falsification is a rationalization of academic competition, but, more significantly . . . it is a device for maintaining the patriarchal status quo. . . . [F]alsificity makes error a punishable form of wrongdoing. (41–42)

In the case of *The Scarlet Letter,* the patriarchal status quo, as I discussed earlier in this book, has not only determined readings of Hester Prynne, but also whose work on her should be read and legitimized,

even normalized as the winners of the ongoing but generally unacknowledged academic competition about whose scholarship is "best" or,
at least, not wrong. If some scholarship wins the already predetermined
competition, then the rest of it (and most particularly that of hundreds
of women scholars and critics) can be considered not good enough at
best, and false or full of error, and thus dismissible, at worst.

Hawthorne and Mainstream Scholarship on *The Scarlet Letter*

The Nathaniel Hawthorne we read is a canonical author, his status the
consequence of the authority and power of an academically constructed
gaze at his gaze at Hester Prynne, as Jane Tompkins explained more than
a decade ago, though in somewhat different terms (see *Sensational Designs*). Q. D. Leavis calls him "the finder and creator of a literary tradition" (183); thus, Hawthorne's constructed position as male canonical
author bestows an authority on his representation of Hester Prynne, and
gives him the right first to create an icon of American womanhood and
then to gaze at it, as may all those who read his text across time and
place. Amy Louise Reed reminded readers in 1926 about Hawthorne's
dread regarding

> that coldness of heart . . . that unwillingness to participate in the
> "united life of mankind," that curiosity to know what lies beneath
> the surface of human actions. . . . Yet this analytic inspection of
> his fellow man was the very essence of his art as a writer of psycho-
> logical romance. His notebooks prove that he kept up a ceaseless
> activity of *observation,* motivated by deliberate inquisitiveness and
> a definite intention to use the material for publication. (52, em-
> phasis mine)

Hawthorne gets to have it both ways in *The Scarlet Letter,* just like
his fictional Puritan patriarchy and like patriarchy more generally; that
is, he gets to look, to direct his readers to look, to appear to be sympathetic and knowledgeable about women's issues and rights while holding
an objectifying gaze, and to construct a narrative out of this looking
without reference to or recognition of the absence of the woman's narrative as shaping or informing his narrative (or of the narrative of the fathers and of the consequent generations of his readers). Hawthorne's
text, then, appears not to be gazing while gazing, or appears to be sym-
pathetically gazing. Nancy Roberts calls this the "'stereo-optic' gaze, a
way of looking in two directions at once." She says that

What this means is that [Hawthorne] can adopt either a pre-en-lightenment perspective . . . or a post-enlightenment perspective, which sees some elements of that [Puritan] society as barbarous or inhumane. . . . Each viewpoint unsettles, undercuts, and de-natu-ralizes the other. By maintaining both perspectives, by alternating from one to another, Hawthorne provides himself with the means of "having it both ways." He can be condescending and derisive about the ways of his forefathers and never lose his own obsession with those ways. He can censure and judge the events of Puritan Massachusetts while at the same time maintaining the ability to experience them through fiction. (58–59)

The appearance of sympathetic gazing supposedly neutralizes the power of the Puritan father's gaze—making it seem, as Naomi Segal puts it, "a gaze at once background and formal" (*Adulteress's Child* 150)—while remaining complicit in the act of gazing, which inevitably captures and controls its object—in this case, the representation called Hester Prynne. Thus, although Hawthorne has been seen as allowing his creation a kind of unheard-of freedom and expression, his text ultimately controls the construct of Woman (even as it appears to be re-thinking and revising that construct), or as Emily Miller Budick says, Hawthorne, "despite his fondest wishes, [does not] exceed his own male prejudice" ("Hester's Skepticism" 206). This construct and Hawthorne's appropriative relationship to it are emphasized first in "The Custom-House" sketch; as Carlanda Green says, the Hawthornian persona that discovers the scarlet A is "almost hypnotize[d] . . . with its strange power and [it] seems to sear his breast with its heat. . . . And like Hester, from the moment the scarlet letter touches his breast, he cannot change his role" (191). (See also Christine Brooke-Rose, Ursula Brumm, Jane Don-ahue Eberwein, Elise Miller, Sandra Tomc, Linda Wagner, and Roberta Weldon on "The Custom-House.")

In earlier chapters, I have generally categorized the "malestream's" re-sponse to Hawthorne's Hester Prynne as sexually transgressive and thus morally inadequate and/or defeminized, or as sexually transgressive and thus politically radical. Perhaps the mainstream's continuously intense focus on Hester Prynne—as both a consequence of male desire and of patriarchal logic (bad women get punished, but good women, especially mothers, can overcome their badness by recognizing patriarchal rules and then self-punishing)—reveals that the "other" feminine, women's sexual difference, which is mysterious and hidden to the eyes of men, "cannot be fully controlled within the terms of phallic law. As Jacqueline Rose explains, this other feminine . . . is the place where representation

is obscured and where interpretation fails" (Benstock 291). Each interpretation, then, becomes another attempt to control Hester Prynne, just
as Hawthorne's text attempts to control what the fictional Puritan community could not by making Prynne eventually share their view of her:
she is a sinner who cannot therefore be a spokeswoman; she is tainted
and must return to the site of her sin, doing endless penance. "Under
[the] auspices [of the letter] Hester must relinquish her individuality (as
woman) to become a generalized symbol of 'woman's frailty and sinful
passion'" (Benstock 299). Also, each subsequent representation of Prynne
(and other "scarlet" women) can likewise be read as attempts to control
female sexuality.

The Tradition of Women's Scholarship
on *The Scarlet Letter*

Some women scholars and critics have examined Prynne's strengths
rather than her weaknesses, sometimes ignoring the fictional fact of her
self-punishment and focusing instead on the authorial fact of Hawthorne's
personal and artistic choice to punish her. Many have focused on her
emotional transgressiveness, her intellectual lawlessness, and her insistence on keeping Pearl. Most have discovered ways to make their work
on Hester Prynne reflect the concerns of women, rather than merely in-
dulging in reverential rhapsodies about Hawthorne's ability to create a
female character. Some women have critiqued Hester Prynne as a female
representation, taking her creator to task for his male fantasizing about a
strong woman whom he will later subdue completely. Segal says that
women readers are "teased with some proto-feminist pearls" but are, for
the most part, "deeply unintended" by Hawthorne's text (*Adulteress's
Child* 147).

Although the critical relationships to Hester Prynne and Hawthorne
are varied among the more than two hundred essays and books I examined, much of the women's scholarship that discusses Prynne can be
generally categorized as follows: (1) strongly negative critiques of the
representations of Prynne and of Hawthorne as her creator; (2) celebra-
tions of Prynne's strength and of Hawthorne's courageous portrayal; (3)
ambivalent relationships to Prynne and Hawthorne; (4) examinations
of Prynne's relationships to historical figures, particularly to Anne
Hutchinson, and of Hawthorne's relationship to history; (5) discussions
of Hawthorne's artistry and discussions of his characters as artists; (7)
analyses of the convention of the "fallen" woman; and (8) positionings
of *The Scarlet Letter* and its female protagonist inside genre conventions

and expectations, particularly those of the romance and of novels of adultery (see the listing of women's scholarship on *The Scarlet Letter,* a section in the bibliography; see also DeSalvo's categories of feminist criticism on Hawthorne's romances 25ff).

Many of the arguments of these women scholars, whatever their conclusions about Prynne and Hawthorne, are generally rooted in women's and feminism's issues, concerns, and critical methodologies. Many of the essays and books also cross, even explode, all categorical boundaries, making us aware, as much women's writing does, that such categories are at best only roughly descriptive. For example, the discussion of Prynne's relationship to the institutional and psychic constructions of motherhood cross all the categories, as do revisionings of the concepts of literary heroes and heroines and explorations of American individualism, freedom, and otherness.

Moreover, each category of relationships to Hester Prynne spans the generations of twentieth-century critics and scholars. In other words, the women of a particular critical generation do not all share a relationship to Hester Prynne that can be seen as simplistically reflective of cultural or academic concerns of that time; however, it is true that there are more overtly feminist readings of Prynne and Hawthorne after 1960. That is not to say that women prior to 1960 did not recognize the feminist/womanist potential in the character of Hester Prynne or in critiques of her, especially when these women were writing scholarship and criticism in restrictive (often punitive) academic environments that did not recognize, admire, or encourage women (and often failed to hire, tenure, and promote them; see n9, n10 chapter 3). For example, as early as 1927, Lucy Lockwood Hazard recognized Hester Prynne not as a feminist subject, but as a "faint precursor of the feminist type" (38). In the 1960s, Millicent Bell said that "Hester Prynne's Romantic self-realization stirs Hawthorne's sympathies but not his ultimate sanction" (*Hawthorne's View* 24), and Carolyn Heilbrun described Hawthorne as not only "ultraconventional in his view of the proper destiny of the sexes" but even "strongly antifeminist in his opinions" (67). In the 1980s Mary Suzanne Schriber recognizes Hester Prynne as a "radically imaginative characterization" that "challenged the culture's ideology," yet she also sees that Hawthorne "seemingly suffers a failure of nerve, investing his narrator with a series of speculations that serve to undermine the meaning of Hester's character and the unity of romance" (46), and Margaret Olofson Thickstun claims that Hawthorne "circumscribes Hester's political power by giving her a self-defeating, because literally interpreted, version of Margaret Fuller's prophetic feminism" (153).

Louise DeSalvo more severely indicts Hawthorne in relationship to feminists and feminism:

> Hawthorne's criticism of Hester's behaviour suggests not only that women cannot accomplish *feminist* reform, but also that women, by their very nature, cannot ever hope to accomplish reforms of *any* sort. . . . The views Hawthorne held about the nature of women and men reflected the most conservative of the prevailing stereotypes of his time rather than the feminist challenge to those stereotypes. (6, 12)

About Margaret Fuller, DeSalvo shows, by quoting from Hawthorne's personal letters, what she calls his "arrogant" and "brutal" judgments and the "persecutory nature of his tone. . . . Hawthorne believed that Fuller *deserved* to die as she did . . . because Fuller had overstepped her bounds as a woman, and because he had ascertained that her nature was evil" (11).

In the 1990s Lauren Berlant examines the context in which a national self is constructed; about Hawthorne she says that his

> national work, in its defamiliarizing drive, runs up against a set of limits within hegemonic political culture. . . . But his critical analysis of the technology of modern citizenship also runs into personal, perhaps more banal obstacles, at the social axes on which his self-privileging takes place: I refer to the racial and gendered sites of his entitlement, which superintend the emancipated ethnic identity Hawthorne lives, that of a white man in a culture that sanctions this conjunction of identities. (209)

And Elizabeth Aycock Hoffman argues that "by having [Hester] undergo lifelong retribution for her adultery, [Hawthorne] indicates an inability to render a completely independent individual" (202). As this brief list demonstrates, such critiques occur across the critical generations.

The work of all the women of the bibliography shapes the rereading of Hester Prynne in this chapter because that female tradition allowed me to resee and reread mainstream scholarship as fundamentally gendered, exclusionary, and self-perpetuating. During the course of this chapter, I will engage with and quote as much of the women's work as possible in order to demonstrate the collaborative nature and extent of this body of scholarship. However, as I use it, collaboration does not mean consensus. Sosnoski explains:

> Literary criticism calls for intellectual collaboration. The form of

critical collaboration I have been advocating converges upon the apprehension of a problem and the critics involved band together to seek solutions to it. This form of collaboration in literary criticism occurs when a group of differing intellectuals . . . concur about a possible reading of it. By concurring they do not seek conformity; they seek the coincidences among their differences. . . . In this form of collaboration, intellectual subject positions are not configured competitively. Differences are crucial. Reading is not an appropriation by an individual; it is the political concurrence of a group. Inescapably, collaboration is the heart of the practice of literary study, despite the patriarch's insistence upon individualistic readings. . . . [Collaboration] takes place within the polis, the aggregate of communities. An intellectual community is a concurrence of intellectuals. Intellectual communities engender different and sometimes competing collaborations . . . [in other words,] communities are not unities . . . critical inquiry is the . . . accommodation of difference. Such inquiries are, by this definition, collaborative. (52–54)

A Collaborative Rereading of Hester Prynne

Hester Prynne as literary spectacle, as object of the Puritan patriarchal gaze. From the moment Hester Prynne crosses the prison threshold to venture onto the scaffold—with the scarlet A attached and Pearl clutched to her breast—she functions as a spectacle. According to Judith Mayne, the "term *spectacle* [in classic cinema] is fairly straightforward in its designation of subject/object relationships, defining the object of the look as possessed and controlled by the subject of the look" (13). Or, as Shari Benstock argues about the literary text of *The Scarlet Letter*, "This spectacle of womanhood, the female body dressed as icon or effigy, wards off patriarchal fears of female sexuality" (291). Naomi Segal goes even further by saying that "Hester becomes something out of the control of the visible-invisible that would make her phallic" (*Adulteress's Child* 148), and Nancy Roberts draws attention to Foucault's chapter in *Discipline and Punish* called "The spectacle of the scaffold" as she discusses *The Scarlet Letter.* Drawing from such feminist film and literary theory, I will show in this chapter that Hester Prynne is to be looked at—is *spectacle* in Hawthorne's novel, what Laura Mulvey calls the female object's "to-be-looked-at-ness":

> The determining male gaze projects its phantasy on to the female figure which is styled accordingly. In their traditional exhibitionist role women are simultaneously looked at and displayed, with their appearance coded for strong visual and erotic impact. . . . Woman

displayed as sexual object is the leit-motif of erotic spectacle . . .
she holds the look, plays to, and signifies male desire. (62)

In fact, how Prynne looks (especially in relationship to how other Puritan women appear) and how she is looked at supersede any other consideration or description of her. As Lois Josephs argues, "Hester's beauty is constantly described in *The Scarlet Letter*" (185). Even her mood, described as wild and reckless, is merely manifested in her choice of clothing that defies their social constraints, but on which is imposed the scarlet A, "[t]he letter—as Hester's 'mark of shame'"—that Jenny Franchot likens to "religious spectacle, with the shameful and redemptive branding of the stigmata, and the 'marks' of the visible church" (262). As Hawthorne's narrator says,

> The young woman was tall, with a figure of perfect elegance, on a large scale. She had dark and abundant hair, so glossy that it threw off the sunshine with a gleam, and a face which, besides being beautiful from regularity of feature and richness of complexion, had the impressiveness belonging to a marked brow and deep black eyes. She was ladylike, too, after the manner of the feminine gentility of those days; characterized by a certain state and dignity, rather than by the delicate, evanescent, and indescribable grace, which is now recognized as its indication. And never had Hester Prynne appeared more lady-like, in the antique interpretation of the term, than as she issued from the prison. Those who had before known her, and had expected to behold her dimmed and obscured by a disastrous cloud, were astonished, and even startled, to perceive how her beauty shone out, and made a halo of the misfortune and ignominy in which she was enveloped. It may be true, that, to a sensitive observer, there was something exquisitely painful in it. Her attire, which, indeed, she had wrought for the occasion, in prison, and had modelled much after her own fancy, seemed to express the attitude of her spirit, the desperate recklessness of her mood, by its wild and picturesque peculiarity. But the point which drew all eyes, and, as it were, transfigured the wearer,—so that both men and women, who had been familiarly acquainted with Hester Prynne, were now impressed as if they beheld her for the first time,—was that SCARLET LETTER, so fantastically embroidered and illuminated upon her bosom. It had the effect of a spell, taking her out of the ordinary relations with humanity, and inclosing her in a sphere by herself. (*SL* 53–54)

Gabriele Schwab redescribes this scene:

> At the onset of the novel, Hester is established as an outcast
> woman. The scene is the Puritan performance of public punish-
> ment. Exposed to the gaze of the collected community, Hester
> stands at the pillory bearing both emblems of her disgrace: . . . the
> scarlet letter A for adulteress, and in her arms, her illegitimate
> daughter Pearl. (180)[1]

Maxine Greene calls such scenes "tableaux, 'set pieces'" (125). This spec-
ular objectification allows the viewer—and more significantly, a
reader—to make determinations about Prynne's thoughts and feelings
by examining her external appearance, as if she is part of a picture, as
Elissa Greenwald suggests (57). Moreover, it allows Hester Prynne to be,
even on the scaffold, separated justifiably from the community and common humanity—and from Roger Prynne (soon-to-be-Chillingworth)
who gazes from the edge of the crowd: "At his arrival in the market-
place, and some time before she saw him, the stranger had *bent his eyes*
on Hester Prynne. It was carelessly, at first. . . . Very soon, however, his
look became keen and penetrative" (*SL* 61, emphasis mine).

It is not *her* gaze, then, driven by her desires, motivations, and fears,
that counts or is accounted for, but rather Prynne as object of the socially and religiously constructed gaze of Puritan men and women and
Hawthorne's nineteenth-century readers; as Hawthorne puts it, "she was
the most conspicuous object" (57). Or, as Segal says, "Hester is in excess
of the regulations of the colony by her presence in its gaze" (*Adulteress's
Child* 149). Every textualized gazer and every complicit reader watch
Hester Prynne. Their gazes, locked on her, are intertwined ideologically,
despite the gaps in time and place and in fiction and reality, as if to say,
here, before us, is a sinful woman who needs to be punished and instructed. According to Schwab,

> *The Scarlet Letter* foregrounds the dominance of the gaze in the his-
> torical formation of the witchcraft pattern. The gaze, in fact, be-
> comes the organizing principle for the whole text: as puritanical
> gaze, it steers the dynamics of the narration; as the gaze of the narra-
> tor, it inserts a normative perspective to guide the reader's response.
> Thematically, the gaze becomes a medium of social formation, be it
> through the dynamics of seductive or of punitive exposure to the
> gaze, or even—as in Hester's interaction with the community—
> through a dialectic of seduction and punishment. Finally, as aes-
> thetic device, the gaze is used as metaphoric visualization, as an

exposure of images to the gaze of the reader. All the central symbols
in the book are visual images derived from the puritanical gaze-
mediated code. The text presents the gaze of the scopophilic community, fixed on the marked woman and her child, as a social ritual
staged in order to establish the power of social consensus via visual
interactions. (181–82)

Ann Douglas has argued that the "cruelest aspect of the process of
oppression is the logic by which it forces its objects to be oppressive in
turn, to do the dirty work of their society in several senses" (11). Thus,
other Puritan women, whom Monika Elbert describes as "matriphobic,"
gaze at Hester Prynne with disdain, even calling out abusive, "venomous,
patriarchal judgments," making these women a co-opted voice against
themselves as well as Prynne: "In emphasizing Hester's Eve-like sexuality, [they] deny her motherhood, and thus, their own past" ("Hester's
Maternity" 175–76).

> A lane was forthwith opened through the crowd of spectators. Pre-
> ceded by the beadle, and attended by an irregular procession of
> stern-browed men and unkindly-visaged women, Hester Prynne
> set forth towards the place appointed for her punishment. A
> crowd of eager and curious schoolboys, understanding little of the
> matter in hand, except that it gave them a half-holiday, ran before
> her progress, turning their heads continually to stare into her face,
> and at the winking baby in her arms, and at the ignominious letter
> on her breast. (SL 54–55)

Even schoolboys who do not yet understand "the matter in hand" are
undergoing instruction, as they are ideologically shaped by the experience: women must not be allowed their sexuality or to transgress sexually, even beautiful ones, although they garner far more interest from the
male Puritans than old or unattractive ones. The constructions are also
mired in "the tales men invent of women—adored as virgins, feared as
witches, despised as spinsters, or exploited and abused as wives and
prostitutes—[that] assume new meanings according to these 'other'
terms" (Benstock 291); Itala Vivan sees witchcraft "enter[ing] the text
through the letter, signature and seal of the covenant and the contract"
(157). (See also Swartzlander 227–28.)[2]
  Consequences of the patriarchal gaze for Hester Prynne. The constructions of male power within the community, as well as the more secretive
constructions of male desire, allow for the Puritan gaze, then, to be both
sexual and punitive, forcing Hester, as Wendy Martin argues, to "forfeit

her sexuality" (260). Hester Prynne has had illicit sex, making her sexuality "threatening," according to Judith Fryer (72)—in other words, threatening "with destruction the society in which the Dimmesdales and the Hawthornes do live and serve" (84). Knowledge of this illicit sex can elicit vicarious fantasies and titillations, or, as Benstock claims, "The female body is . . . the locus of patriarchal fears and sexual longing, its fertile dark continent bound and cloaked" (300). For Jennifer Fleischner, "Hawthorne locates female eroticism at the origin of meaning— his contact with the 'secrets' of female eroticism is the enabling force of his imagination. Faith, Hester, Zenobia, Miriam—they are the focus of the interpreter's stare at the center of Hawthorne's narratives" ("Female Eroticism" 515–16). Hawthorne represents his Puritan fathers as desiring Hester Prynne's punishment, which of course she is seen as deserving. Prynne has been fearfully transgressive, and the combination of fear and desire that this generates in the male Puritan community, along with their need to punish and instruct her, create a space in which a focused gaze on her is seen as both legitimate and necessary—what Deborah Madsen calls "the whole issue of 'Fathers' and their right to determine identity" (258) and what Louise Barnett sees in "the condemnation of Hester [as] a ritual of collective self-validation" (*Authority* 52). Even more specifically, Elbert argues that the "worst sin against patriarchy is to bear a child and not disclose the identity of the father" ("Hester's Maternity" 179).

Their kind of focused gaze frees these Puritans—and Hawthorne's many generations of readers—from responsibility for their gaze, because it is socially and religiously sanctioned, and from accountability for the sexual desire with which it is inevitably mingled, given the repressive constraints at work in Puritan society (and in nineteenth-century, even twentieth-century America). The sexual desire is also mingled, as I say above, with the kind of power that accrues through the appropriated right both to gaze at and punish another, or, more accurately, stated, an Other. In the very deliberative action on the scaffold, Hester Prynne's humiliation is set in motion, based on her act(s) of female sexuality and desire; she is intensely conscious "of being the object of severe and universal observation" (*SL* 60).

Susan Elizabeth Sweeney sees Hester as identified "not only with the Virgin Mary [compared "not to the Madonna, but to a painting of the Madonna"], but also with Mary Magdalene—so that [Hester] . . . seems to embody spiritual purity and eroticism simultaneously" (416). Hester Prynne "unites within herself both Eve and Mary, the Fallen Woman and the Divine Mother," to put it slightly differently, as Judith Armstrong does (103). Viola Sachs says that "Hester is the Adulteress, the Babylonian whore of *The Book of Revelation;* she is also the Virgin Mary." ("Gnosis" 131–32). And Kristen Herzog extends this list when she says that "Hester is not just a fallen Eve; she is a divine mother, a Sister of Mercy, a nun, a saint, an angel, a potential prophetess or foundress of a religious sect, and a martyr. . . . Hester, then, is an example of a new American Eve" (13, 16; see also Judith Ruderman). Jessie Lucke more specifically locates Hawthorne's Madonna image in the historical irony that Hawthorne would have learned from his wife Sophia's "reminiscences about Cuba" and from Sophia's sister's (Mary Peabody Mann's) novel *Juanita* when, according to Louisa Hall Tharp, "Mary mentioned the Cuban custom of referring to a slave mistress and her children as a 'holy family,' a bitter Spanish jibe at both private morality and the Holy Church itself" (Tharp 330).

In any case, Hester is transformed "from person to pedagogical tool for Puritan ideology" (Benstock 299), and the humiliation and separation engendered by the letter and her actual physical banishment to the fringes of community life, it is hoped, will break her spirit, her intellect, her will, and her desire.

> Of an impulsive and passionate nature, she had fortified herself to encounter the stings and venomous stabs of public contumely, wreaking itself in every variety of insult; but there was a quality so much more terrible in the solemn mood of the popular mind, that she longed rather to behold all those rigid countenances contorted with scornful merriment, and herself the object. Had a roar of laughter burst from the multitude,—each man, each woman, each little shrill-voiced child, contributing their individual parts, —Hester Prynne might have repaid them all with a bitter and disdainful smile. But, under the leaden infliction which it was her doom to endure, she felt, at moments, as if she must needs shriek out with the full power of her lungs, and cast herself from the scaffold down upon the ground, or else go mad at once. (*SL* 57)

Whatever spirit is left in Hester Prynne, and whatever possible intellectual freedom will manifest itself in her separation from the community, she is, in this first scaffold scene, the spectacle, the object, whose very body and its sexuality, as well as its procreative capacity (misused in the community's eyes to produce Pearl) are deemed dangerous, fearful, sinful, and Hester Prynne is branded and marked, as Marjorie Pryse argues—the direction of her life forever altered—or as Jan Stryz says,

"Hester's badge does shape her character" (428). Pamela Banting explains that "[t]he law has unnamed her with its sentence that she must wear the letter. It has even deprived her of the dubious name of adulteress by reducing that name to the letter A alone" (36). Jane Flanders is more negative in her assessment, seeing Hester as "pathetic" and "destroyed" (97), and Anna Balakian describes her as acquiescing in the Puritans' punishment of her, in their "correcting a morality gone astray" (165).

The next time Hester Prynne emerges from the prison, she moves to the "outskirts of the town, within the verge of the peninsula, but not in close vicinity to any other habitation . . . [to] a small thatched cottage . . . out of the sphere of that social activity which already marked the habits of the emigrants" (*SL* 81); Rosemary Franklin sees this place as a "microcosmic landscape within the larger [pastoral] one," which includes "the western wilderness, the town, and Europe" (65). Hester's choices are limited to this alienated sphere of existence understood by the community in terms of its separate and unequal status. Sarah Davis describes Hester as "living her lonely, reflective life with Pearl, the barrier of the A between her and the town . . . [her] dynamic self full of the vital strength that destroyed the role she once played as wife and afforded only that of scapegoat and nurse" ("Self" 75). And, Joanne Feit Diehl explains this alienated sphere as a place where Prynne can

> lead a socially constructive, if psychically restrictive, life while she simultaneously marks, with the wearing of the letter, the barrier against future temptation, or (given her sociocultural milieu) against "sin." Hester's identifying A not only lends her freedom by separating her from the community; it also leads her, in the narrator's view, dangerously close to chaos. Hester's marginalization, for all its apparent freedoms, subdues her even as it becomes the source of her strength. While bestowing compassion, motherhood blocks her full intellectual development. In Hester, Hawthorne . . . combines a vision of motherhood rendered inviolate with the portrait of the dangerous woman deprived of her full capacity to threaten the community or contemporary standards of femininity. (665; see also Segal)

Hester Prynne as Othered object of the gaze affirms and teaches community's ideology. Ironically, Hester Prynne is out of eyeshot of the community, separate and isolated, but she is also under "the license of the magistrates, who still kept an inquisitorial watch over her" (*SL* 81). This gaze is necessary because, as Elbert argues, "To Hawthorne and to the Puritan mind, a woman alone meant trouble" ("Hester on the Scaffold" 238). The magistrates' gaze extends to that which they cannot daily see, but maintain watch over through the letter and Prynne's very absence from the community. In other words, the surveillance is maintained in its actual physical absence, although the children of the community peer and peek at her at will:

> Children, too young to comprehend wherefore this woman should be shut out from the sphere of human charities, would creep nigh enough to behold her plying her needle at the cottage-window, or standing in the door-way . . . and, discerning the scarlet letter on her breast, would scamper off, with a strange, contagious fear. (*SL* 81)

The ideological conditioning of the children continues, then, in Hester Prynne's absence from the community and the scaffold, as the children learn the power of the gaze and the fear of the Other. Hester Prynne has been a far more powerful tool than Puritan rhetoric, but no matter how much she may generate the children's (and the Puritan father's) fear and desire, she is still trapped as the object of their constructed gaze. Likewise, Hawthorne's text directs his reader's gaze through the cottage windows to watch her sew and embroider. Like the children and the fathers, we are invited to watch her, furtively and without access, except through Hawthorne's also constructed male gaze, to see how and what he thinks a woman in such a set of circumstances might think and feel.

As Hawthorne directs his readers' gaze into the windows of her isolated cottage, he shows us that what allows Hester Prynne the pretense of inclusion into the community is her handiwork, commodified because it *appears* to fulfill an absence (no one else is making and selling her kind of product) and because buying her goods keeps her in the public gaze, as Hawthorne's narrator says, as a consequence of their "morbid curiosity" (82). Thus, an absent presence, Hester Prynne, fills an absence in the community's economic structure, while continuing to function, as Millicent Bell puts it, as "one of the great American isolatoes, who cannot speak the language of the community" ("Obliquity" 22), or as an "intruder" and "outsider," according to Carol Wershoven (162–63).

Then, equating financial responsibility with morality, as capitalistic ideology has shaped its constituencies to assume, the community, created by nineteenth-century Hawthorne, begins to gaze somewhat differently at Hester Prynne in the light of the goods she produces, although as Hawthorne says of Prynne: "In all her intercourse with society, however, there was nothing that made her feel as if she belonged to it" (84). Her sewing products are separate from her other, also artfully adorned "product": Pearl. Although Prynne gives her goods to the poor, who "often reviled the hand that was stretched forth to succor them" (*SL* 84), the economically and socially privileged members of the community can buy her elaborate fashions, giving them legitimacy as indicators of their dignity, rank, and power, and especially for clothing babies, already the products of the power of paternity. This puts Prynne in the double bind of patriarchal logic: accepted and not accepted simultaneously; legitimized and illegitimized at the same time. This position is even more complicated by Hester's earlier sanction as a married woman—the property of Roger Prynne, who has now rejected her because of her betrayal of their marriage, but who still exerts power. As he tells her during the prison scene: "No matter whether of love or hate; no matter whether of right or wrong! Thou and thine, Hester Prynne, belong to me" (*SL* 76). Most particularly, he has elicited a promise from Hester that she will "[b]reathe not, to any human soul, that thou didst ever call me husband!" (76).

Pearl is somewhat outside the power of all the gazers' commodifying legitimations, because her father's name is not known. She remains the symbol of her own and Prynne's patriarchally construed illegitimacy, even if later Hawthorne will reduce her character to a quest for paternity that will legitimize and socialize her, doubly achieved through Dimmesdale's kiss and admission of paternity and Chillingworth's legacy of land and money. At this point in the novel, however, "Mother and daughter stood together in the same circle of seclusion from human society" (*SL* 94); that is, as Hawthorne's narrator says, Pearl "was the scarlet letter in another form; the scarlet letter endowed with life!" (102). (See also Mary Jane Hurst on Pearl.) This remains so, despite Prynne's hand-worked goods as the symbol of her entrance into possible societal acceptance: "In this manner, Hester Prynne came to have a part to perform in the world" (*SL* 84). Some women critics, for example, Roberta Weldon, have seen Hester's artistic performance (however commodified it may be) as connected with Hawthorne's own notion that creative growth is the consequence of freedom from "a locale that seems . . . a part of external [communal] life"; as Weldon argues further, Hawthorne "is aware that without this freedom there can be no art" ("From 'The Old Manse'" 43).

While this was certainly so for Hawthorne's own artistic endeavors, I see that Prynne, unlike Hawthorne, must struggle with the double message of patriarchy that can be seen in the distinction the Puritans make between her artistic products. She can sew for all occasions, even for babies' christenings, but the community refuses to allow Prynne "to embroider the white veil which was to cover the pure blushes of a bride.

The exception indicated the ever relentless vigor with which society frowned upon her sin" (*SL* 83). Because Hester Prynne has violated her marital vows, she cannot produce even "the finer productions of her handiwork" for brides (82). Thus, despite her performing her part in their world, she

> stood apart from mortal interests, yet close beside them. . . . It was not an age of delicacy; and her position, although she understood it well, and was in little danger of forgetting it, was often brought before her vivid self-perception, like a new anguish, by the rudest touch upon the tenderest spot. (*SL* 84)

In other words, no actions of Hester Prynne, not even her entrepreneurial artistic productions, will free her from the gaze, not even from that of most academically constructed readers.

Endless variety of gazers and gazes at Hester Prynne. Hester Prynne as object of the seemingly endless variety of gazes and gazers is often emphasized by Hawthorne's narrator. Of particular anguish to her, the narrator explains, is "the gaze of a new eye. When strangers looked curiously at the scarlet letter,—and none ever failed to do so,—they branded it afresh into Hester's soul" (79). And combined with the "cool stare of familiarity" of an "accustomed eye," she "had always this dreadful agony in feeling a human eye upon the token; the spot never grew callous; it seemed, on the contrary, to grow more sensitive with daily torture" (*SL* 86). Even when there are no Puritans around to gaze at Prynne, the reader's gaze is directed at her and the letter A. For example, when she and Pearl go to Governor Bellingham's—a character Hawthorne based on the historical Bellingham who became governor of Massachusetts in 1641—Pearl notices that Hester is reflected in the shiny breastplate of a suit of armor hanging on the governor's wall. In this way, Hester comes to gaze at herself, looking at herself looking—or to complicate the picture, as in a cinematic gaze: the reader looks at Hester's looking at herself. In films, as I shall discuss in chapter 5, such mirror scenes have functioned to capture a woman's gaze at herself so that even her gaze is controlled by the onlooker, making her the object of her own gaze. Sometimes the mirror scenes in films create distortions in the image reflected or the woman's body is fragmented, with only pieces or parts seen in the mirror.

In the scene at the governor's, as Hester is reflected, her image is vastly distorted by the convex shape of the breastplate:

> [S]he saw that, owing to the peculiar effect of this convex mirror, the scarlet letter was represented in exaggerated and gigantic pro-

portions, so as to be greatly the most prominent feature of her appearance. In truth, she seemed absolutely hidden behind it. (*SL* 106).

Thus, Hester's image is reduced to the scarlet letter as the consequence of her own gaze, and readers are complicit in the distortion. And for modern readers, the breastplate mirror functions like mirrors in a carnival fun-house or house of horrors. There, however, we often laugh at our images; here, at Governor Bellingham's, Hawthorne's distortion functions to foreground yet again the scarlet A and its inevitable alteration of the image of Hester Prynne. She has literally disappeared behind its patriarchal power, even to her own eye. That this occurs in the home of the most powerful man in the Boston community emphasizes the nature of the Puritan control over Prynne's position.

Interestingly, however, at this moment she does not succumb to their power; she maintains some measure of agency, insisting that she be allowed to keep Pearl and that Dimmesdale speak in her behalf:

> "God gave her into my keeping," repeated Hester Prynne, raising her voice almost to a shriek. "I will not give her up!"—And here, by a sudden impulse, she turned to the young clergyman. . . . "Speak thou for me!" cried she. . . . "Look thou to it! I will not lose the child! Look to it!" (*SL* 113)

It must be said, however, that it is not Hester's shrieking insistence that allows her to keep Pearl; it is the decision of the men, including Chillingworth who has insinuated himself into the life of the community, as well as into Dimmesdale's. They "look to it" after looking at her. Just as Pearl's earlier screams and shrieks at the children of Boston who taunt her have no real consequence, Hester Prynne's overt anger and anguish reveal her to the Puritan men as hysterical or even mad. As Cynthia Jordan has argued about Hester (and Hepzibah from *The House of Seven Gables*), when they "break their embittered silence, there is no sense of lasting release. Their speech [like Pearl's] recapitulates the psychology of authority that has kept them so long in bondage" (156–57).

Thus, at Bellingham's, it is Dimmesdale's earnestness, as Chillingworth names the emotion that feeds the minister's pleas to the governor, as well as the power of his argument, that convinces. Bellingham says that Dimmesdale "hath adduced such arguments, that we will leave the matter as it now stands; so long, at least, as there shall be no further scandal in the woman" (*SL* 115). Moreover, Pearl is to receive instruction from the minister, just as her mother is being continuously instructed via her exclusion from the community and the scarlet A as sign of their punitive rights.

Dimmesdale and Chillingworth in relation to Hester Prynne as Object of the gaze. Because, as Gretchen Graf Jordan explains, Dimmesdale has "drop[ped] from our sight intermittently while we [have] focus[ed] for far longer periods on Hester"—that is, the text does not "keep a steady eye on Dimmesdale" (74), four chapters intrude at this point into Hawthorne's, his narrator's, the Puritan community's, and a reader's gaze at Hester. Even so, these chapters reinforce the power of that gaze, in part by the difference in the manner in which readers are directed not to look with or at Chillingworth, who looks at Dimmesdale. A reader's gaze could even be said to be repelled by Chillingworth—whom Ellen Moers describes as "clearly . . . the villain . . . [but a]t bottom . . . a conventional romantic figure" (60–61), Sister Jane Marie Luecke calls "Hawthorne's greatest villain" (556), Hena Maes-Jelinek describes as one of Hawthorne's "heartless inquisitors" (341), and Sheila Dwight sees as a character who has "chosen a prolonged journey into evil" (391). Hawthorne's text calls for a looking away from Chillingworth, while a reader is directed to look *with* Dimmesdale, not at him. The gaze at Hester is also reinforced by a short scene that occurs within these chapters when Dimmesdale and Chillingworth are conversing:

> Before Roger Chillingworth could answer, they heard the clear, wild laughter of a young child's voice, proceeding from the adjacent burial-ground. Looking instinctively from the open window,—for it was summer-time,—the minister beheld Hester Prynne and little Pearl passing along the footpath that traversed the inclosure. (*SL* 133)

Perversely repeating the opening scene when Dimmesdale, along with the Puritan elders, is situated on a balcony looking down at Hester on the scaffold—and Roger Chillingworth is on the edge of the crowd looking up at her, trapping her between them, this time Hester's two "husbands" stare down at her while she is framed in the window with her child. As in the cinema, when such framing shots indicate impending danger for the female characters captured in the hidden camera's gaze, this scene represents the male power of this Puritan community, rearticulating its right to gaze. This power structure does not question or even notice that Chillingworth's growing concentration on the minister has evil intentions. Such men are above questioning, as is Dimmesdale, for the community's socially and theologically sanctioned gaze is always at the Other. Interestingly, here Hester and Pearl, as the powerless

Other, look up, and the four characters lock gazes—while the reader gazes at them gazing, until Pearl's knowing laughter breaks the moment: "'Come away, mother! Come away, or yonder old [Chillingworth] will catch you! He hath got hold of the minister already. Come away, mother, or he will catch you! But he cannot catch little Pearl!'" (*SL* 134). Readers are also told in these chapters that Dimmesdale's inner gaze of self-hatred is different from that of the community's toward him, which is respectful, even reverent:

> [T]he Reverend Mr. Dimmesdale had achieved a brilliant popu-
> larity in his sacred office. He won it, indeed, in great part, by his
> sorrows. His intellectual gifts, his moral perceptions, his power of
> experiencing and communicating emotion, were kept in a state of
> preternatural activity by the prick and anguish of his daily life. His
> fame, though still on its upward slope, already overshadowed the
> soberer reputations of his fellow-clergymen, eminent as several of
> them were. (*SL* 141)

When Dimmesdale appears on the scaffold in chapter 12, "The Minister's Vigil," he is, at first, alone—his gaze turned inward in what Susan Donaldson describes as his "introspective egotism linked with self-contempt" (71). Readers are told that this moment is indicative of his ongoing solipsistic focus:

> He kept vigils . . . night after night, sometimes in utter darkness;
> sometimes with a glimmering lamp, and sometimes viewing his
> own face in a looking-glass, by the most powerful light he could
> throw upon it. . . . On one of those ugly nights, which we have
> faintly hinted at, but forborne to picture forth, the minister
> started from his chair. . . . Walking in the shadow of a dream, as it
> were . . . Mr. Dimmesdale reached the spot, where, now so long
> since, Hester Prynne had lived through her first hour of public ig-
> nominy. (*SL* 144–47)

In this scene particularly, readers are told they have been spared the "picture" of Dimmesdale's self-gaze, and are instructed to look *with* Dimmesdale, as Hawthorne does, rather than *at* him, as Chillingworth does, and as everyone does at Hester Prynne. This difference in the construction of a reader's gaze is possible because of Hawthorne's choice to show Dimmesdale on the scaffold alone in the night, lost in an agony that elicits sympathy; whereas Hester's appearance on the scaffold in the second chapter is part of a public spectacle, where disdain or pity, rather than sympathy, might be evoked—although it must be noted, as Sylvie Mathe argues, for Hawthorne "[s]ympathy is . . . not a reciprocal bond

but a unilateral arrangement to suit the writer's needs" (606). Naomi
Segal says that

> Dimmesdale's falsity hides something that is truth, and all the
> scalpels with which he is penetrated only recharge our sympathy.
> The pillory that opens the story is a brothel-window for [Hester],
> the one that closes it will be a crucifix for him. This is the real dif-
> ference in which she is caught. (*Adulteress's Child* 151–52)[3]

It may also be that because Chillingworth's gaze is so obsessively focused on Dimmesdale, reading every outward sign as evidence of his
guilt and feeling no sympathy or pity for the minister's guilty plight,
readers are asked to feel even stronger sympathy for Dimmesdale who is
not strong, as Hester is, nor obsessively determined, as Chillingworth
is. Parsons and Ramsey emphasize the role of Chillingworth's potions
for tormenting [Dimmesdale's] conscience" (205). Or, in Hawthorne's
narrator's words: "Chillingworth scrutinized his patient carefully" (*SL*
124)—in Diana Mae Sims's words: Chillingworth recognizes "obvious
evidence" (292)—much as Hawthorne scrutinizes Hester Prynne, or as
Agnes McNeill's Donohue's puts it: "he probes Hester's mind and heart"
(53). Dimmesdale is not presented as intellectually arrogant, as
Hawthorne will later claim about Hester, nor does he object to the community's laws and punishment, although by his silence he refuses to face
public shame and by his refusal to marry shakes off the community's
pressure. According to Carol Bensick, "Dimmesdale is not merely free
to marry; he is positively under pressure to do so. He is not accidentally
celibate; he is obstinately so" ("Bachelorhood" 103). Hawthorne's narrator describes Dimmesdale's "characteristic humility" (*SL* 120), which
will also later be contrasted with the fact that Hester is not humble. For
her, the "scarlet letter had not done its office" (*SL* 166), but for
Dimmesdale, his self-torture and guilt burn in him, the "letter" and its
"office" complete and self-imposed: "His form grew emaciated; his
voice, though still rich and sweet, had a certain melancholy prophesy of
decay in it; he was often observed, on any slight alarm or other sudden
accident, to put his hand over his heart, with first a flush and then a
paleness, indicative of pain" (*SL* 120). In Ann-Janine Morey's words,
Dimmesdale is consumed "from within, marking him without" (61),
while Marilyn Mueller Wilton sees him as a traditional literary heroine
rather than hero. Gillian Brown goes so far as to say that it "is in the
story of Dimmesdale's expiation, rather than Hester's, that the plot of
victimage runs its course." (113)—and DeSalvo notes that he becomes

"more sinned against than sinning—he is described as the 'victim'" (64). Ann French Dalke goes even further: "Hester was as clearly Dimmesdale's seducer as he is clearly [made] the ultimate victim of their sexual encounter" (197). Millicent Bell, as well as many other women critics and scholars of *The Scarlet Letter*, argues that "the essential drama is . . . between the two men, and not in Hester" ("Obliquity" 23).

Dimmesdale's sensitivity and inability to deal with his breaking of the social and theological codes—or with the consequences he assumes are imposed by the transcendental signifier—also mark him as deserving not only of sympathy, but also in need of specific care. Claudia Johnson views Dimmesdale as a child: "not only in his dependence upon the Puritan elders and in his rejection of fatherhood, but in his failure to emerge from the closed circle of his own heart. He is a striking example of the self-centered, unperfected man as he is described on the scaffold under cover of darkness" ("Hawthorne and Nineteenth-Century Perfectionism" 591). Reinforcing this view, Baym sees Dimmesdale as requiring "authority over him" (*Shape* 136). Elbert argues that while Dimmesdale is "the character who has become most enchained in patriarchal definitions of manhood, [he] is looking for a mother. In this unresolved Oedipal conflict, he resembles Hawthorne, the narrator of the 'Custom-House,' not looking for a father figure, but rather for a mother figure" ("Hester's Maternity" 191). Betty Kushen agrees, explaining that

> Dimmesdale's hidden orgies of perverse and painful physical sensation carry the emotional tone of masturbatory guilt characteristic of that period of early childhood when he must have struggled with his romantic infatuation for his mother or some other forbidden and loved woman. It is Dimmesdale's incapacity to settle his childhood conflict, to set aside the taint of original sin, that determines his mode of repeated secret scourging. (112)

As with Hester, although oppositely, Dimmesdale's inner turmoil manifests itself in his appearance, which deteriorates steadily. He looks as though he needs help, whereas Hester looks as though she grows stronger and more independent; she reacts strongly to the change in him:

> In her late singular interview with Mr. Dimmesdale, Hester Prynne was shocked at the condition to which she found the clergyman reduced. His nerve seemed absolutely destroyed. His moral force was abased into childish weakness. It groveled helpless on

the ground, even while his intellectual faculties retained their pristine strength, or had perhaps acquired a morbid energy, which disease only could have given them. With her knowledge of a train of circumstances hidden from all others, she could readily infer, that, besides the legitimate action of his own conscience, a terrible machinery had been brought to bear, and was still operating, on Mr. Dimmesdale's well-being and repose. Knowing what this poor, fallen man had once been, her whole soul was moved by the shuddering terror with which he had appealed to her,—the outcast woman, — for support against his instinctively discovered enemy. . . . Hester saw—or seemed to see—that there lay a responsibility upon her, in reference to the clergyman, which she owed to no other, nor to the whole world besides. . . . Here was the iron link of mutual crime, which neither he nor she could break. Like all other ties, it brought along with it its obligations. (*SL* 159–60)

It is interesting that Hawthorne's narrator does not seem to consider such obligations, which are for Hawthorne the consequence of feminine sensibilities, to have been felt by Dimmesdale for Hester when she is punished and ostracized, "allowing Hester to bear the burden for their joint responsibility in conceiving little Pearl," as Eileen Dreyer says (78). In order to keep himself from public shame and to inflict his own brand of self-punishment, Dimmesdale evidently has rarely seen or been seen by Hester. If it were otherwise, she would not have been so shocked by his deteriorated condition. As Joyce Rowe argues, "Each of the characters is engrossed in a self-preoccupation so acute that for seven years they are barely aware of one another's presence . . . this mutual blindness . . . complemented by . . . self-suppression" (28). Dimmesdale's "obligations" have manifested themselves in a guilt and angst-ridden, but purely self-focused form—or as Peggy Kamuf says of Dimmesdale's reading of the "sign" of the letter in the sky:

The minister's act, which conceives a written sign in the closed narcissistic circle from the guilty subject back to itself, is a failure of discretion in the sense that it does not discern the difference between the interpreter/subject and an exteriority of the material world on which that subject imposes itself as image. At that moment, the whole differentiated expanse of nature becomes the subject's likeness, or, rather, repeats the sign whereby the subject acknowledges his identity to himself, his secret interiority. (77)

Likewise, Dimmesdale's narcissism, shot through with his desire, can make no gestures toward Hester to help or comfort her, other than that enforced by Hester's passion years earlier: Dimmesdale's argument to Bellingham that she be allowed to keep Pearl. Dimmesdale seems heartened, though, for a time by joining hands with Hester and Pearl on the scaffold; Cynthia Jordan claims that Hawthorne "uses feminine sympathy as a metaphor for the only corrective to patriarchal legalism. . . . When Dimmesdale joins hands with 'the mother and the child' he feels what Hawthorne has called elsewhere in the book 'the softening influences of maternity'" (164). DeSalvo argues that such a novelistic move by Hawthorne "subtly shifts the blame for what happens to Chillingworth and to Dimmesdale onto the shoulders of Hester. The effect of this is to render Hester completely responsible for the physical, emotional and spiritual well-being of the men in her life" (65). And complicating this picture, Barbara Garlitz concludes that "[i]n accounting for Pearl's character, the physiological psychology of the period must have appealed to Hawthorne; for it enabled him to shift the responsibility for her evil to Hester" (699).

"Another View of Hester" as more gazing. In the chapter that follows, "Another View of Hester," readers' gazes are refocused on her, now in the context of an awareness of the deterioration of Dimmesdale and with the knowledge of passing time:

> Hester Prynne did not now occupy precisely the same position in which we *beheld* her in the earlier periods of her ignominy. Years had come, and gone. Pearl was now seven years old. Her mother, with the scarlet letter on her breast, glittering in its fantastic embroidery, had long been a familiar *object* to the townspeople. . . . She never battled with the public, but submitted uncomplainingly to its worst usage; she made no claim upon it, in requital for what she suffered; she did not weigh upon its sympathies. (*SL* 160, emphasis mine)

Amy Schrager Lang emphasizes Hester as object, arguing that the "more self-sufficient Hester grows, the more exclusively a symbol she becomes until, no longer a self at all, she is, even to herself, an object" (169). Haipeng Li calls Hester "an art form that is everlasting" (85).

Moreover, Prynne's life has been "pure" during her exile, and she has shown compassion for anyone in need: "Such helpfulness was found in her,—so much power to do, and power to sympathize,—that many people refused to interpret the scarlet A by its original signification. They said that it meant Able; so strong was Hester Prynne, with a woman's strength" (*SL* 161). Betty Kushens claims this as Hester's sublimation of her "shared eroticism" with Dimmesdale. They "sublimate [it] in loving and Christlike affection and dedication to the community. . . . In Hester's case it involves the suppression of retaliatory impulses for injuries endured" (113). Janis Stout sees this as a superficial reconciliation, as it occurs at "precisely the time when she is more fully divorcing herself psychologically" (98), and Elizabeth Hardwick worries that even though such heroines can be seen as heroic, "the heroism may turn into an accusation and is in some way feared as the strength of the weak" (185).

The shifting nature of the community's gaze is complicated at this point by narrative gestures toward the meaning of Hester's refusal to participate in the changes: "Meeting them in the street, she never raised her head to receive their greeting. If they were resolute to accost her, she laid her finger on the scarlet letter, and passed on. This might be pride, but was so like humility, that it produced all the softening influence of the latter quality on the public mind" (*SL* 162). Hester's silence continues; "[f]emale expression is either inadequate—castrated—or indecent," as Barbara Bardes and Suzanne Gossett explain (59). The narrator goes on to note that "[i]nterpreting Hester Prynne's deportment as an appeal of . . . [human] nature, society was inclined to show its former victim a more benign countenance than she cared to be favored with, or, perchance, than she deserved" (162). Then, he further complicates the community's gaze by saying that the town's magistrates are not so quick to forgive, of course, but eventually even they "were relaxing into something which, in the due course of years, might grow to be an expression of almost benevolence" (162).

Readers of Hawthorne's text are thus faced with an awareness that, although the community's gaze has changed, he still considers it as wrong, as missing the point of Prynne's need for instruction and punishment. Hester has failed to do actual moral penance, complying only with the social penance demanded of her—what Marjorie Elder calls an outward "conform[ity] to society's requirements" while in the "unholy light of her impenitent soul" (128). Instead, as Sarah Davis argues, "in her alienation [Hester Prynne] achieves the individual perspective that marks the Romantic self" ("Self" 78), and unlike Dimmesdale, she does not recognize that "the expectation of an ideal consonance of self and social role is romantic delusion" (80). Louise Barnett notes Hawthorne's emphasis that this intellectual freedom is Indian-like: "Her intellect and heart had their home, as it were, in desert places, where she roamed as freely as the wild Indian in his woods" (*SL* 199; see my chapter 5 for analysis of Hawthorne's relationship to Native Americans); as Barnett puts it, "Hester . . . substitut[es] intellectual for physical freedom" (*Ignoble* 159). Marianna Torgovnick views Hester's "presence [as] strong, but demonic" (96).

The Puritan community, of course, has assumed that social and moral penance are interconnected and that social isolation and punishment, as well as the wearing of the scarlet A, would lead her to recognition and acceptance of her social role as well as to moral penance. However, as Donohue has explained, "Hawthorne's crowds are almost always wrong" (40), and as Hawthorne's narrator tells us, "The scarlet letter had not done its office" (*SL* 166). It has sheltered Hester, as well as torturing her, according to Dorena Allen Wright (118). This office, as described by Rosemary Stephens is to "cause Hester as artist to grow regretful, to mend herself, to become socialized. It is punitive and potentially corrective" (24), and described by Janet Gabler-Hover, it "does not reform; it preserves: by privileging the adulterous moment of Hester's life over all other moments, the legal letter reduces Hester's significance to 'passion' and preserves that passion in an unchanging magical state" (100). In Zelda Bronstein's words, Hester is seen as "beyond the pale of legitimacy" (204)—and in Torgovnick's, Hester is operating in terms of a "moral individualism and, as such, [to Hawthorne is] dangerous" (96).

Ellen Moers describes Hester Prynne at this point in the novel as one "whose condemnation to despised and alienated solitude has the effect of turning her life from one of passion to one of thought, though at variance with 'the world's law'" (61–62), and Nina Baym says that Hester "has become altogether self-reliant" (*TSL: A Reading* 80). Hester's growing strength and independence—the consequence, as many women critics have argued, of her life of the mind—are described by Hawthorne's narrator, as in the opening chapters, in terms of her appearance, although now as a loss of beauty, femininity, and an ability to nurture and love. Gone is the nineteenth-century feminine ideal; as Deborah Gussman explains, "Nineteenth-century . . . rhetoric . . . sanctified marriage and idealized 'true womanhood'" (61). "By devoting herself to a man and living through him, or to the spiritual sacrifice of a higher love, woman could forget her untenable position on earth and ascend to the top of the pedestal (which often meant actual death)," according to Thelma Shinn (4). And, significantly, as DeSalvo points out, "real problems, like want of food, shelter, and clothing, need not concern her if she is a true woman" (5). Joyce Warren explains that Hawthorne "apparently believed that it was possible for women to possess talent and even genius, but he was concerned that the public exercise of talent would destroy what he regarded as the essence of a woman's femininity" (190).

Thus, Hawthorne sees Hester Prynne's feminine essence as destroyed (or at least hidden); she is not only no longer desirable, but even more fearful. It will take a meeting in the forest with Dimmesdale to bring back outward physical evidence that she is worthy of male desire. The narrator points readers toward this possibility when he says, "She who has once been woman, and ceased to be so, might at any moment become a woman again, if there were only the magic touch to effect the transfiguration. We shall see whether Hester Prynne were ever afterwards so touched, and so transfigured" (*SL* 164). In other words, readers are to gaze at her, noting particularly her appearance for signs of the return of her "womanliness." This particular act of gazing is limited to readers, who, unlike the community, are privy to the absence of her moral penance, to the presence of her intellectual lawlessness, and to the loss of what constitutes a femininity that is constructed as desirable. Hawthorne and readers contemporaneous to him would have also understood the implied ideas of "coverture" and "domestic dependence." "Coverture . . . erased the woman's legal identity"; a wife "assumed her husband's name and rank, and came under his 'protective cover'" (Gussman 61). As Deborah Gussman argues,

> Hawthorne represents Hester Prynne as a woman ruled by her passions and with a highly developed intellectual sense, who is also a gifted and loving mother. This representation effectually sabotages her independent political identity, inasmuch as it upholds traditional notions about republican virtue and simultaneously reinforces antebellum notions about true womanhood that worked against the assumption of women's rights. . . . The 'unquiet elements' that distracted Hester, in other words, her passion and her intellect, can only be 'softened' by 'maternity,' [and] by the fulfillment of her woman's role. . . . The inalienable passion of Hester and Pearl is both natural to them and inseparable from them. It alienates them from society at large, and from the self-possession required for contributing to the public good as citizens. (68, 71–72)

Millicent Bell claims, though, that "Hester's public shame, her very ostracism, establishes her for a sounder connection with the social whole than does Dimmesdale's secret self-chastisement" (*Hawthorne's View* 23).

Gazing at Hester and Arthur in the forest. Possibly the most famous scene of *The Scarlet Letter* occurs in the forest; Constance Rourke says that "some may call it the single great scene in American literature where love is dominant" (190). It is in the forest where, as Janice Daniel tells us, "[i]ronically, the most pronounced sensitivity emanates, not from the human community, but from the natural environment" (310), and as Patricia Carlson argues, "the forest . . . is made the metaphor for the thematic movement by becoming a synecdoche of the 'moral wilderness' in which all the characters grope for meaning" (24). There, Dimmesdale and Prynne speak, not as minister and parishioner, but as former lovers who have produced a child, to attempt a "reconciliation of opposites," according to Charlotte McClure (72).

And despite Dimmesdale's "dead-beat dad" status and what Johnson calls his "de-sexe[d]" state ("Impotence" 609), Hester's desire for him has not abated. As the text tells us, she also is determined to reveal Chillingworth's identity to Dimmesdale, atoning for her "sin" of silence to him. The narrator puts it in strong terms: "Such was the ruin to which she had brought the man" (*SL* 193); thus, Hester Prynne is set up to beg Dimmesdale's forgiveness, and readers gaze at another scene of her humiliation. Dimmesdale's anger is self-righteous and hot; Donohue calls his response "hysterical" (58), and DeSalvo points out that Hester, "the person with the least amount of real power in the novel is made, symbolically, the person with the most power, and the most responsibility for the outcome of the tale" (65). Dimmesdale cries out to Hester:

> "I might have known it. . . . Was not the secret told me in the natural recoil of my heart, at the first sight of him, and as often as I have seen him since? Why did I not understand. O Hester Prynne, thou little, little knowest all the horror of this thing! And the shame!—the indelicacy!—the horrible ugliness of this exposure of a sick and guilty heart to the very eye that would gloat over it! Woman, woman, thou art accountable for this! I cannot forgive thee!" (*SL* 194).

Hester, however, does not respond with such words about her own years of shame and indelicacy, the consequence of the horrible ugliness of her exposure to all—not just to a single gloating eye, but to *every* eye, all gloating: Hester Prynne as ongoing spectacle; Hester Prynne as object; Arthur Dimmesdale as loved and revered subject. Having earlier cast "Hester into an isolation from which he will redeem her only to castigate for abandoning him" (Segal, *Adulteress's Child* 151), Dimmesdale's temerity in first refusing and then forgiving her (when he has never asked her for her forgiveness for his abandonment of her and Pearl) is exceeded only by the audacity of his plea, "'Be thou strong for me! . . . Advise me what to do'" (*SL* 196).

When the narrator finally mentions Hester's years of shame, despair, and solitude, these trials are seen as ones that have made her strong and even more socially lawless, as Segal says, Dimmesdale's "hypocrisy . . . will always be as forgivable as Hester's generosity is dangerous" (151). The comparisons between her and Dimmesdale continue for pages. But "[once] . . . Dimmesdale accedes to Hester's plan for them to flee the colony together . . . [he] no longer merely postpones his confession but chooses what he as well as his congregation considers a life of sin" (Stephensons 5). Dimmesdale's decision to leave with Hester is, of course, in the context of this narrative of torturous guilt and hideous shame. Thus, many readers recognize the impossibility of their escape, despite Hester's plan of not *looking* back to remember that for seven years she has been the object of everyone's gaze except Dimmesdale who has been gazing only and intently at himself. Even momentarily casting aside the scarlet A does not change the future to which the Puritan patriarchy has assigned her, nor does it—or their plans—slow the impending death of Dimmesdale. He has escaped in life by gazing inward, by not facing the community or Hester Prynne, and he will escape again in the death he chooses, even embraces. "Dying is the only thing left for Dimmesdale to do. It is the supreme evasion of responsibility, the final negation" (Wershoven 173).

During the momentary relief from patriarchal pressures felt by Hester and Arthur, Pearl then becomes Hester's mirror, reflecting the absence of the A, which ironically means Mother to Pearl: "Pearl . . . stood . . . gazing silently at Hester and the clergyman" (*SL* 207). Hawthorne's own cinematic eye complicates the gaze by having Pearl stand on one side of the brook, reflected in it, while gazing at Hester and Arthur. Thus, they are captured in her gaze twice: "Just where she had paused the brook chanced to form a pool, so smooth and quiet that it reflected a perfect image of her little figure . . . [t]his image, so nearly identical with the living Pearl . . . [she] stood, looking so stedfastly at them. . . In the brook beneath stood another child,—another and the same" (*SL* 208). And as at earlier moments in the text, a reader's gaze is refracted through the gaze of another character; in other words, readers look at two Pearls looking at Hester Prynne, this time without her badge.

> Now [Pearl] fixed her bright, wild eyes on her mother, now on the minister, and now included them both in the same glance. . . . At length, assuming a singular air of authority, Pearl stretched out her hand, with the small forefinger extended, and pointing evidently towards her mother's breast. And beneath, in the mirror of the brook, there was the . . . image of little Pearl, pointing her small forefinger too. (*SL* 209)

Hester is of course accustomed to the gazes of others, and understands Pearl's gestures immediately. Arthur, however, cannot bear the look, and as he did earlier, makes strong demands: "'Pacify her, if thou lovest me!'" (*SL* 210). Anne McNamara argues that Pearl "tells [Dimmesdale] in her wordless language that his acquiescence to Hester's will to escape is a false answer to his problem and is distasteful to her" (542). Whatever communication occurs between Pearl and Dimmesdale, neither is cognizant of the pain Hester feels when she pins the A upon her chest again: "[T]here was a sense of inevitable doom upon her. . . . She had flung it into infinite space!—she had drawn an hour's free breath!—and here again was the scarlet misery" (*SL* 211), nor do either of them attempt to feel empathy or sympathy for her plight. Hester Prynne is to make them feel comfortable, just as it was her task to adjust to the punishments of the community, find a way to earn her own wage, raise her child alone, and endure under the probing, unsympathetic gazes of all and, harder for her, in the absence of Dimmesdale.

Another public spectacle for Hester Prynne and Dimmesdale's death.
Hester Prynne's ordeal is not over, however, as she is soon to discover. Nor is she any less an object of the text's or the community's gaze, although for at time she believes that these townspeople have looked their "last on the scarlet letter and its wearer" (*SL* 227). Again perversely repeating an earlier scene—another one of Hester's "chastisement" (Torgovnick 97)—Hawthorne stages another public spectacle, this time with the gaze, although quite differently motivated and manifested, on Dimmesdale. First, he enters as part of the Election Day procession:

> It was the observation of those who beheld him now, that never, since Mr. Dimmesdale first set foot on the New England shore, had he exhibited such energy as was seen in the gait and air with which he kept his pace in the procession. . . . Yet, if the clergyman were rightly viewed, his strength seemed not of the body . . . so abstracted was his look . . . so he saw nothing, heard nothing, knew nothing. (*SL* 238–39)

Hester Prynne, always perceptively aware of the other person's pain or fears, recognizes that he is now "utterly beyond her reach" (*SL* 239). She needs him to look back at her, but he does not: "One glance of recognition, she had imagined, must needs pass between them . . . [but] there could be no real bond betwixt the clergyman and herself. And thus much of woman was there in Hester, that she could scarcely forgive him,—least of all now" (*SL* 239–40). He has abandoned her again. Pearl is not even sure she sees the same man as in the forest: "'I could not be sure that it was he; so strange he looked'" (*SL* 240).

While Dimmesdale delivers the greatest sermon of his life—one written in the aftermath of the "sexually charged" day in the forest (Johnson, "Impotence" 609), one Bensick also sees as "energized by his sexually stimulating encounter with Hester . . ." ("Bachelorhood" 108)—she is further objectified: "During all this time Hester stood, *statue-like*, at the foot of the scaffold" (*SL* 244, emphasis mine), and those who are left in the marketplace stare at her; there "were many people present . . . who had often heard of the scarlet letter." They

> thronged about Hester Prynne with rude and boorish intrusiveness . . . [in] a circuit of several yards. At that distance they accordingly stood, fixed there by the centrifugal force of the repugnance which the mystic symbol inspired. . . . [T]he inhabitants of the town (their own interest in this worn-out subject languidly reviving itself, by sympathy with what they saw others feel) lounged idly . . . and tormented Hester Prynne. (*SL* 246)

Her humiliation is not complete, nor is she done with the gazes of all, including almost 150 years worth of readers and critics.

This absence of sympathy in the gaze at Hester—replaced by the community's sympathetic gazing with the others gazing at Hester as Other—and the contrast with how Hawthorne has constructed the responses to Dimmesdale will be reaffirmed a few pages later by the narrator as he describes Dimmesdale's final and dramatic self-immolation, what Dreyer calls his "public pseudo-confession" (80):

> Partly supported by Hester Prynne, and holding one hand of little Pearl's, the Reverend Mr. Dimmesdale turned to the dignified and venerable rulers; to the holy ministers, who were his brethren; to the people, whose great heart was thoroughly appalled, *yet overflowing with tearful sympathy,* as knowing that some deep life-matter—which, if full of sin, was full of anguish and repentance likewise—was now to be laid open to them. (*SL* 254, emphasis mine)

Even in his moment of dying, Dimmesdale asks the crowd to "look again" at Hester's scarlet A, but to understand that his pain and "his own red stigma" are worse. Hers is "but the shadow of what he bears on his own breast" (*SL* 255). And he cries out, "Behold! Behold" (*SL* 255). Or as Donohue puts it, "Not content to be a great sinner, Dimmesdale has to be *the one sinner of the world* . . . the rigid Puritan speaks his dying words of incomparable spiritual pride and bares his breast to the multitude, triumphantly. Selfish in death, as in life, he gives Hester no assurance of God's mercy to her" (60).

Yet those who looked with disgust at Hester Prynne in the same spot years before, seeing only sin and degradation, now look at Dimmesdale but cannot see:

> It is singular . . . that certain persons, who were spectators of the whole scene, and professed never once to have removed their eyes from the Reverend Mr. Dimmesdale, denied that there was any mark whatever on his breast, more than on a new-born infant's. Neither, by their report, had his dying words acknowledged, nor even remotely implied, any, the slightest connection, on his part, with the guilt for which Hester Prynne had so long worn the scarlet letter. (*SL* 259)

He dies and becomes a legend, whereas Chillingworth is "withered up, shrivelled away, and almost *vanished* from moral *sight*" (*SL* 260, emphasis mine). Not only does Hawthorne not make Chillingworth the object of the community's gaze at this point, but also, as earlier in the text, directs their gaze away from him, this time because he can no longer be seen.

Pearl also is offered an escape from the gaze as she is legitimized by paternity and paternalism: Dimmesdale's confession and Chillingworth's legacy. According to Laurie Sterling, "Pearl is legitimated within the community and given the possibility of gaining a legitimate, conventional, and paternalistic name by Chillingworth . . . [who] re-translates her according to society's values" (27). Her eventual escape from this community and further legitimation through marriage render her finally free from the gazes of all, including any readers who do not resist the narrator's invitation to celebrate Pearl's entrance into patriarchal society; as Sterling puts it, "With her disappearance from Boston, Pearl escapes the community's re-estimation of her, her potential renaming" (27). Gussman says that "the narrative cannot accommodate Pearl, even after she is presumably transformed by Dimmesdale's acknowledgment of her. Pearl, along with her inherent passion, is removed to an 'unknown' region. Then, as if reluctant to leave her uncontained, the narrator rumors her status as finally secured through marriage and motherhood" (74). However, some women critics read Pearl's fate as "Hester's legacy to [her which] deeds her daughter entry into future narratives of property" (Brown 116), or as Pearl's marriage and Hester's presence at the end of the novel historically ensuring the "female line, at once representative and accepting of the body . . ." (Thickstun 156).

The return of Hester Prynne for Hawthorne's final gaze. When, at the end of the novel, Hester returns to Boston, she resumes her place as object of the gaze of the community, the narrator, Hawthorne and generations of readers—this time, though, humbly replacing the letter and supposedly changing its signification. In order to do so, however, she must now admit her own sin and shame, giving up her dreams and her voice in service to the community: Gussman argues that

> [i]n the end, Hester consents to her own submission, publicly accedes to state discipline, internalizes the community's condemnation of her passion and, to a great extent, repents for her "sins." . . . While the narrative leaves open the question of whether women's passions and desires *can* be contained by the state, what seems more significant is the sense it leaves us with that such passions and desires *should* be contained. (75)

Amy Schrager Lang says that "Hester *is* contained" (191, emphasis mine), and Carol Gilligan explains that

> [i]n the end, then, [Hester] must be corrected—and unlike Dora, Freud's later patient who flees from what had become the iron framework of his treatment, leaving her analysis in mid-stream, Hester, in the dark conclusion to Hawthorne's brooding novel, takes on the Puritan mantle[, a]ssuring the women who come to her for counsel and comfort that a new truth will reveal a new order of living and that "the angel and apostle of the coming revelation must be a woman." . . . Thus, the very woman who is able to envision a new order of human relations is, by the same token, unable since the experience which enables her also adulterates her in the eyes of the community. Released from goodness, she is imprisoned in badness, within the iron framework of a puritanical order. (506–7)

Lucy Maddox discusses the larger issue framing Hawthorne's decision for his literary character: "For Hawthorne, then, the necessity of bondage and the consequent need to choose one's bondage carefully are components of all civilized life, but the need is especially great in America, where the tempting illusion of freedom in a new and open country can lead the unwary or the willful straight into the most dangerous kinds of captivity" (124). Moreover,

> the life story of Hester Prynne . . . grossly distorts the fate of women who committed adultery in Puritan New England. In one very important sense, depicting Hester's strength and her resilience in the face of her punishment serves to nullify the effects

of such persecution. If Hester could endure, and triumph (as women who were persecuted for adultery surely did not), then the negative consequences of the persecution itself are blunted, and the persecuting fathers are rendered less virulent than they in fact were. (DeSalvo 63)

For example, Laurie Rozakis discusses the real "case of Hester Craford, punished for 'fornication' with John Wedg. She confessed, and was ordered severely flogged. In addition, her father, Mordecaie Craford, had to provide security to save the town from the charge of keeping her child. The judgment of her being whipped was postponed for a month or six weeks after the birth of her child" (64; see also St. Martin's "Case Studies" of *TSL* 12–13). Likewise, Elizabeth Pain (on whose life, Rozakis argues, Hawthorne may have at least partially based Hester Prynne) was ordered to be "whipt with twenty stripes," and her gravestone in King's Chapel Burial Ground in Boston is engraved with a large A (67–68). In Boston in 1644, Mary Latham and her partner James Britton were executed for adultery.

Thus, while Hawthorne may not, as Phyllis Jones explains, have "endorse[d] the 'grim rigidity' that occasioned such ignominious public punishment" (64), as that of Hester Prynne, he, consciously or unconsciously, imagines and writes a book in which a woman who resists Puritan orthodoxy and discovers love and sex—and effectively parents her child alone—also must eventually self-punish, doing self-imposed penance similar to that which she had escaped when she left Boston with Pearl. To understand the fate Hawthorne chooses for his female character, Hester Prynne, then, is to say, as White does, "Hester's true character can be appreciated only as she lives out her punishment and comes to an intellectual understanding of it" (141). And Hawthorne's readers, across time and place, gaze at Hester gazing at herself as though she has become the scarlet letter:

> Earlier in life, Hester had vainly imagined that she herself might be the destined prophetess, but had long since recognized the impossibility that any mission of divine and mysterious truth should be confided to a woman stained with sin, bowed down with shame, or even burdened with life-long sorrow. The angel and apostle of the coming revelation must be a woman, indeed, but lofty, pure, and beautiful; and wise, moreover, not through dusky grief, but the ethereal medium of joy; and showing how sacred love should make us happy, by the truest test of a life successful to such an end! So said Hester Prynne, and glanced her sad eyes downward at the scarlet letter. (*SL* 263–64)

Putting his words into the mouth of his already punished character was a masterful act on Hawthorne's part, having consequences and implications that still play out in the lives of real women—an act celebrated by much of the "malestream" and critiqued by much of the women's scholarship on *The Scarlet Letter.*

Hester-Prynne-ism, Hester Prynne's "daughters," and the tradition of women's scholarship. Hester-Prynne and Hester-Prynne-ism are reborn continually in re-representations of her, whether they are named Hester Prynne in subsequent narratives and visual images or renamed in a film, a novel, a drama, a song, a cartoon, a political struggle, or a courtroom. These women consistently self-silence, give up, accept punishment or self-punish, or are proven wrong, often by another woman who functions in the socially constructed role of the "true woman." In this way, new generations of gazers are ideologically shaped, like the children of Boston peering into Hester Prynne's cottage windows, and society's messages and lessons about female sexuality are learned anew and well. The scarlet woman, in whatever individual shape she takes—but always seen as the resisting embodiment of the good/bad woman dichotomy and always in need of punishment and instruction—continuously returns as the spectacle of the cultural repressed. Thus, only through continual rereadings that destabilize the familiar and the normalized will women resist the objectification and the roles assigned to, and eventually accepted by, Hester Prynne. Hawthorne could not have known—despite his supposed concerns about the "medium of joy"—that, as Alice Walker has told us, "Resistance is the secret of joy" (279).

The tradition of women's scholarship has not practiced self-silencing, however, and whether intentionally or not, has resisted an all male response to a male-authored, canonical text. So, as I mention in my introduction, despite the academic reality that women's scholarly work on *The Scarlet Letter* has received almost no attention or engagement from that text's mainstream critics and scholars, and despite the gendered, often unsafe, potentially victimizing territory where they have had to work, women have continued to write about the text, producing a stream flowing beneath the mainstream in chasms and crannies, unnoticed or viewed as inconsequential. And, significantly, these women have quoted, noted, and engaged with each other's scholarship. Thus, all attempts to damn up this stream, redirect it, or connect it with the mainstream for full assimilation and appropriation have failed. These women have confirmed Tillie Olson's insight that "[e]very woman who writes is a survivor." This chapter, then, has been my attempt to offer a rereading of Hester Prynne, shaped and informed only by the extensive, ongoing tradition of women's scholarship on *The Scarlet Letter.* This rereading does not, of course, unseat or attempt to erase the mainstream tradition; instead, it shows what can happen when the women's scholarship is engaged with, rather than ignored or a few merely cited. My rereading also shows how the long-term, various gazes at Hester Prynne can be destabilized through rereadings that recontextualize and reinterpret the gaze and its consequences, not just for Hawthorne's textual Prynne, but also for all "daughters" of Hester Prynne, including real women, which includes academic women scholars and critics.

5

Demi's Hester and Hester's Demi(se): *The* (New) *Scarlet Letter* and Its Spectators

*T*he 1995 cinematic adaptation of *The Scarlet Letter,* produced and directed by Roland Joffé (*Killing Fields, The Mission, City of Joy*), is the eighth in a line beginning with silent versions in 1911, 1913, and 1917.[1] Before it was released, I assumed it would participate in the Hollywood tradition of translating Hawthorne's novel to the screen—a tradition that partakes primarily of the melodrama, sometimes with added comic scenes and sometimes deviating completely from Hawthorne's "script." For example, the 1911 film, starring Gene Gauntier as Hester Prynne—also adapted for the screen by Gauntier—ends, as "the censors required," with the marriage of Hester and Arthur; Edward Wagenknecht says in response, "one wonders what the story can possibly have been about" (*Movies* 54). And the official description of the 1917 film, starring Mary Martin as Hester Prynne, says that it "tells the story of a noble but poor woman who arrives at Boston in the seventeenth century. There she marries an old but quite rich doctor but does not become happy" (Boehm).

Having read many of the prerelease reviews, I also assumed the new film, because it stars Demi Moore, would function, like the literary text, in terms of Hester Prynne as spectacle (see chapter 4)—her threat contained at the level of narrative by her punishment and alienation from the community, allowing for voyeuristic containment, and at the level of cinematic apparatus by fetishizing her, allowing for scopophilic containment; in other words, the pleasure in looking *at* Demi Moore:

> [V]oyeurism . . . has associations with sadism: pleasure lies in ascertaining guilt . . . asserting control, and subjecting the guilty person through punishment or forgiveness. This sadistic side fits well with narrative. Sadism demands a story, depends on making something happen, forcing a change in another person, a battle of will and strength, victory/defeat, all occurring in linear time. . . . Fetishistic scopophilia, on the other hand, can exist

outside linear time as the erotic instinct is focused on the look alone. (Mulvey 64)

Early feminist film theory, like that of Laura Mulvey, long ago argued that both kinds of containment are necessary because the "female figure as spectacle can . . . provoke the very anxiety [in the male viewer] it was intended to contain" (Penley on Mulvey, *Future* 42). As illustrative of this anxiety, one prerelease reviewer from *Newsweek* wrote in an essay entitled "Hester Prynncesse" that "[t]he producers, presumably, had chosen [Demi] Moore knowing that the audience would spend 90 percent of the movie staring right at the big red 'A' on her chest" (Adler 58).

Further, I assumed, following some of Mary Ann Doane's work, that the film would probably not attempt to construct a female spectator beyond the one who would become, rather than resist or reject, the classical image of Hester-Prynne-ism; in other words, "[f]or the female spectator . . . to possess the image through the gaze is to become it" ("*Caught*" 199). The image of Hester-Prynne-ism is that of the bad/good woman—bad, because she violates society's codes of confession and paternity, and good, because of her

> inherent virtue and her indomitable will . . . transcend[ing] society's view of her; she achieves an heroic stature because of her good works. . . . She does not become self-pitying, spiteful, or hostile. She endures and, by so doing, using Faulkner's phrase, she prevails. (Sochen 12; see also my chapter 2)

And, finally, I assumed that the new film would compound the containment already at work in Hawthorne's text—a containment of the objectification and sexual violence that exist at its core and are replicated in the mainstream academic critical tradition I have discussed so far in this book (see chapter 3). However, once I saw it, I realized that something much more complicated and interesting occurs in this film I now call *The* (New) *Scarlet Letter*.

Thus, in this chapter I will reread *The* (New) *Scarlet Letter*—in part, a prequel to Hawthorne's text; in part, an historical contextualizing of the novel; and in part, a revisioning of its ending—as an attempt to rewrite Hester Prynne by exposing the literary text's implicit violence and voyeurism. That is, the film represents the historical and sexual excesses that a Hawthornian semiotics tries to contain. Containment, as I am using it, is an attempt to hide the failures of cultural repression—the excesses. As Penley says, "repression is never complete. For, in fact, we only know of repression through its failures; if repression were total, nothing would remain to make us aware of what had been repressed or the act of repression itself" (52). The practice of containment was also attempted, I will show, in earlier film versions of *The Scarlet Letter,* not only at the level of the content and technique, but also in the choice of actors who have portrayed Hester Prynne. I will also argue that *The (New) Scarlet Letter* functions to destabilize and disrupt—to trouble the cinematic frame—rather than to reinscribe male desire. Jacqueline Rose has argued that "cinema appears as an apparatus which tries to close itself off as a system of representation, but that there is always a certain refusal of difference, of any troubling of the system, an attempt to run away from the moment of difference, and to bind it back into the logic or perfection of the film system itself" (qtd. in Penley 44). But, using Constance Penley's use of Rose's phrase, then, I am saying that the film attempts to refuse the "refusal of difference," or following Tania Modleski, I would say that this film disrupts the "fetishistic disavowal in the male . . . the means by which the psyche avoids facing the fact of woman's difference, the fact of her *being* a woman" (22). I am arguing further that all of the reviews and critiques, in an effort to re-contain what the film exposes, do reinscribe male desire by fetishizing Demi Moore, and by extension, Hester Prynne, and thus participate in the established tradition of Hester-Prynne-ism (see chapter 2). These reviews, along with my discussion of the old films and actors, as well as the feminist film theory, function as part of the context in which I reread *The (New) Scarlet Letter.*

The critics' hysteria, nostalgia, and fetishization of Demi Moore. The examples of the critical hysteria and efforts at containment that introduced this film to the viewing public are numerous. In addition to the *Newsweek* article I just quoted, other critics discuss Demi Moore's chest and body, derisively dismissing actor, producer, director, and film, perhaps oblivious to its attempts (though Disneyized at times, as Joyce Carol Oates suggests) to expose rather than participate in the ongoing American pastime of fetishizing Hester Prynne. This time the critics had two targets, Prynne and Demi Moore, but they missed the revelation of their own nostalgia and desire as they cried out for the "real" Hester Prynne of Hawthorne's text, the beautiful but silent one who is fully clothed, her body forever imaginary. For example, one review calls Demi Moore's Hester a "pious hoochie-koochie girl" and the film a "superficial story [with] cardboard characters who are about as complex as the imbeciles on 'Melrose Place.'" Unable, seemingly, to stop himself, this reviewer goes on to say that Moore's Hester Prynne "turns the New World into the Nude World" and further, that "from the looks of Hester's chest, her doctor husband must be a plastic surgeon." Marjorie Rosen, in the *New York Times,* reveals even more (about herself) when she says that Demi "tripped up in 'The Scarlet Letter' and 'Striptease'" and thus, "might give her thoroughbred thighs and perky implants a rest" by doing a female film version of *The Nutty Professor* in the style of Eddie Murphy (37).

Some critics decry the loss of Hawthorne's classic story; for example, Jim Welsh in *Film and Lit Quarterly* calls the film "Roland Joffé's foolishly updated . . . version of . . . *The Scarlet Letter.*" Welsh goes so far as to call the film "an insult to literature of the highest order." He says, "Only an ignoramus would advise stuffy purists to 'lighten up' when confronting this film. Anyone who really cares about literature will be upset when an important novel is corrupted beyond endurance and almost beyond recognition" (299). And Rita Kempley of the *Washington Post* called it a "dumbed down version of Nathaniel Hawthorne's tale of sexual misadventure among the Puritans." Anthony Lane, in the *New Yorker,* also regrets the loss of Hawthorne's text when he says that "Roland Joffé's film is, in the words of the opening credits, 'freely adapted from the novel by Nathaniel Hawthorne,' in the same way that methane is freely adapted from cows." He goes on, after saying that he doesn't "object to films that take liberties," to say that there "is more suspense, more dramatic torque, in one page of Hawthorne's heart-racked ruminations on the Christian conscience than in all Demi Moore's woodland gallops and horizontal barn dancing" (114). Joyce Carol Oates in the *New York Times* calls the film "a backlash against every great American prose classic in which happy endings are denied"; she adds that the film "represents American filmmaking at its most spectacularly superficial" and Hester Prynne as changed "into a patronizing, predictable figure whose independence and single-mother feistiness would have been absurd in Hawthorne's theocratic, thoroughly patriarchal Puritan community: anyone who behaved as she does would have been broken, driven away, her baby taken from her."

Interestingly, these reviews echo the textual nostalgia at work in the reviews of the 1934 *Scarlet Letter,* a B-movie produced by one of the most reputable and respected B-movie studios, Majestic (which, a year later, merged with five others into Republic Studios; see Balio). This version of Hawthorne's tale, produced by Larry Darmour and directed by Robert Vignola, starred Colleen Moore as Hester Prynne and featured Hardie Albright as Dimmesdale. A review in *Variety* argued that, although the screenplay was well written (including its scenes of comic relief, which features added characters such as Bartholomew Hockins [played by Alan Hale], Abigail Crakstone [played by Virginia Howell], and Samson Goodfellow [played by William Kent]), and argued further that although the originary novel is "dismally dark . . . it is at least one of the most outstanding examples of early American writing and should not be tampered with to make it conform to the Hollywood tradition" (Scharnhorst 252). This reviewer, however, concludes by praising the acting in the film, saying that "[i]t would be difficult to imagine a more happy choice for Hester than Colleen Moore. Her work is informed by gentle humility which gives the part dignity and appeal" (Scharnhorst 252–53). The *Hollywood Reporter* reviewer, however, cries out:

> Pity Nathaniel Hawthorne! The production that Majestic Pictures have given his . . . 'Scarlet Letter' almost succeeds in making the old classic ridiculous. . . . The fault lies primarily with the direction . . . and with the screen play by Leonard Fields and David Silverstein, which treats the old tale with no respect at all and won't even hand it some crutches when it falls down. (Scharnhorst 251)[2]

The Women Who Have Played Hester Prynne in Films

Colleen Moore. Colleen Moore, the star of the 1934 film adaptation of *The Scarlet Letter*—like Lillian Gish and Demi Moore, who also play Hester Prynne and whom I will discuss later—can be seen in the context of her successful status as a woman actor. Like Gish, Colleen Moore's career first began in the "extras ranks" in Chicago (C. Moore 247–48), and then with D. W. Griffith's studio in 1917, when she was still a teenager. Although she never appeared in a Griffith film, she was given a six-month trial contract as a favor Griffith owed her uncle, "Walter Howey, the Chicago *Examiner* editor who helped him clear 'Birth of a Nation' and 'Intolerance' through the censors" (Stephan; see also MacCann 247). Her fame came after years "of playing supporting roles with Tom Mix and others" (MacCann 247), but "only after she had her hair cut and played a 'flapper' in *Flaming Youth*" in 1923 (MacCann 196), the same year "she married the first of her four husbands" (Stephan). Some film historians call her the "original screen flapper . . . who was making $12,500 a week . . . compared with Clara Bow's $2500" (MacCann 204). By 1926 and 1927, according to the Exhibitors Herald Box Office poll of 2500 theater owners, Colleen Moore was judged to be the female actor who brought in the most money (MacCann 9). She invested much of her salary in the stock market, later writing a book on investing, as well as marrying two stockbrokers (Stephan). Moreover, she made fifty-eight films in all—six sound films, the last of which was

The Scarlet Letter, then "separated herself from Hollywood . . . [beginning] a super-elaborate hobby, known as Colleen Moore's Doll House, which . . . became a touring event to benefit crippled children" (MacCann 197).[3] Moore's flapper status, which might have allowed her to be sexually objectified, is mitigated and contained by her comedic status; as Molly Haskell explains:

> [I]n the twenties, perhaps in defense of the assault on the "woman's domain" by silent comedy, there were a great many female comics of varying types . . . mimics, pranksters, and buffoons [such] as Colleen Moore, Gloria Swanson, Bea Lillie, Marie Dressler, Mabel Normand, Bebe Daniels, Clara Bow, and Marion Davies. . . . There was a tradition of the cutup or personality girl, who was more down to earth and (theoretically) less beautiful than the romantic heroine. They, too, were divided by sexual stereotyping into "good girls" and ["bad girls"] but the categories were less hierarchical . . . the "good girl" comedienne . . . actresses like Colleen Moore [particularly in the film *Ella Cinders*] . . . represent[ed] the true, back-home values that were being threatened. (62–65)

Richard Dyer MacCann adds to this description:

> Clara Bow, Joan Crawford, Colleen Moore, and Louise Brooks were the leading bobbed-hair "flappers" of the screen . . . acting out their freedoms in part by smoking, drinking and dancing the Charleston. They were modified vamps, perhaps, not menacing or mysterious like Theda Bara and her ilk, but open and, as they said, "fast." A good title writer could provide them with "wisecracks," and sex was obviously on their minds. (MacCann 137)

Moore was also protected from societal sexualization by her position as an oppressed, long-suffering wife of a manipulative, alcoholic, suicidal husband. In fact, the famous 1937 film *A Star Is Born,* a remake of *What Price Hollywood* (screenplay by Adela Rogers St. John), is "drawn in part from the life of Colleen Moore," as the tragic hero[ine]/top star of First National studio, married to its handsome, but alcoholic publicity man—later to be head of production, John McCormick (MacCann 186, 196).

In such a cultural and cinematic space, the choice of Colleen Moore as Hester Prynne is neither as surprising nor puzzling as some film historians have claimed. Like most films in the 1920s and 1930s, this film version of *The Scarlet Letter* confirms American values; during these decades, as Sochen explains, "[t]he movies did not become a daring medium in which new social ideas were explored or old ideas were challenged. Rather, in a continued effort to be popular and profitable, they confirmed the culture's values" (5). Even the opening credits include this statement: "This is more than the story of a woman—it is the portrait of the Puritan period in American life. Though to us, the customs seem grim and the punishments hard, they were a necessity of the times and [the beginnings] of the doctrine of a nation."

Colleen Moore's Hester Prynne assumes not just guilt and shame about Pearl, but all of the fault and responsibility. In a scene that does not appear in Hawthorne's novel, Dimmesdale visits Prynne shortly after the first scaffold scene, begging her to marry him. Hester, who is not distraught after her day's ordeal, but merely and melodramatically sad, refuses Dimmesdale, saying that "[m]y salvation and yours can come only from heaven." She then pats his hand, asking him to leave her alone. As another example, late in the film, the character of Roger Chillingworth, played by Henry B. Walthall (who also played Roger in the 1926 film *The Scarlet Letter*), tells Hester that the Puritan council has debated whether or not to allow her to take off the scarlet A; she replies, "Were I worthy to be rid of it, it would fall off of its own nature." In the last scene of the film—not of the novel—Dimmesdale's confession occurs on the scaffold on Election Day. As he begins to confess, Colleen's Hester rushes to quiet him, her admonitions echoed by Chillingworth, who of course desires Dimmesdale's silence. Dimmesdale confesses, nevertheless, exposing the A carved into his chest, collapses, kisses and blesses Pearl, and dies. A bell tolls. The community in unison remove their hats and bow their heads—fade to black as the film ends.

Lillian Gish. There is even less of a problem or puzzle in the choice of Lillian Gish as the star of the 1926 silent version of *The Scarlet Letter*. Gish, professionally molded by director D. W. Griffith, played Hester Prynne (not for Griffith, but for MGM) in the wake of her successes with Griffith in *Birth of a Nation* (1915), *True Heart Susie* (1919), and *Way Down East* (1920). It has been argued that Griffith's films often presented "typically Victorian fantasies of delicate, idealized girls tormented by brutish males" (MacCann 78). In Gish, Griffith "constructed a symbol of fragility and he delight[ed] in putting it in the direst jeopardy, fairly tantalizing the audience, capitalizing on the lurid fascination with peril" (Affron 52). In *True Heart Susie,* Gish played "a true-hearted country girl" (Naremore 77), and in *Way Down East* she portrayed a self-sacrificing, long-suffering character named Anna Moore, who is seduced by a scoundrel and abandoned during her pregnancy (Sochen 7;

see also Lucas).[4] The audiences, especially the female ones, were said to have loved this silent, melodramatic film that focused on pregnancy and motherhood, represented as "woman's unique experience, burden, and pain . . . her agony, as well as the sign to the world of immorality, if the mother is without a husband" (Sochen 9). Such a character, who "appeared fragile, [but] was a very tough woman" (Sochen 6), has been categorized by film historians as a version of the Hollywood type, the "Girl-Woman . . . Lillian Gish's portrayal of Anna Moore in *Way Down East* and Hester Prynne in *The Scarlet Letter,* displayed th[is] . . . type: a victim pure of heart who is also strong and enduring, the melodramatic heroine" (Sochen 11–12)—somewhat like Colleen Moore's portrayal of Prynne, but without the comedic or latent flapper attitudes and their suggestion of freedom. As Lucas explains "Gish had the gift for externalizing [an] interior drama. . . . [She had] the physical attributes and skill to convey softness, delicacy, and vulnerability readily; but she also suggests an implicit strength" (40)—or, as Haskell puts it, Gish was "delicate as a figurine but durable as an ox" (qtd. in MacCann 3).

By Hollywood standards, Gish was considered far more beautiful than Colleen Moore, which situates her Hester Prynne differently as well. Richard Dyer argues that even the cinematic techniques of *Way Down East, True Heart Susie,* and *The Scarlet Letter* function to make Gish the "supreme instance of the confluence of the aesthetic-moral equation of light, virtue and femininity with Hollywood's development of glamour and spectacle. She may also be its turning point," he goes on to say, because very "soon, the radiance of femininity came to be seen as a trap for men, not a source of redemption" (4). Gish's version of Hester Prynne was directed by Victor Sjöström (known in the United States as Seastrom) and costarred Lars Hanson as Arthur Dimmesdale. He was a great director, according to Edward Wagenknecht, but

> made the best showing . . . in his two films with Lillian Gish, *The Scarlet Letter,* and *The Wind.* Like Miss Gish herself, Sjöström was a great human being as well as a great artist; each instantly perceived kinship in the other and drew upon their own and each other's deepest resources, and they remained close friends to the end of Sjöström's life. (*Movies* 205–6)

Gish came to MGM, after "her two independently produced films, *The White Sister* and *Romola* . . . Despite the stamp of big studio lavishness and care in production, there is a non-MGM quality about *The Scarlet Letter,* as well as the last Gish-Hanson-Seastrom collaboration, *The Wind* (1928). Both films are deadly serious; neither is designed to appeal to the Saturday-night movie audience out for a thrill or a laugh or a cry" (Affron 66, 78)—unlike Griffith's films. Seastrom's *Scarlet Letter* focuses often on the public spaces of the Puritan community, alternately filling and clearing them of people and using them as the site of conflict and punishment. There is even a scene when Hester Prynne is pilloried that perhaps unintentionally invokes Gish on the brace of the guillotine in her last film with Griffith.

> There is a calm about Gish in these [public] moments that bespeaks her understanding of dramatic potential of situations in which the dynamics of mass pivots around the actress. The hysteria of Griffith's crowd scenes took on contour in the reach of [Gish's] body, which she stretched beyond possibility. The hush of *The Scarlet Letter*'s Puritanism is drawn inside the actress's eyes and enfolding arms. (Affron 80)

As in many of her earlier films, Gish portrays a character who is "the angel of light," redeeming the male character's "carnal yearning" (Dyer 4).[5] Lars Hanson's Dimmesdale in *The Scarlet Letter* is the dark version of carnal desire, saved by the light of Lillian Gish as Hester Prynne. In the scenes between them, the clothing of Gish, and the lighting behind her, envelope her to provide the associations with the strength of redemptive purity and femininity. In some of these films, Dyer claims, the male character, dressed in black, "rears up out of the darkness," but Gish's characters are "already in the light. That light comes from behind his head, magically catching the top of his hair but falling full on her face, itself an unblemished surface of white make-up which sends the light back on to his face" (4). Affron claims that, in fact, the success of *The Scarlet Letter* is

> guaranteed by Seastrom, by the integrity of his vision and the full use of decor, lighting, camera placement, and his sensitivity to landscape and texture. This 'Scarlet Letter' may not be pure Hawthorne, but it emerges with a stylistic unity that sustains the conflict between desire and society. (82–83)

Despite Colleen Moore's also being trained by Griffith for silent films, significant in assessing differences between her 1934 Hester Prynne and Gish's 1926 portrayal is that Gish's film is silent:

> In silent pictures the conception of acting was somewhat different . . . the players were artists by definition, "poets" who suggested through pantomime more than they actually stated. . . . "We are forced to develop a new technique of acting before the camera," Griffith wrote. "People who come to me from the theatre use the

quick broad gestures and movements which they have employed upon the stage. I am trying to develop realism in pictures by teaching the value of deliberation and repose" . . . [an] artless conception of acting. (Naremore 77)

Gish's own version of Griffith's techniques show up most clearly when Hester Prynne is distraught, for example, when Pearl is ill in the prison and Chillingworth comes to visit:

> Gish transforms her face into a succession of symbols for despair. Such gestures as hands freely mingling with and blocking out areas of face are exemplary of Gish's ability and willingness to translate expression into disharmonious physical states. This is not overacting, but acting that is more figurative than purely lifelike. Gish balances these two extremes of representation. . . . (Affron 82)

In these films, as Naremore argues, "Gish specialized in child women with a strong maternal streak—a description which already suggests some of the[se cultural and cinematic] oppositions [embodied in women that] she was able to contain" (79)—both in terms of the roles she played and her position as star, which in that system of filmmaking linked her inevitably to her roles (77). Blake Lucas explains,

> [T]he public would be lured by something they believed to be real in the star's personality; and, that aspect of the star's personality was usually seized upon and became the basis of the star's enduring popularity. . . . Whether by design or personal limitation, stars generally play roles within a relatively narrow range. (38)

Even as a never-married woman, Gish was able to maintain her incredible stardom in a culture that demanded that women marry. As Sochen says:

> The ideal of the New Woman, first announced during the 1910s as a harbinger of a radically different type of woman, did not fulfill its promise (or fear) in the 1920s. . . . Indeed, the vital feminist movement of the first decade seemed dormant during the 1920s . . . The majority of both sexes still believed that the woman's primary adult role was as wife and mother; the majority still believed in chastity for females before marriage . . . [even when some] social realities [i.e., education, credit buying, urban living] were challenging those beliefs. (3–4)

Perhaps Gish's nonmarried status further emphasized the public's image of her as ethereally beautiful, pure and feminine, but strong and enduring.

Like Colleen Moore, Gish began her film career as a teenager, at first helped by Mary Pickford, also a child actor, to get jobs as an extra in films produced by Biograph, then, after she was introduced to D. W. Griffith by Pickford, as a featured actor (Fontana; MacCann 3; see also Sochen 5). Her film career, however, followed her earlier stint as a working child actor, along with her sister Dorothy, in their mother's act, which she began as a way to "support the family . . . where [the] restless father was frequently absent" (Fontana). Gish began working at age five because her father,

> unsatisfied and unsuccessful as the owner of a candy store, had left the family in Baltimore and gone to New York. Her mother tried to join him there, but found herself alone, making a poor living as demonstrator in a department store. She then turned to the theatre, where she made $15 a week. (MacCann 2–3)

Later, Gish toured with another acting company that "needed a child performer"; she was "entrusted to an actress friend" by her mother (3).

But unlike Colleen Moore and Mary Martin, who played Hester Prynne in the 1917 film, Gish did not leave Hollywood after the completion of *The Scarlet Letter*, except to take "the five-day train trip across the country to go to London to be with her mother" (MacCann 7). Gish had a long screen history and life, living until 1993, and she made the last of her more than eighty films in 1987, *Whales of August*, sharing the lead with Bette Davis. In fact, Gish stayed in the film industry most of her life, producing pictures at Metro that made money (quote from Loretta Young in *When Women* 41), and even directing one film—*Remodeling Her Husband* (1920)—although in

> the late 20's, [her] star began to wane [as] sound pictures became the rage with the viewing public. Lillian would resist the new sound pictures as she believed that silent pictures had a greater power and impact on audiences . . . [and she] was released by MGM . . . [making only two films in the 1930s]. In the forties she again appeared in a handful of "talkies" and received a Best Supporting Actress Oscar nomination for her role . . . in "Duel in the Sun" (1946). (Fontana)

Gish made three films in the 1950s and five in the 1960s. "In 1970 she received a special Academy Award 'for superlative artistry and distinguished contributions to the progress of motion pictures'" (Fontana).

Gish's status in Hollywood allowed her always to claim "the right to make her roles over to suit" herself, as Edward Wagenknecht wrote in 1927 (qtd. in Naremore 77).

Demi Moore. Demi Moore's status in Hollywood is both similar to and different from that of these earlier cinematic "daughters" of Hester Prynne, though no less connected to her particular cultural moment. She is like them in that she enjoys immense box-office success: from 1981 to 1997, Demi Moore made thirty films and produced five. However, she is not a construction of the purified, rarefied, even comedic good girl; instead, she is an object of desire, often of derision, as well as an object of controversy in her subject-position as a strong-willed, capable woman. As one newspaper reporter put it, "It's no accident that Demi Moore is the highest-paid actress in Hollywood. You can tell by the way she walks . . . that she's a woman in control of her own destiny . . . She [now] runs her own production company and served as producer on *Now and Then*" (Uricchio 1). Moore thus follows in the footsteps of other, earlier female actors, such as Mary Pickford, who also set records for her salary and established her own studio, The Mary Pickford Company, an affiliate of Adolph Zukor's Famous Players Company. Moore's marriage to Bruce Willis and their status as doting parents has only minimally complicated the culturally constructed sexualization of Demi Moore, especially after *Vanity Fair*'s "attempt to boost sales with [its] . . . controversial cover photograph of the nude and heavily pregnant Demi Moore" (Francke 149).

Interestingly, with Colleen Moore, Demi Moore shares an interest in dolls and dollhouses; she has a collection of two thousand dolls (Cerio et al.). With Gish, she shares the experience of an unstable life as a child:

> Her father left her mother . . . before Demi was born. Her stepfather Danny Guynes didn't add much stability . . . either. He frequently changed jobs, made the family move a total of 40 times. The parents kept on drinking, arguing, and beating, until Guynes finally committed suicide. (Zoerner)

Moore has called herself a

> trailer park kid . . . [but p]overty wasn't Moore's only problem. At 12, she developed a crossed right eye, which required two operations to correct. At 14, she discovered that Guynes was not her biological father. . . . That revelation, and the constant drinking and fighting of her parents, set her adrift. "I got lost," she [said]. . . . "I had an essence in my life that I was nothing." (Cerio et al.)

Like both Colleen Moore and Gish, Demi Moore began working early; she "quit school at the age of 16 to work as a pin-up girl" (Zoerner). Another biography of Moore says that she left high school at age sixteen, "got a job at a debt collection agency, took her own apartment and did some modeling" (Cerio et al.).
By eighteen she was married to rock musician Freddy Moore, but her marriage lasted only four years.

> At 19 she became a regular on the TV show "General Hospital" (1963). From the first salaries she started celebrating parties and sniffing cocaine. That lasted more than 3 years, until director Joel Schumacher fired her from the set of *St. Elmo's Fire* (1985) when she turned up high. She got a withdrawal treatment and returned clean after a week . . . and stayed clean. (Zoerner)

Cerio et al. claim that after Moore was clean, she

> never looked back. Her mother, who has a long record of arrests for crimes, including drunken driving and arson, has not been so lucky. Virginia [Guynes] posed nude in 1993 for *High Society* magazine, imitating her daughter's *Vanity Fair* pregnancy cover. Through it all, Moore tried to get help for her mother, but when Virginia walked from a rehab stay Moore had paid for . . . Moore broke off contact with her.

Moore's consistent refusal to deny or apologize for her past, ambition, outspokenness, power, and sexuality also contextualizes her Hester Prynne as completely as those of Lillian Gish and Colleen Moore. Part of Demi Moore's context is, of course, the locating of male desire in and on her body rather than in men who objectify her through their desire and in women whose gaze at other women is also constructed by male desire. Unlike Gish or Colleen Moore, but like Hester Prynne, Demi Moore has been blamed for her own objectification, choices, and resistances; she has also, like Hester Prynne, been publicly demeaned. So, despite academic and media claims to the contrary, Moore seems quite the perfect choice for this role in the late 1990s.

Rereading *The* (New) *Scarlet Letter*

Significantly for this study, Demi Moore's status and sexuality are not contained in *The* (New) *Scarlet Letter*. In fact, the film's content and cinematic apparatus expose the attempts at containment in the earlier films, as well as the containment of a radical woman by Hawthorne in his novel and by "malestream" academic critics who have written about

Hester-Prynne-as-woman while excluding women's scholarship. Director Joffé's insistence on Demi Moore as Hester Prynne recontextualizes the earlier cinematic versions and Hawthorne's text, and thus allows for a rereading of the actors Colleen Moore and Lillian Gish in relation to Demi Moore. Such a rereading destabilizes the picture of these actors as fully contained by directors, studio codes and rules, and social constructions, and recognizes them as women who were personally and professionally trapped inside the cultural economy of Hester-Prynne-ism, but also outside it because of their life choices, rebellions and resistances, public positions and status. These three women actors—Moore, Gish, and Moore—play Hester Prynne differently. Colleen Moore's and Lillian Gish's versions of Prynne participate in the cultural conditioning of women to accept all responsibility and blame and then to redeem men, yet did not reflect their own lives. Demi Moore plays Hester Prynne in ways similar to her own life, as she pursues her career goals, remains single-minded, and resists all attempts to contain her, her out-spokenness, or her self-styled sexuality. Joffé's casting of Demi Moore, then, inevitably rewrites Prynne, and thus, Hester Prynne-ism.

In fact, Joffé's film rewrites most of Hawthorne's novel, and this rewriting has been the basis for much of the negative response to the film. Therefore, in order to reread the film against the critical responses and in terms of the cultural, psychological, literary, and cinematic gender issues I have so far set up—particularly Hester-Prynne-ism—I must also examine *The* (New) *Scarlet Letter's* rewriting of Hawthorne's text through its representation of the Wampanoags (the Algonquin nation most closely associated with the Plymouth colonies), as well as its representations of Mituba (a mute slave woman), Harriet Hibbins, Mary Rollings, and a Quaker woman. The film's twentieth-century representations, which are suggestive of the historical contexts that informed American Puritan communities of the seventeenth century, have been attacked and demeaned by the critics of Joffé's film, in part because of their significant differences from Hawthorne's nineteenth-century relationship to the historical and social issues, incidents, and persons that shaped his representations. In examining and discussing these differences I am not claiming that Joffé's twentieth-century film is an accurate version of seventeenth-century historical and social conditions in the Plymouth colonies and that Hawthorne's nineteenth-century novel is not. Neither am I claiming that Joffé transcends his own time, and Hawthorne could not—or that Joffé cannot and Hawthorne did. Instead, my examination of the film allows me to destabilize and recontextualize Hawthorne's novel and his character Hester Prynne—as I have been doing throughout this book—particularly as his text assiduously avoids the contexts that Joffé's film articulates. Their differences cannot be simply explained by their differing personal, aesthetic, and political sensibilities, nor merely by twentieth-century artistic freedoms and nineteenth-century restrictions, although of course these issues inform the representations by Joffé and Hawthorne. Significantly for my project, though, I am not making claims about the intentions of either of these male artists—or deciding who is better or worse, but rather examining particular kinds of consequences for marginalized individuals and groups that are exposed by avoidances, absences, and uncontained excesses in artistic renderings. These discussions will allow me to make claims about the extent to which Joffé's film functions as a revisioning of Hester-Prynne-ism—whatever his intention, about the critical and cultural efforts to recontain what his film exposes, about the fear and desire that a new representation of Hester Prynne elicits, and about the ways readers/viewers of various versions of *The Scarlet Letter* have been constructed.

Rereading the film in its context of Native American history. By beginning his screenplay at the funeral of Massasoit—his death dated in various historical accounts as 1660, 1661, and 1662—followed by Hester Prynne's arrival in the Massachusetts colony in 1666 (rather than in the 1640s as in Hawthorne's novel), Douglas Day Stewart (known best for *An Officer and a Gentleman*) can represent the unstable environment within and without the Massachusetts Bay Colony. He can also imagine Prynne's and Dimmesdale's early connections, as well as Hester Prynne's strength and outspokenness (or as Dimmesdale puts it during their second meeting: "Your tongue knows no rules, Mistress Prynne"). Moreover, Stewart can set up an eventual avenue of escape for them during Metacomet's raid on the colony to free the imprisoned "praying Indians." His screenplay also depicts how the community reacts to Hester prior to her emergence from the prison onto the scaffold (the point at which the novel begins), how the Puritan communities are inevitably contextualized by their dependence on and relationship with the Algonquin nations, particularly the Wampanoags (a point the novel ignores), and how Hester Prynne suffers and endures (a point the novel eventually trivializes, as do earlier films).[6]

For example, in the opening scene of the film Dimmesdale and Governor Bellingham express to Metacomet their appreciation for earlier assistance by the Wampanoags and their condolences on his father's, grand sachem Massasoit's, death. Metacomet responds, through an interpreter—Johnny Sassamon, one of Dimmesdale's converted "praying

Indians"—"My father should have let you die." He turns then to
Dimmesdale and says, "You are the only one who comes to us with an
open heart, but your people have murdered my father with their lies."
One history of Native Americans tells us that the English who landed at
Plymouth in 1620 would not have survived if the Indians had not saved
them:

> A Pemaquid named Samoset and three Wampanoags named Mas-
> sasoit, Squanto, and Hobomah became self-appointed missionar-
> ies to the Pilgrims. All spoke some English, learned from explorers
> who had touched ashore in previous years. Squanto . . . and the
> other Indians regarded the . . . colonists as helpless children. . . .
> By the time Massasoit . . . died in 1662 his people were being
> pushed back into the wilderness. (Brown 3)[7]

Another historical account of the Wampanoags adds information
about the death of Metacomet's older brother, Wamsutta, renamed
Alexander by the General Court at Plymouth. Wamsutta became grand
sachem after his father's death, but the English, who "were not pleased
with his independent attitude . . . invited him to Plymouth for 'talks.'"
After one of the meals offered during the "talks," Wamsutta died. "The
Wampanoag were told he died of a fever, but the records from the Plymouth Council at the time make a note of an expense for poison 'to rid
ourselves of a pest.'" The English were not much happier with Metacomet, "King Philip," when he became grand sachem, although they
did not poison him.

> Philip does not appear to have been a man of hate, but under his
> leadership, the Wampanoag attitude towards the colonists under-
> went a drastic change. Realizing that the English would not stop
> until they had taken everything, Philip was determined to prevent
> further expansion of English settlement, but this was impossible
> for the Wampanoag by themselves since they were down to only
> 1,000 people by this time. Travelling from his village at Mount
> Hope, Philip began to slowly enlist other tribes for this purpose.
> Even then it was a daunting task, since the colonists in New Eng-
> land by this time outnumbered the natives better than two to one
> (35,000 versus 15,000). Philip made little attempt to disguise his
> purpose, and through a network of spies (Praying Indians), the
> English knew what he was doing. (Sultzman)

Running Moose, renamed Johnny Sassamon, Dimmesdale's friend and
primary convert in the film, also has an historical counterpart in John

Sassamon, "a Christian Indian informer" whose murdered body was discovered in January 1675:

> Three Wampanoag warriors were arrested, tried for the murder, and hanged. After this provocation, Philip could no longer restrain his warriors, and amid rumors the English intended to arrest him, Philip held a council of war at Mount Hope. He could count on the support of most of the Wampanoag except for those on the off-shore islands. For similar reasons, the Nauset on Cape Cod would also remain neutral, but most Nipmuc and Pocumtuc were ready for war along with some of the Pennacook and Abenaki. The Narragansett, however, had not completed preparations and had been forced to sign a treaty with the English. (Sultzman; see also Gussman's parable of "A Good Indian's Dilemma")

By mid-1675 the tensions between the colonists and the Native Americans increased. Metacomet's men began to kill livestock near Swansea, "convincing many that an assault was imminent. After a Swansea boy killed a warrior, the Indians attacked the town" (Mandell 375). "King Philip's War" escalated and included an alliance of Native nations; even the Narragansetts "joined the uprising after English forces attacked their village" (375). When, overpowered by the increasingly effective colonial forces and ravaged by disease and hunger, the alliance began to break apart by the spring of 1676, Metacomet "headed for home after his allies threatened to send his head to the English as a peace offering" (375). In August, he was killed by colonial forces and beheaded; his head was "exhibited in the fort at Plymouth, Massachusetts, for twenty-five years" (374).

These accounts are pertinent to the film's narrative because they discuss the general historical context that was used to shape *The* (New) *Scarlet Letter's* specific narrative action. For example, although Johnny Sassamon is not killed in the film, Roger Prynne (Chillingworth) commits a murder and attempts to make it look as though it was committed by Indians. Chillingworth mistakenly assumes he is killing Dimmesdale, as well as mistakenly assuming he is functioning like a Native warrior. Instead, Duvall's Prynne/Chillingworth has "gone native" in the worst sense of that phrase; that is, Prynne releases his own repressed savagery, naming it (and blaming it) on his association with the Tarantines and the Wampanoags. In one particularly memorable scene, Prynne so completely loses his inhibition and dances so crazily with a dead deer on his head during a Native ceremony that it frightens the Wampanoag. One

of the Native women says, "He has a ghost in him," and another answers, "He'll bring us bad luck. Send him home." But, as a consequence
of the murder (and scalping of the victim), the "praying Indians" who
live inside the confines of the Puritan community are accused of savagery and murder and imprisoned. Dimmesdale sends Johnny to urge
Metacomet to free them. In the ensuing skirmish between the Puritan
soldiers and the Wampanoag warriors, Dimmesdale, Hester Prynne,
Harriet Hibbins, and the other women are saved from hanging.

Hawthorne and the Native Americans:
Containment and Excesses

Hawthorne lived in Salem, Boston, and Concord, and spent time as a
child at Nahant, a nearby seaside resort, as well as in Raymond, Maine,
with his uncle Richard Manning. Although he seems to have developed
a deep respect for nature, he, like most nineteenth-century white, privileged Americans, does not appear to have had extensive knowledge of
the histories and struggles of the native populations who had been de-
feated in order for him to roam freely in nature and for his family to
own property in these locations. He seems locked in a romanticized notion of Native American freedom from all restraints, in contrast to the
restrictiveness of Puritan life. Hawthorne did not acknowledge Native
Americans to any great extent in his narratives (see Barnett, *Ignoble*),[8] although he often included Puritan historical figures and incidents that
shaped his stories and informed his characters' lives. In other words, his
historical context was primarily white and colonialist. When Native
Americans appear in Hawthorne's narratives, they are most often background figures steeped in the sensationalized fear of the "savage," "barbarous," "heathen" Other, even if and when Hawthorne may have been
problematizing such racist labels. For example, in Hawthorne's "Mrs.
Hutchinson"—first published in 1830 and the tale most often assumed
as precursor to *The Scarlet Letter*—his narrator sensationalizes Hutchinson's death, along with a group of like-minded colonists, at the hand of
Indians:

> Her final movement was to lead her family within the limits of the
> Dutch Jurisdiction, where, having felled the trees of a virgin soil,
> she became herself the virtual head, civil and ecclesiastical, of a lit-
> tle colony. . . . Her last scene is as difficult to be portrayed as a
> shipwreck, where the shrieks of the victims die unheard along a
> desolate sea, and a shapeless mass of agony is all that can be
> brought home to the imagination. The *savage* foe was on the

watch for blood. Sixteen persons assembled at the evening prayer; in the deep midnight, their cry rang through the forest; and daylight dawned upon the lifeless clay of all but one. It was a circumstance not to be unnoticed by our stern ancestors, in considering the fate of her who had so troubled their religion, that an infant daughter, the sole survivor amid the terrible destruction of her mother's household, was bred in a *barbarous* faith, and never learned the way to the Christian's Heaven. (24, emphasis mine)

In Hawthorne's *Scarlet Letter,* the Native Americans are a shadowy presence—staring with "their snake-like black eyes" (*SL* 246), more absent than present, appearing only occasionally on the fringes of the narrative action—as also, for example, in "Roger Malvin's Burial," "The May-Pole of Merry Mount," "Old Ticonderoga," and "Young Goodman Brown," where the focus is on the whites in relation to Indian battles or incidents. As Louise Barnett argues, although

> Hawthorne usually sees the Indian as one of the many victims of Puritanism. . . . Like other Americans, [he] could not repudiate white conquest. In his history of Salem, he writes: "Even so shall it be. The payments of the Main Street must be laid over the red man's grave." The same sketch encapsulates in the figure of a drunken Indian "the vast growth and prosperity of one race, and the fated decay of another." (*Ignoble* 155)

Lucy Maddox says that at the end of *The Scarlet Letter* "Hester chose submission and assimilation, and the 'race' of American womanhood has flourished; the Indians refused assimilation, and their race is, in Hawthorne's view, well on its way to predictable extinction" (120). Barnett reminds us, too, of Hawthorne's words in "The Old Manse":

> Finding an arrowhead in the vicinity of the Old Manse establishes a rapport between Hawthorne and the red hunter whose hand touched it centuries ago: "Such an incident builds up again the Indian village and its encircling forest, and recalls to life the painted chiefs and warriors, the squaws at their household toil, and the children sporting among the wigwams, while the little wind-rocked papoose swings from the branch of the tree. It can hardly be told whether it is a joy or a pain, after such a momentary vision, to gaze around in the broad daylight of reality and see stone fences, white houses, potato fields, and men doggedly hoeing in their shirt-sleeves and homespun pantaloons. But this is nonsense. The Old Manse is better than a thousand wigwams."
> (*Ignoble* 156)

That Native Americans appear at all in Hawthorne's texts—that he found it necessary to romanticize and appropriate them—is evidence of the kind of excess I am discussing, an excess represented by the Other that most American historical and fictional narratives have attempted to contain through omission, disregard, stereotyping, and marginalization. As Julia Kristeva and others have argued, various texts contain "the *excess* of meaning that constantly threatens to disrupt the boundaries of . . . defined identities and expose the fiction of any imposed 'truth'" (Morris 138, emphasis mine). Such containments have functioned to normalize the narrative of white, male Americanness (see chapters 1 and 2), making it seem progressive or radical when an author like Hawthorne bothers to include references to Native Americans—or as Barnett explains, even "conjures up the Indian Wappacowet" in "Main Street" (*Ignoble* 157)—or when he focuses on a woman condemned by the dominant Puritan community, such as Anne Hutchinson or Hester Prynne.

The omissions and containments are repeated in much of the critical mainstream's historical contextualizings of *The Scarlet Letter,* which consists primarily of additional Puritan history or that of other white settlers in Massachusetts. The history of the Other, like women's history and their scholarship discussed throughout this book, has been generally omitted, although sometimes the Antinomians and witch trials are mentioned—not in terms of the women who were victims of that particular cultural moment, but, instead, as the cultural hysteria implicating Hawthorne's ancestors, such as William Hathorne, a judge who persecuted Quakers, and John Hathorne, a judge involved in the witch trials in Salem in 1692. Even in textbooks used in classrooms—for example, St. Martin's "Case Studies" of *The Scarlet Letter*—the section entitled "Biographical and Historical Background" discusses Puritan history as the novel's context, but fails even to mention the Puritan attempts to convert to Christianity the indigenous populations of America, whom these Puritans called "savages." The "Viewer's Guide" to the 1979 PBS film of *The Scarlet Letter,* directed by Rick Hauser and primarily shown in classrooms, gives extensive Puritan history as "background" to the textual narrative and the film, explaining religious, social, and family life in New England with almost no references to the Other.[9]

Moreover, this film's depictions of Native Americans further calls into question Hawthorne's romanticizings and omissions in relation to nineteenth-century white America's responses to the "Indian question"— a reductive phrase that supposedly considered the lives and futures of Native Americans. One of the answers to that "question" was calculated genocide and another was the policy of removal. For example, in the 1830s, just a decade before Hawthorne wrote *The Scarlet Letter,* the "Five Civilized Tribes"—the Cherokees, Choctaws, Chickasaws, Creeks, and Seminoles—were forcibly removed "from their ancient homeland in the East to present-day Oklahoma" (Hoxie 639). The removal, known as "The Trail of Tears" because thousands died of exposure and smallpox, began in 1831 and continued throughout the decade, although the removal of the Seminoles, who "fought when federal authorities insisted they honor [a] fraudulent treaty," was not completed until 1859, when the "last band of Seminoles were forced westward in chains" (Hoxie 640). By 1850, the year of publication of *The Scarlet Letter,* all land east of the Mississippi, as well as in the states that formed the western borders of that river, had been transferred to the U.S. government (Edmunds 291). These few examples barely touch the extent of the savage and brutal treatment of Native Americans during Hawthorne's lifetime, but which was ignored or considered necessary by most of white America, including Hawthorne. By denying the savagery perpetrated on millions of Indians—and instead projecting savagery onto them—white America could avoid accountability and responsibility.

In the film *The* (New) *Scarlet Letter* the issue of savagery is explored through various namings and manifestations; for example, Thomas Cheever, newly arrived from England, says to Dimmesdale: "So like home. And yet beyond those trees, I suspect a savage land with savage passions, dark and untamed." More significantly, the issue of savagery is focused, as I earlier mentioned, on the character of Roger Prynne/Chillingworth—chillingly portrayed in terms of his most evil potential and worth by Robert Duvall. The film's version of Chillingworth represents the excesses that are implicit in the novel's version of him. Lucy Maddox argues that in the novel, in the Election Day scene, Hawthorne equates Native Americans with the "sun-blackened sailors." According to Maddox, quoting Hawthorne, as

> "wild as were these painted barbarians, [they] were [not] the wildest feature of the scene. This distinction could more justly be claimed by some mariners,—a part of the crew of the vessel from the Spanish Main." . . . These sailors are "the swarthy-cheeked wild men of the ocean, as the Indians were of the land." . . . The very color of the . . . sailors in this scene links them with the dark-skinned Indians in what is apparently for Hawthorne a sinister opposition to the whiteness of Puritan Boston, since the dark physiognomies are an index of the moral nature of both the sailors and the Indians. (122)

Maddox argues further that Hawthorne also links the Indians and sailors with Chillingworth, "whose own complexion has darkened from dusky to black as he has pursued his campaign of revenge against Dimmesdale. . . . Chillingworth has apparently learned two things during his Indian captivity . . . herbal medicine, and the pleasures of revenge" (122–23). Thus, Chillingworth's cold, calculating obsessiveness, his complete lack of compassion, his desire for revenge, and his constant surveillance of Dimmesdale in the novel are characteristics and actions that attempt to contain, even hide, his underlying anger, resentment, bitterness, loss, fear, and desire, and his potential for brutality. All are exposed in the film as physical, rather than only mental, actions, delinking him from Native Americans. It is as though the film literalizes Hawthorne's words: "a terrible fascination, a kind of fierce, . . . necessity seized the old man within its gripe, and never set him free again, until he had done all its bidding" (*SL* 129).

Hawthorne's own fears of becoming isolated—of functioning only in terms of a morbid curiosity and without sympathy, of committing the "unpardonable sin"—are well known. His series of male characters (besides Chillingworth, for example, Hollingsworth, Ethan Brand, Rappaccini, Judge Pyncheon, Westerfelt, Wakefield, Aylmer, the painter in "The Prophetic Pictures," Peter Hovenden, and to a lesser extent Coverdale, Clifford Pyncheon, Holgrave, Kenyon, Reverend Hooper, Young Goodman Brown, Owen Warland, Drowne, Giovanni Guasconti, even Dimmesdale) are, then, exposed as representations of the excesses that threatened Hawthorne, ones that he attempted to theorize and contain, particularly by creating these male characters with sensibilities varying along the spectrum from sympathetic and involved to cold and calculating (see also Amy Louise Reed). The excessiveness of his worries and fears about failures of sympathy and human engagement were perhaps also recognition at some level—certainly not consciously—of the immensity of his, and the rest of white America's, denial of its failure of common humanity, of its ongoing commission of the unpardonable sin in the name of democratic ideals.

Rereading the Film in the Context of Slavery and Witchcraft

The absent presence of slavery in American literature. Containment in relationship to the slavery of Africans was also most severely practiced in canonical American literature, including that written by Hawthorne in the nineteenth century. In seventeenth-century America, the time of

Hawthorne's *The Scarlet Letter*—as well as in Hawthorne's own time—slavery was the legal and social norm. In fact, the first Africans—three of them women—were brought to Jamestown, Virginia, in 1619 and sold as slaves (Davidson and Wagner-Martin 950). In the year of publication of *The Scarlet Letter,* 1850, the Fugitive Slave Act was passed. This act, which confirmed the legal condition of slaves as chattel, allowed slave owners or their representatives to enter free states and seize freed and escaped slaves. Only two years later, Hawthorne's friend Franklin Pierce was elected as president.

> Hawthorne did his share by writing the official campaign biography, in which he extols Pierce as "the statesman of practical sagacity—who loves his country *as it is,* and evolves good from things *as they exist"*—and he defends Pierce's support of the Fugitive Slave Act. (Bercovitch, "Hawthorne's A-Morality" 7).

In the campaign biography, called *Life of Pierce,* Hawthorne explains that slavery is

> one of those evils which divine Providence does not leave to be remedied by human contrivances, but which, in its own good time, by some means impossible to be anticipated, but of the simplest and easiest operation, when all its uses shall have been fulfilled, it causes to vanish like a dream. (qtd. in Bercovitch, "Hawthorne's A-Morality" 8).

As Bercovitch argues, "Only the security of commonplace could allow for this daring inversion in logic, whereby slavery is represented, symbolically, as part of the 'continued miracle' of America's progress. Like the scarlet letter, Hawthorne's argument has the power of a long-preserved cultural artifact" (8).

Yet slavery is never mentioned in Hawthorne's novel, and no slaves or black characters appear, even as shadowy background figures like the Native American characters. As Toni Morrison argues,

> For some time now I have been thinking about the validity or vulnerability of a certain set of assumptions conventionally accepted among literary historians and critics and circulated as "knowledge." This knowledge holds that traditional, canonical American literature is free of, uninformed, and unshaped by the four-hundred-year-old presence of, first, Africans and then African-Americans in the United States. It assumes that this presence—which shaped the body politic, the Constitution, and the entire history of the culture—has had no significant place or consequence in the origin and

development of that culture's literature. Moreover, such knowledge assumes that the characteristics of our national literature emanate from a particular "Americanness" that is separate from and unaccountable to this presence. There seems to be a more or less tacit agreement among literary scholars that, because American literature has been clearly the preserve of white male views, genius, and power, those views, genius, and power are without relationship to and removed from the overwhelming presence of black people in the United States. This agreement is made about a population that preceded every American writer of renown and was, I have come to believe, one of the most furtively radical impinging forces on the country's literature. The contemplation of this black presence is central to any understanding of our national literature and should not be permitted to hover at the margins of the literary imagination. (*Playing* 4–5)

In Joffé's *The* (New) *Scarlet Letter* slavery is made evident in the character of Mituba, a mute slave woman. From the slave narratives by women, as well as the historical, critical, and theoretical work done on them, we have learned that

the institution of slavery subverted and deformed all aspects of black female life in the attempt to colonize the African woman as worker and as producer of workers in a grand experiment of transportation of free labor . . . they were obliged to take on the role of "surrogate men" and to become "breeders." (Scott 814)

Early in the film, after Hester Prynne has *chosen* her land and house on the cliffs overlooking the sea (rather than, as in the novel, forced to live away from the community), she buys the time of two indentured men who can help her clear her land and plant crops. The trader, after insulting Hester Prynne about her gender, offers to "throw in" Mituba as part of the deal. When Prynne objects, saying that Mituba is a slave, the trader explains how she "don't speak, if that be a problem—born that way." Demi's Prynne decides to take Mituba, who is not only mute, but cowering and fearful. Although there is no further direct dialogue about Mituba's condition, the next time we see her, she is no longer cowering or dirty, and, later, we see that she lives in the house with Hester Prynne, both of them sharing the domestic duties, as well as sharing the farming duties with the two indentured male servants. The film, then, seems to be working against another recurrent problem of slavery—that slave women "had no protection and little pity from their mistresses. The slave woman became the scapegoat in the domestic politics of the master" (Scott 816). Whatever the film's partial successes in exposing earlier attempts at containment, as Bercovitch argues, in Hawthorne's *The Scarlet Letter,* "[n]o doubt, the overall tendency is toward evasion" ("Hawthorne's A-Morality" 8) of the issue of slavery.

Female sexuality and desire in relation to Mituba and Hester. In addition to repressing slavery and racial and gender opposition as the shaping force of canonical American literature and its national narratives and characters, that literature—and for my purposes here, specifically Hawthorne's *The Scarlet Letter*—has also repressed female sexuality as feared and desired (and therefore rendered taboo), as I discuss more fully in chapter 4. In the film female sexuality is represented and played out in relation to both Hester and Mituba—once, in a scene I will discuss more fully later, Hester's bathing and mirror scene, and, again, during the love scene between Hester and Arthur. In the first scene, Mituba stands with a container of hot water, prepared, yet afraid, to fill Hester's bathing tub (already part of the community's myth about Hester; one of the women sarcastically says when she hears of the bathing tub: "What is she? French?"). In answer to Mituba's fear, Hester explains that it is only a bathing tub, not a "toy of Satan."

While Hester bathes, Mituba watches through the keyhole, although not voyeuristically. She sees Hester's desire ignited as she thinks of Arthur and examines her own reflection in the mirror. Later, when Dimmesdale and Prynne make love for the first time—after receiving word that Roger Prynne has died during a Tarantine attack on his ship (although his body is not recovered)—Mituba is aware of them in the barn. She uses the time to bathe in the water that she has drawn for Hester. The scene moves between the lovemaking of Hester and Arthur and Mituba's eroticized bath. By using extremely close-in camera shots, Joffé avoids objectification of their bodies and refuses to offer the spectator voyeuristic opportunities and satisfaction, yet he also manages to represent something of female desire and sexuality, both denied by the Puritan society and condemned, misunderstood, or reinscribed as male desire in nineteenth-century America, and ever since.

By showing that Hester's and Mituba's desire and sexuality are similar and strong, Joffé's film also exposes the received belief of slaveholders and citizens throughout the history of slavery in the United States who claimed slave women to be, like Native American women, "savage" and "oversexed"—different from white women. This received belief of course justified slave owners' systematic rapes of slave women, placing the blame for the rapes on the women's sexuality. Joyce Hope Scott adds to this abusive picture:

Generally, slave plantations were structured in such a way as to reflect a type of extended family. The master served as master-father
to his own family as well as to his slaves, with his wife assuming
the role of mistress-mother. Given their precarious positions
within such a "dysfunctional" family, slave women experienced in-
cestuous rape, child abuse, and neglect. (816)

Mituba and Tituba. Mituba's presence in the film calls to mind a particular slave woman, Tituba—

> sold in Barbados to the Reverend Samuel Parris, and brought to
> the American colonies to serve his family. Alleged to have be-
> witched the minister's daughter and his niece, causing the children
> severe fits of hysteria, and initiating the accusations, interroga-
> tions, and executions of the Salem witches, Tituba has become in-
> separably linked with the beginning of this notoriously odious
> chapter of American history. (Dukats 325–26)

Reconstructing Tituba's silenced story, Maryse Condé's first-person
narrative *I, Tituba*

> has inserted extracts from Tituba's official deposition—the one
> safely deposited for posterity in the Essex County Archives in
> Salem, Massachusetts. Ironically, this recontextualization of Titu-
> ba's interrogation and of the words she is recorded as having
> spoken, serves to underscore her voicelessness—her lack of access
> to a voice at the very moment when she is called upon to speak.
> (Dukats 326)

As Dukats says of Condé—that she "allows Tituba a new hearing"
(327)—one could say of this new film version of *The Scarlet Letter,* as it
allows for the visual representation of the muted history of a slave
woman, particularly of one later implicated in witchcraft, as Mituba will
also be. Representing Mituba as mute in the film could, of course, be
read (as some critics have) as evidence of Joffé's further silencing. In my
rereading I see it instead as exposing and depicting the attempts at historical silencing of slave women. It exposes as well attempts by canonical
authors like Hawthorne to contain the significance of slavery and racial
opposition—though repressed and misrecognized by whites—as allowing for the creation of a self-narrative of the (so-called) white race in the
United States. As I argue in my introduction, the space for the creation
of self-narrative of whites in the United States has been in the opposition between their freedom and the enslavement of Africans, and the

space for the creation of the self-narrative of white men has been in the opposition between their public power and women's domesticity and reproductive capacity. That is, without the opposition of the Other, always tautologically defined as the absence of the privileged defined, the privileged defined cannot be defined—nor its narratives told and retold (see introduction). As Dukats argues, quoting from Morrison's *Playing the Dark*, "the Africanist presence has provided the 'arena for the elaboration of the quintessential American identity'" (329)—whatever century has been depicted.

Dukats goes on to say that "*I, Tituba* presents itself as a corrective for historical oblivion" (329). In her novel, Condé incorporates Hester Prynne into the narrative, saying that Hester "enabled [her] to think about the way that her heroine, Tituba, had enabled Hawthorne to produce the 'true beginning of American prose fiction.' Condé thus returns to this canonized 'point of origin . . . in order to reclaim Tituba's part in this origin, and to reaffirm Tituba's presence in what inevitably becomes a 'wider landscape,'" following Morrison (Dukats 331). In *I, Tituba*,

> Tituba strives to follow Hester's recommendations and give the magistrates "their money's worth" . . . describing to them exactly what they believe, even if it has nothing to do with the truth. Hester thus advises Tituba to legitimate the beliefs of her persecutors, and not without good reason, because, by law, the life of a witch was spared if she confessed. By confessing then, Tituba escapes death, yet legitimates the authority of her oppressors. (331)

The opposite occurs in the film for Mituba. After delivering a note to Dimmesdale from Hester and while returning with a note for Hester, Mituba is stopped in the woods by Chillingworth. He slaps at her, verbally tortures her, and then takes her to the Puritan ministers who interrogate her about Hester Prynne's activities and about the presence of the devil—that is, women's sexuality and desire. The interrogation is brutal, motivated by their desire for titillating information, although their self-narrative concerns the discovery and elimination of witchcraft in their community. In fact, they have interpreted all of the community's problems, at the suggestion of Chillingworth—harsh weather, bad crops, Hester Prynne's adultery, threats of Native uprisings—as evidence of witchcraft. Joffé's depictions, however, leave no doubt of the desire and the sexual excitement felt by these ministers as they overpower Mituba until she confesses. Of course, since Mituba is mute, they must interpret her signs, putting words into her mouth, as it were, as they hover over her. One says, "[the devil] made you strip naked before him," and the

other cries out, in obvious excitement, "Totally naked." Finally, Chillingworth stops them as they sweat, pant, and yell (reminiscent of the
Senate committee at the Thomas/Hill hearing).

Mituba later consents to meet Chillingworth when he summons her,
because she wants to undo any damage she might have done to Hester
Prynne and because she is called as a witness against Mistress Hibbins,
known in the film as Harriet Hibbins (played by Joan Plowright), who
is seized as a witch. Chillingworth, however, kills Mituba; her "confession" to Chillingworth and the Puritan ministers ensures her death. The
ministers and magistrates, as well as the community—hysterical by this
point in the witch trial—interpret Mituba's death as further evidence of
witchcraft. The fate of Hibbins is sealed, though, when at that moment
Chillingworth, who knows of Pearl's birthmark on her stomach, exposes
it as a witch-mark—the consequence, he says, of Hibbins's midwifing
at Pearl's birth. As Marjorie Pryse says of the town's interpretation of
Hester in the novel: they "disregard Hester as a symbol of human im-
perfection . . . and view her instead as the actual flaw. She possesses
their 'birthmark,' which must be revealed, in an attempt to erase it in
themselves" (23). Pearl is also marked, becoming the flaw that must be
erased.

Pearl's birth and her mother; Una Hawthorne and her father. In the
film, there is a rather remarkable and lengthy depiction of Pearl's birth
in the prison, where Hester has been held without examination or trial
for five months; this scene functions as another exposure of the excesses
almost contained in the novel. The painful birth in filthy conditions is
attended only by Hibbins, who is both solicitous and efficient; she tells
Hester that she must have a "will of iron." During labor Hester cries out
to ask Harriet if God is punishing her. How simple it has always been
for readers not to consider what Hester must have faced during her imprisonment and childbirth, or any real woman who faced similar circumstances in the Puritan colonies. As Delese Wear explains, "Women,
especially midwives . . . attended deliveries. The patriarchal society,
church, and government, which had assigned strict domestic roles to
women, regarded pregnancy as a private women's matter" (111). Wear
continues,

> [T]he presence of pain during labor represented to men and
> women alike an infliction by God for women's assumed perdition
> and moral frailty. As Cotton Mather's solemn and frightening
> words to expectant mothers suggest, childbirth was a serious tra-
> vail with high infant mortality rates: mother might "need no
> other linnen . . . but a *Winding Sheet,* and have no other chamber

but a *grave,* no neighbors but *worms."* Private writings show an acceptance of pain as punishment and the fear and terror it inspired. (111)

Anne Bradstreet, though, in her poetry shows that the pain of birth "can't be told by tongue." For centuries, even women writers like Anne Bradstreet accepted the supposed sinfulness of sex and the guilt imposed on them by unrelenting patriarchs. (Wear 111)

Although Hawthorne was confined by social values and rules, it is unlikely, given his temperament, fears, sexual guilt, "addict[ion] to passive enjoyment" (Herbert, *Dearest* 123) and intense focus on sensitive, creative, intelligent, fearful, guilty (in other words, super-ego-driven) men like Dimmesdale (like himself) that he would have, even without the social constraints, included the scene of the birth or the sex between Dimmesdale and Prynne that necessarily preceded the pregnancy. In fact, Herbert argues in *Dearest Beloved* that the "Hawthornes' marital relation bears a striking analogy to the adultery portrayed in *The Scarlet Letter*" (115). Herbert also explains that the

> erotics of middle-class purity were inherently precarious, and for the Hawthornes the characteristic tensions were unusually strong, so that Sophia envisions sexuality as an all-but-forbidden fruit of wonderful deliciousness that is available only when the purity of the sexual partners is absolute. . . . Sophia believed Nathaniel as pure as she herself, having a communion like her own with absolute right, which canceled merely private will. . . . Nathaniel's insistence on Sophia's absolute pond-lily purity aided him in overcoming his dread of sexual pollution through her; and her insistence on his 'heavenly health' allayed her own sharp misgivings at the threat of subordination to him, including sexual subordination. (146–48)

With regard to childbirth and children, Herbert notes that for the Hawthornes,

> to contemplate having a baby brought unacknowledged conflicts to a new pitch of intensity. . . . The Hawthornes met the anxieties of parenthood through a massive deployment of their characteristic strategy, sublimating discord into an exaltation of their union. . . . The baby administered a powerful shock to the Hawthorne's relationship, as revealed by Sophia's abrupt announcement that Nathaniel is sending her home to her mother. (150–51)

Although Sophia invented justifications for Nathaniel's desire for her to go home for a fortnight,

[b]oth Sophia and Nathaniel were temporarily confounded, and each ascribed the collapse of their oneness to the other. . . . His letters to Sophia during her absence indicate how acutely he desired a restoration of the exclusive relation he had enjoyed before the child was born. . . . The fusion of contraries that was present in the union of Sophia and Nathaniel was thus focused on their newborn child. Una is made to represent the central tension of her parent's relationship. (152)

Hester Prynne's Pearl is of course based on Una, just as the relationship between Dimmesdale and Prynne reflects Sophia and Nathaniel Hawthorne's.

The time of the writing of *The Scarlet Letter* was further troubled for Hawthorne because of his firing from the Salem Custom-House and the death of his mother: "Nathaniel's mental life was shaken to its foundations by his mother's death. His literary identity, with its fragile aura of sacred privilege, was grounded in a prior selfhood that still bound him to her" (Herbert, *Dearest* 167). When she was dying,

after his sobbing ended, Hawthorne stood at the window . . . "[and] saw . . . Una . . . then I looked at my poor dying mother; and seemed to see the whole of human existence at once . . . Oh what a mockery!" . . . Looking to Una for divine consolation, Nathaniel is startled by glimmers of the fiendlike. Not only does the child speak bluntly of death, but she is also fascinated by the slow failure of his mother's body. Nathaniel is appalled. . . . Returning Nathaniel to the darkest hour he ever lived, Una appeared to him an unaccountable compound of the divine and the demonic . . . carried forward into the writing of *The Scarlet Letter*. . . . In modeling the character of Pearl on Una, Hawthorne sought to make sense of the enigma he saw in her . . . [and] [t]he "hell-fire" in which the book was written had cast its glow on the hearthside of his Salem household. (Herbert, *Dearest* 169–70).

Hawthorne's attempts to control and contain his grief about his mother's death and the loss of his job and family income—as well as his attempts to repress his revulsion about women (including his wife and daughter[s]), marriage, and sex—are also exposed in *The Scarlet Letter* in the excessive exaltedness of the relationship between Hester and Arthur, in the presence of Pearl as devil and daughter, and in the absent presence of sex and childbirth, never mentioned, but always there shaping the narrative.

Rereading the film in the context of women's history. The (New) *Scarlet Letter* also provides us with a site for contestation and debate about other gender issues that remain merely implicit in Hawthorne's text, in the older films and their female stars, in the critics' responses, and in the cultural constructions and views of women. As Roland Joffé, the director, stated, "the book is set in a time when the seeds were sown for the bigotry, sexism, and lack of tolerance we still battle today . . . yet it is often looked at merely as a tale of nineteenth-century moralizing, a treatise against adultery" (qtd. in Ebert)—or, I would add, as a tale of nineteenth-century moralizing, which was far more about social propriety and middle-class manners than moral issues like genocide, removal policies, slavery, and the subjugation of women of all races. In fact, Hawthorne's kind of nineteenth-century moralizing depended on denial of these moral issues. Further, by displacing his moralizing onto his mythical Puritan community, he could escape accountability yet remain complicit, as was discussed earlier.

The film opens up the site of contestation and debate about gender issues and female sexuality and subjectivity through its representation of the male Puritan's community's fear of (but desire for) Hester, and its depictions of rape and sexual abuse, including the legally sanctioned processes by which women were accused of witchcraft, brutally interrogated, and indicted—even killed. Thus, this film allows us to examine how typical social and cinematic constructions of the male and female generate and perpetuate notions of desire and desiring and of the female imago. At the level of narrative content, not only does this new film represent the community's sexual violence directed at Hester Prynne, but also at Mistress Hibbins, at the prostitute Sally Short, at Mary Rollings who was a captive of Native Americans, and at Mituba. By focusing on the persecution of more women than Hester Prynne—and by making fully explicit the hatred and desire directed at her in the punishments she endures—Hawthorne's efforts in his novel to contain Hester's agony and the community's violence are revealed, as well as Hawthorne's primary focus on Dimmesdale's angst-driven, self-tortured, over-determined, over-valued phallus, and on his own nineteenth-century privileged position as a member of various dominant groups, including that of white, educated men. In this film a small community of heretical and ostracized women, which includes Prynne and Hibbins, provides a marked contrast to the male-Puritan-identified women, who (as Hawthorne does show) accuse and persecute out of fear and in order to justify and maintain their own social and religious subject-positions. In the film, it is such a woman, the wife of a minister, who thinks up the punishment of the scarlet A, and (Nancy Reagan–like) whispers her plan into the ear of her husband; she gets his attention first, though, by telling him to release Hester from prison after Pearl is born. She says,

"You don't put her in the prison; you put the prison in her, so that each time someone sets eyes on her, her sin will be marked into her soul afresh." Later, Hester confirms the power of this punishment when she says to Hibbins (who is perhaps based on Ann Hibbins, executed as a witch in Boston in 1656): "I never imagined how cruel and cunning their punishment could be . . . [men] preaching at me in the streets, the people pointing and shouting, even the children, and that horrible drummer boy following me everywhere." In despair, she continues: "I wonder if existence as a woman is worthwhile at all, even for the happiest of women." She pauses, then says, "What if everything I believed so strongly was a lie?"

The film's Hester Prynne, like the male characters and Mituba, can be reread in light of historical incidents, not only in terms of birth statistics and witch trials, persecution, and hangings, but also in terms of education and intellectual work—for example, when Demi's Hester brings books to Arthur, a scene set against their earlier, brief encounter in the town's library. This library is primarily full of tracts, pamphlets, religious treatises, and books on animal husbandry, all of which both Hester and Arthur have read. Hester also displays her knowledge of the Bible, quoting occasionally from it—first, in a scene just after she arrives in the colony, upsetting the ministers who do not allow women publicly to display their knowledge (or even to have it)—and, later, she theorizes its teachings, particularly in the film's scene of the women's gathering at Hester's home.

Anne Hutchinson. In the film, the gatherings in Hester Prynne's home may be based on those held after church by Anne Hutchinson, beginning in 1635 until she was expelled from the Massachusetts Bay Colony in 1637 (see Davis, DeSalvo), unlike Hawthorne's novel in which, as Amy Schrager Lang argues, "Hester Prynne is not the antithesis but the fictional embodiment of a 'fictional' Anne Hutchinson . . . a figure bearing her name, created by the Puritan chroniclers and kept alive by their heirs" (165). Not twice-removed historically from Anne Hutchinson, Demi's Hester further displays her knowledge of the scriptures during her various trials and hearings before the Puritan ministers and governor, just as Anne Hutchinson did when she was tried for heresy and banished from the colony and the church. Hutchinson

> aroused the suspicion of John Winthrop and other political and
> clerical leaders when she began holding "prophesyings" to discuss
> the sermons of her minister, John Cotton. Through these informal
> meetings of lay members of the church, Hutchinson became the
> head of a religious faction that believed in direct revelations from
> God or, in their own terms, "assurance of grace." (Kibbey 410)

Like Demi's Hester, "Hutchinson was vilified as a monstrous threat to public order, the epitome of evil female sexuality unwilling to submit to male authority. . . . The language of Hutchinson's enemies linked female sexuality and antinomianism," as does the film (Kibbey 410). The language of the enemies of women's rights in the nineteenth century linked their fears of women to their laws, social codes, and representations—for example, in their vilifications of the suffrage movement, especially when Elizabeth Cady Stanton and Lucretia Mott rewrote the *Declaration of Independence* as the *Declaration of Sentiments,* calling for social and legal reforms for women, and presented it at the 1848 Women's Rights Convention in Seneca Falls, New York (see earlier discussions of Hawthorne's relationship to Margaret Fuller and to the women's movement).

Mary Rowlandson's story and other captivity narratives by women. In the film, at the gathering at Hester's house—later used as evidence against Hester at her hearing for heresy and adultery—various women speak, including Mary Rollings, a Native captive, who says that the Indians treated her "real fair and square. If truth be told, what's cruel is how you folks have treated me since I come home." Perhaps this character is loosely based on Mary Rowlandson, although it was not until February of 1676 that Rowlandson was taken captive by Metacomet when the Wampanoag burned Lancaster, Massachusetts. Her eleven-week captivity was chronicled in her "principal work, *The Soveraignty and Goodness of God, Together, with the Faithfulness of His Promises Displayed (1682)*" (Amore 770–71). Unlike the film's Mary Rollings's verbal account, captivity narratives, especially early ones, "emphasized God's role in spiritual conversion and deliverance; later ones focused more on woman captives' attempts to cope or to flee through their own wits" (Amore 148). As Amore explains about Mary Rowlandson, she saw

> herself as part of the New Israel's Elect. Thus, when she and her three children were captured . . . she turned to God and the Scriptures for mercy and deliverance. She records events in the same way biblical scholars did, and presents the wilderness as hell and the Indians as kin to Satan . . . her religious sense dominates all she experiences. Throughout her trial, Rowlandson prays for deliverance, and when it is granted through ransom [her husband pays twenty pounds ransom], she sees her freedom as an act of God. (148)

Accounts of captivity were also written and published by other women, for example, Hannah Duston, Susannah Johnson, Elizabeth

Hanson, and Jane Adeline Wilson, although not all followed Rowland-son's tone or shape. And as Amore reminds us, "History fails to provide a clear record of Indian women who were killed, held captive, or suf-fered at the hands of white men" (148–49). Laura Tanner complicates this when she argues that a

> revelation of culture's double standards emerges in Sarah Win-nemucca Hopkins' *Life Among the Piutes* (1883). This Native American perspective on frontier life reveals the Indian woman's fears of rape by white frontiersmen, and thus provides an impor-tant counter to a genre of Indian captivity narratives in which the virtue of white women is repeatedly threatened by the savagery of their captors. (741)

For example, in Hawthorne's essay on Hannah Duston, Lucy Maddox argues that

> by the end of the essay Mrs. Duston and the Indians have changed places: she is the one who is "raging" and "bloody" while the Indi-ans have become a "copper-colored" version of what the Dustons once were, a peacefully sleeping family. Although Hawthorne does not explain *how* the good woman becomes a savage (hence the reader's surprise), the essay does at least suggest that the transfor-mation begins at the moment Mrs. Duston is forced to "follow the Indians into the dark gloom of the forest. . . ." When Mrs. Duston is removed from her domestic place and separated from her hus-band and children, she is simultaneously removed from all the constraints that made her the good woman. Forced to exchange the cottage for the dark forest, she rapidly ceases to be "woman" (since "woman" does not, *by definition,* kill children, even Indian ones) and becomes "hag" or witch, capable of out-Indianing the Indians: they killed one of her children, but she kills six of theirs. Their savagery pales before hers. (118)

In the film, representing such fears of white Puritan women, Goody Hunter says, almost wistfully—and certainly not convincingly, "The thought of being taken by a savage. It makes me sick to my stomach." In fact, in 1639 Mary Mandame was "convicted of a 'dallyance' with a Na-tive American in Plymouth, Massachusetts, and after being whipped, [was] sentenced to wear a badge of shame on her sleeve" (Davidson and Wagner-Martin 950; see also Lydia Marie Child's novel, *Hobomok; Gussman*).

Quaker women and heresy. As history has recorded, the Quakers were persecuted, even killed, with state sanction by the Puritans. In 1656

Quakers first arrived in Massachusetts and were quickly banished. By 1658 there was a death penalty for Quakers that stayed in place until 1661, when Charles II stopped such executions in New England. Mary Dyer, a Quaker woman who was Anne Hutchinson's friend, was imprisoned for preaching in Boston. "She wrote *A Call from Death to Life* (1660), in which she reports her last-minute reprieve from hanging. She continued her preaching, faced a second trial, and was hanged" (Amore 754). Many other Quakers, like Ann Curwen and her husband, were "beaten and imprisoned . . . [for] preaching equality. Curwen defended the right of slaves as well, and demanded they be allowed to attend Quaker meetings" (Amore 754). Hawthorne's relationship to the Quakers can be seen in his story, "The Gentle Boy," in which

> the Quaker woman Catherine allows her religious "fanaticism" to draw her away from her child; the abandoned boy is taken in by a Puritan family, but they cannot protect him from the abuse of other children, who despise him because he is a Quaker. While her child suffers and declines, Catherine continues to "wander on a mistaken errand, neglectful of the holiest trust which can be committed to woman." She leaves the domestic place to wander, physically and intellectually, and the ultimate result is the death of her child. (Maddox 118)

In the film, also present at Hester Prynne's gathering is an unnamed Quaker woman who says, during the women's discussion of the Bible: "We Quakers believe that the scriptures be not religion in themselves, but only the ceremony and history of it." Hester agrees with this description of the scriptures, saying, "For are not the laws of men but the imagination of mortals, and our inner spirit the true voice from Heaven." Her comment is considered blasphemous because it implies that Hester speaks "directly to the Diety," as one woman then queries Hester. In response, Hester admits that she has talked to God since she was a small child, and Hibbins warns her to be careful or "they will be talking of thee the way they talk of me."

During the gathering, the women also use humor, even sexual humor, and offend Goody Hunter so completely that she leaves. Later, it is she who tells the Puritans about Hester's gatherings and her probable pregnancy, and testifies against Hester. At Hester's hearing for heresy and adultery, when one of the ministers says that the kind of talk that has gone on at these gatherings is "what comes when there is no qualified man present to guide these women in their untutored chatterings,"

Hester answers that if the "discourse of women is untutored chattering, why, then, does the Bible tell us that women shall be the teachers of women?" The ministers ask Hester to cease the gatherings, but she refuses, functioning not like Hawthorne's version of Anne Hutchinson, but like the historical Hutchinson.

Mrs. Hopkins, Anne Bradstreet, Mary Oliver, Mary Hammon, and Goodwife Norman. The film's fictional scenes are played out in relationship to many historical moments and figures, including writings such as Governor John Winthrop's 1645 account of "the sad fate of a Mrs. Hopkins, who was driven mad by 'giving herself wholly to reading and writing'" (Perkins, Warhol, and Perkins 8). As a fictional intellectual, Hester Prynne, then, like a real Anne Bradstreet, had "reason to be wary of 'each carping tongue who says my hand a needle better fits'" (qtd. in Perkins, Warhol, and Perkins 8). But like Bradstreet who was "writing poetry within a year of her arrival in the New World and [who] continued to write verse and prose throughout her life" (8), Demi's Hester Prynne refuses to give up her intellectual life or its consequences.

The film's representation of Prynne also evokes Mary Oliver, "Salem's own heretic," eventually banished by William Hathorne (Davis 193). Unlike Hawthorne's novel, in which Hester's intellectualism is turned into a problem and a marker of her loss of femininity, in the film her abilities and knowledge serve her well, not only because they are depicted as partial reasons for the attraction between Hester and Arthur, but also because they allow her to argue her case and to stand up for the other women who are accused of witchcraft. Of course, the more these women logically and wisely present their cases and positions, the more persecuted they become. Because their abilities belie the social constructions of women as lesser than men, the women threaten the attempts at containment at work in those constructions. And like all fictions about women imposed on them by dominant paradigms and social codes, these fictions must be continually protected and shored up, like a dam with holes that must be plugged again and again. It can only be imagined how frightened the Puritans must have been of lesbian sexuality; there is a recorded case of Goodwife Norman and Mary Hammon who were tried for lesbianism in the Massachusetts Bay Colony in 1649. Norman was "forced to make a public confession" and found guilty. Her confession allowed charges to be dropped against sixteen-year-old Mary Hammon. "Norman is believed to be the first women in America convicted of lesbianism" (Swade's Tribal Voice 2; see also Davidson and Wagner-Martin 950).

Arthur suffers; Hester endures. As in the book, Dimmesdale suffers in the film, though not to the same extent. During the film's scene where Mistress Hibbins is captured while hiding in Hester's house and accused of witchcraft, Arthur arrives. Other than the scene in which he stands on the scaffold, rubbing his hands raw against its post, the one in Hester's house is the only other scene in the film in which Arthur is presented as weak and self-flagellating as he is in the novel. As Louise DeSalvo says of the novelistic Dimmesdale:

> [E]ven rendering the character of Dimmesdale as so pathetic, so ineffectual, so self-destructive effectively serves to dim the ferocity of his historical counterparts: it is impossible to read Hawthorne's Dimmesdale and conceptualize the Puritan oligarchy as avenging avatars. . . . And so, in the context of *The Scarlet Letter,* in a fascinating reversal of the facts of history, Dimmesdale, the representative of the Puritan state and Puritan power in the novel, becomes more sinned against than sinning—he is described as the "victim. . . ." Hawthorne, in his revisionist history, thus substitutes a portrait of a male victim for an accurate portrait of a female victim of the Puritan oligarchy. (64; see also my chapter 4)

At Hester's house, just as Hibbins is captured by the Puritan militia, Dimmesdale shows his power and his complicity in the Puritan patriarchy. He asks Hester Prynne why she continues to risk "further anger from the elders." She replies, "Because Mistress Hibbins is no witch, and she has committed no crime beyond speaking her mind." Dimmesdale argues, then, that if "she is innocent, I assure you no harm will befall her." Astounded, Hester responds, "Arthur, after all that has happened, how can you still trust these iron men? Do you not see what is happening. Last night, they took Sally Short in for questioning." She continues her list. Growing defensively angry, Dimmesdale cries out that the elders are "just questioning them. What is the crime in that?" Hester answers that the crime is that "they had done nothing. Do you not see that this is all part of some malevolence. What has become of you?" Arthur begins then a tale of self-pitying woe, shouting at Hester about the hell he is in, ending with "I am a pollution, Woman. I am a lie." Hester says, "*They* are the pollution. *They* are the lie. But you are allowing them to destroy everything that is good in you. What has happened to the man I loved? Does he not still live inside thee?" Arthur then repudiates Hester and their love, saying quietly but with angry passion, "Our love, Woman, was a folly, and that voice we heard . . . we have been justly punished for listening to it." Not content with what he has thus far said to hurt Hester, he looks out the window to see that Hibbins has been captured and turns to Hester, insinuating her complicity with witchcraft by saying, "What have *I* become?" Yet, amidst threats, her first imprisonment, punishment, isolation, brutal words and actions from Roger Prynne, and, finally, Dimmesdale's repudiation, Hester endures. Even after the murder of Mituba and after Hester and Arthur reconcile in a later scene in the forest, where Arthur states his undying love for her and claims Hester and Pearl as his family, Hester endures an attempted rape by a soldier, a witch trial, her second imprisonment, and a verdict of hanging, and grows stronger—and more outspoken. In direct opposition to Hawthorne's Hester, Demi's Hester does not remain silent, except about Arthur Dimmesdale's identity. Throughout this film, he implores her to be silent to avoid incurring the wrath of the Puritan fathers. Each time she answers him with such comments as: "I had to speak out; I couldn't stop myself." And when he asks her how far she will go, she says, "As far as my strength will take me." This new Hester never assumes, guilt, shame, or blame, consistently resisting the Puritans' constructions of women and of her. During the first scaffold scene, she claims, when asked if she believes she has sinned, "I believe I have sinned in your eyes."

The only time Dimmesdale speaks for her or about his relationship to her, she is again on the scaffold, gagged and ready to be hanged, convicted finally of witchcraft, along with Sally Short, Mary Rollings, and Harriet Hibbins. When Arthur confesses to the crowd at that moment, taking the noose from her neck, the crowd calls out for his hanging, and Hester's rope is placed around his neck. At the end of the film, after she, Dimmesdale, and the other women escape their hangings because of the Wampanoag's freeing of the imprisoned "praying Indians," and after Governor Bellingham decides to pardon Hester—allowing her to take off the A, she says, "This letter has served a purpose, but not the one they had intended. So, why would I stay here, to be accepted by them, to be tamed by them?" She leaves, and Dimmesdale finally hops aboard the little cart holding Pearl and their possessions. As they drive away, Pearl drops the scarlet letter on the ground, and the wheels of the cart roll over it. The relationship to the scarlet letter for Demi's Hester is far different from that of Colleen Moore and Lillian Gish, and certainly from that of other actors who have played Prynne, including Gene Gauntier (1911), Mary Martin (1917) and Meg Foster (1979). Thus, even though Joffé's film and Stewart's screenplay could be, and have

been, accused of also romanticizing historical and cultural problems—
and particularly of idealizing the love between Prynne and Dimmesdale—in this film narrative they rewrite Hawthorne's rewriting of history, retold in this film by Pearl in a voice-over (see also Welch).[10]

Some Cinematic Techniques of *The* (New) *Scarlet Letter*

The bathing and mirror scene. Although many of the film's scenes function to destabilize and reread Hawthorne's original narrative, as I have so
far described, many also destabilize the cinematic frame, especially calling attention to those techniques typically used to direct the gaze of the
spectator at women on the screen. One instance of this revisioning occurs in the scene where Demi/Hester gazes at herself in a mirror while
bathing. Typically, the spectator would look at the mirror image of the
female character—that is, look at what she looks at—the mirror-image
of the film's image of her. This gaze is made possible by positioning the
spectator psychically between the camera's gaze and the mirror image. In
this scene, however, the spectator's gaze is directed at Hester looking,
but never into the mirror, never seeing the image she sees; in fact, the
camera is positioned behind the mirror, which mostly blocks the spectator's view of her body. The spectator watches Hester's desire, excited by
her own body and by her memories of Arthur. For most of that scene—
itself interrupted by cuts to Arthur, as she remembers him in certain instances, and to Mituba, who peers through the keyhole—the spectator's
view of Demi/Hester is from her shoulders up. Finally, though, the camera swings to a long upward side shot of her, allowing a quick but gratu-
itous glance at one side of her naked body.

The scaffold scene. Another instance of cinematic revisioning occurs
in one of the only scenes that attempts to follow Hawthorne's text: the
first scaffold scene. As such, this scene disrupts nostalgic memories of
Hawthorne's novel and his constructed reader. In his text, Hawthorne
describes the platform of the pillory on which Hester must stand before
the gathered crowd; he says,

> above it rose the framework of that instrument of discipline, so
> fashioned as to confine the human head in its tight grasp, and thus
> hold it up to public gaze . . . the Governor, and several of his
> counsellors, a judge, a general, and the ministers of the town . . .
> sat or stood in a balcony of the meeting-house, looking down on
> the platform . . . the crowd was somber and grave. The unhappy
> culprit sustained herself as best a woman might, under the heavy
> weight of a thousand unrelenting eyes, all fastened upon her, and

concentered at her bosom . . . she was the most conspicuous object. (55–57)

When Dimmesdale speaks to her in the novel, Hawthorne says, "the eyes of the whole crowd [were] upon the Reverend Mr. Dimmesdale" (66), as he leans over the balcony to speak down to her. The perspective shifts from the crowd to ministers to governor to Hester and finally to Chillingworth who arrives at the edge of the crowd. Consistently, though, Hester is the spectacle on whom all gazes rest. She is positioned between the crowd and the Puritan patriarchs, and all, including the constructed reader, look at her (see chapter 4).

In the film, however, the differences are noticeable: Hester Prynne stands on a platform above the Puritan fathers, who are seated in front of, but below her, yet on the scaffold—as is Dimmesdale. Behind her are other people in the Puritan community, including wives. Most significantly, the camera follows Hester Prynne's gaze. Even when Dimmesdale speaks, he is slightly below her, as though the gaze remains hers. And his back is to the crowd and to the other ministers and governor. Even during one shot when she is captured in his beseeching gaze, the perspective is hers, and the shots of the crowd remain in the context of her looking at them rather than their looking at her. We can even see Pearl's head and the edge of her blanket intruding onto the images of Dimmesdale and the crowd—demonstrating that the camera's gaze is from the Hester's perspective; that is, we sees what she sees. The whole sequence is one of the film's most disruptive uses of a version of the shot-reverse-shot technique, which has generally functioned to objectify the female image. Although Hester Prynne is objectified by the crowd and the Puritan patriarchs, in this scene the camera functions to displace the spectators' voyeuristic and fetishizing gaze.

The (New) Scarlet Letter and Feminist Cinema

Thus, Demi's Hester, as Beverle Houston argues about women characters in other films, "asserts a will to subjecthood" (273). The very different plot, dialogue, and representation of Hester Prynne in this new version of The Scarlet Letter function to interrupt the cultural and discursive hegemony of Hawthorne's novel, without even having to stray from representing the excesses that his novel, his avoidance of the history of the Other, his other texts, and his life attempt to contain. Although I do not want to suggest that The (New) Scarlet Letter functions as what Sandy Flitterman-Lewis calls feminist cinema, I think, as I have said, that it disrupts traditional classical constructions of the male and female spectator (as well as the constructions of the reader of Hawthorne's novel that are already implied in the cinematic constructions). To discover such disruptions, it is necessary to examine the historical and social context of the films and their producers, directors, actors, and viewers, as well as examine, as Flitterman-Lewis urges, the entire cinematic apparatus, what she describes as "its functioning, and its specific determinations for figuring female sexuality. This apparatus," she argues, "is designed to produce and maintain a fascinating hold on the spectator by mobilizing pleasure—the unconscious desire of the subject—through interlocking systems of narrativity, continuity, point of view, and identification. But it is not simply an individualized and self-contained process . . . [because of] the social inscription of the cinema," what Christian Metz has called its "'dual kinship' with the psychic life of the spectator" (Flitterman-Lewis 3). *The* (New) *Scarlet Letter,* then, I am claiming, demobilizes the pleasure of the look and destabilizes the point of view of the novel and of the classic film versions of *The Scarlet Letter.* Thus, what E. Ann Kaplan has called "historical spectators" come to this new film with layers of expectations generated by the novel and by earlier films, and find themselves unseated, so to speak, by the deconstructing of the "hypothetical" spectator-position, and without the means to control and consume this film-product. Further following Kaplan, the "contemporary female spectator whose reading of the film might be inflected by a female consciousness" may not be unseated, but instead resituated by this disruption of classic cinematic techniques (Flitterman-Lewis on Kaplan 9).

Not surprisingly, the film has been soundly rejected by unseated academics, film critics, and in their wake, the general viewing public. Although the film manages to expose the excesses of barbarism, savagery (not in the Native Americans but in the Puritans), slavery, violence, witchcraft trials, and a profound fear and hatred of, but desire for, women (Hester-Prynne-ism), the critical commentary and academic response has attempted to recontain them. The success of these efforts can be seen in the loss of acclaim and revenue (only $10.3 million). Roland Joffé's (New) *Scarlet Letter* has been named a failure. Demi Moore has been refetishized, carrying on her body the scarlet mark of the woman. Hester-Prynne-ism prevails, and Hester Prynne is in her place once again, as the spectacle, the image, not the bearer or maker of the gaze (Mulvey 62–63).

6

Conclusion: Implications of Hester-Prynne-ism and ReReading Women

*B*ourdieu and others have explained that a field, such as literary studies, is a "dynamic concept in that a change in agents' positions necessarily entails a change in the field's structure" (6). Although the women's scholarship discussed in this book has inevitably affected, even disrupted, the sub-field of Hawthorne studies—just as women's and feminist scholarship have inevitably marked the patriarchally structured field of literary studies—these disruptions and markings, as I have argued, have necessitated the closing of ranks in mainstream scholarship, rather than changing the structure and logic of the field of literary studies enough to include or engage with the Other, or even acknowledging their agency. The closed ranks are exposed in part by the pretenses about the lack of quality in women's work and the fear-based perceptions and myths about takeover by women and minorities. This process allows for continuing exclusion while simultaneously claiming progress and inclusion. Such excessive attempts to contain the dynamic, the shifts in agents' positionings, and the consequent (and constant) restructuring of habitus and field, when exposed, acknowledged, recontextualized, and reread, as I have done throughout this book, cause further markings and disruptions.

For example, the social and psychic construct of Hester-Prynne-ism—which I have defined, explained, and demonstrated as it has played out in literature, other print media, drama, film, television, courtrooms, schoolrooms, and academe, as well as in daily life—can be shown as a construct and logic, then re-exposed as it continues, even increases, its own production as more women-as-agents enter the field and sub-fields of literary studies and as more women-as-agents disrupt other cultural fields. The problematic of the originary exclusion is further exposed by the excessiveness of the attempts to contain the disruptions. In other words, although women-as-agents within the field of literary studies inevitably disrupt the structures of the field, Hester-Prynne-ism continues because part of the structure of that field is its own internal logic of self-defining and self-narrativizing as the binary opposite of the (con-structed) Other, as well as the exclusion inherent in such logic. Thus, any alterations in the field and the agency such activity engenders can be at least partially hidden from view within the field or sub-field, or it can be publicly devalued inside a set of standards that inevitably exclude it, or inside a construct like Hester-Prynne-ism. Those few women who are granted inclusion as tokens can be set in competition with other women.

Already Othered rereaders who expose such logic (and its conse-quences), as well as the agency of the agents, are constantly reposition-ing themselves within the field, and thus causing even further disrup-tions and exposures (which necessitate further closing of ranks and protection of the turf of the field). For example, in a rereading like mine, the significance and logic of symbolic capital becomes apparent rather than hidden—"[the] degree of accumulated prestige, celebrity, consecra-tion of honour . . . founded on a dialectic of knowledge . . . and recog-nition"—as does the "competition for control of the interests or re-sources which are specific to the [literary studies] field" (Bourdieu 7).[1] We can begin to see, as an example, that our academic star system, which grants some women great celebrity status—as a consequence of their symbolic capital in the form of certain numbers of published arti-cles and books—can be reread and critiqued as a symptom of the patri-archally structured field of literary scholarship, which maintains itself by co-opting women and by proclaiming itself as radical and progressive (see also Nelson and Shumway). This star system, as it co-opts women and feminists, creates further divisions between women and creates an illusion of a kind of change or alteration within the field that instead is merely an adjustment that keeps the logic of the field intact. That is, gaining a position as a star in the field of literary studies offers the illu-sion of equality, and the field itself appears to be inclusive, radical, pro-gressive, and, most significantly inside my rereading, appears to be af-fected, even changed by women and their work. Offering the star position to some women and feminists makes it seem as though *any* woman could achieve such status if only she would work hard enough and were good enough. Just as insidiously, some women and feminists who have achieved star status have begun to function in terms of this patriarchal logic, turning their backs to other women who continue the struggles without possibility of (or desire for) star status.

As a consequence of my rereadings—and others that are suggested by mine—I am not therefore simply arguing for the inclusion of women in the body of scholarship on *The Scarlet Letter* or in other bodies of scholarship within the field of literary studies, for unproblematic inclusions (like women in the star system) only keep the model and its power and practices intact, as I have suggested. Women's scholarship must continue to destabilize and disrupt the body(ies) of scholarship so that it presses us all to examine academic and cultural assumptions and practices that objectify, exclude, or nominalize the Other. Rather than call for women to exercise the power that men have traditionally held, I urge instead that power be continuously reread and critiqued, because, as I have discussed above, the fields and sub-fields function dynamically, constantly shifting to accommodate, include/exclude, and reposition agents, as well as the definitions of agency. Continuous rereading is necessary, as I have been arguing, because the dynamic "nature" of fields is not as dynamic as some culture studies and social scientific analyses have claimed. That dynamic is always already located in and potentially contained by the structuring structures. Thus, agents within a field have already internalized its logic and can be trapped within its codes and grids, as Luce Irigaray has cautioned us against. Put in other words, the dynamic possibility can be as insidious and problematic as the structure and its capacities to continue structuring institutions, ideas, and individuals, but without the dynamic (and the rereadings) there would be no possibility of agency and change.

Therefore, while recommending that we eschew Hawthorne and Hester Prynne as radical models in the late twentieth century, and while urging that we examine the dynamic of change, I do not recommend the elimination of Hawthorne, *The Scarlet Letter,* and Hester Prynne—or new versions of Prynne—as subjects of study. Neither do I call for the elimination of canonical texts in other sub-fields of literary studies, nor for the elimination of the body of male mainstream scholarship in Hawthorne studies as a sub-field or in the larger field of literary studies. All these texts/contexts must continue to be reread. Hawthorne scholarship has, through its exclusions and often intimidating and silencing impositions, exposed the excessive fears that these exclusions and impositions have attempted to hide. When such texts/contexts are continuously recontextualized and reread, they become sites where identity, agency, and power dynamics are contested, and where differences are allowed to emerge, rather than already claimed territory where identities of the Other can be rigidly constructed and maintained by the dominant group.

We can begin to reread and rethink our way to new conditions and circumstances that might make literary criticism and scholarship function differently: including rather than excluding (and then actually engaging with the included voices); allowing for an "explicit and implicit interplay of . . . voices" (Bauer 671); and rereading and recontextualizing ourselves as critics as well as the authors and texts/contexts we study. I believe that we cannot prosper or claim change, alteration, and progress if we continue to function in terms of Othering and that literary scholarship ought to represent the diversity of people who work together under its rubric. If we recognize the kind of professional and intellectual impoverishment that occurs when there is a refusal to engage with the Other, then mainstream literary criticism, like that on *The Scarlet Letter,* will experience various immeasurable and as yet unknown gains.

Notes

Bibliography

Index

Notes

1. Introduction: Self-Defining Narratives and the Racial and Gendered Other

1. Bourdieu defines "habitus" as

> durable, transposable dispositions, structured structures predisposed to function as structuring structures, that is, as principles which generate and organize practices and representations that can be objectively adapted to their outcomes without presupposing a conscious aiming at ends or an express mastery of the operations necessary in order to attain them. Objectively "regulated" and "regular" without being in any way the product of obedience to rules, they can be collectively orchestrated without being the product of the organizing action of a conductor. (5)

Randal Johnson further explains,

> The habitus is sometimes described as a "feel for the game," a "practical sense" . . . that inclines agents to act and react in specific situations in a manner that is not always calculated and that is not simply a question of conscious obedience to rules. Rather, it is a set of dispositions which generates practices and perceptions. The habitus is the result of a long process of inculcation, beginning in early childhood, which becomes a "second sense" or a second nature. According to Bourdieu's definition, the dispositions represented by the habitus are "durable" in that they last through an agent's lifetime. They are "transposable" in that they may generate practices in multiple and diverse fields of activity, and they are "structured structures" in that they inevitably incorporate the objective social conditions of their inculcation. (5)

2. Randal Johnson explains,

> Bourdieu's theory of the cultural field might be characterized as a radical contextualization. It takes into consideration not only works themselves, seen relationally within the space of available possibilities, but also producers of works in terms of their strategies and trajectories, based on their individual and class habitus, as well as their objective position within the field. It also entails an analysis

of the structure of the field itself, which includes the positions occupied by producers . . . as well as those occupied by all the instances of consecration and legitimation which make cultural
products what they are. . . . Finally, it involves an analysis of the
position of the field within the broader field of power. (9)

I am focusing specifically on raced and gendered aspects of habitus and
of symbolic positionings as constructed and perpetuated within the field
of literary studies, as well as its relation to other fields of artistic production and analysis—for example, film and film studies—and the positionings and functionings of these fields "within the broader field of
power," which is inevitably classed, gendered, and raced.

2. What's Black and White and Red/Read All Over? Hester-Prynne-ism

1. For example, in 1979, Hyatt Waggoner proclaimed Hester Prynne
as the "first great tragic heroine in American fiction" (*Presence* 121). In
1980, Davitt Bell saw Hester as "[v]ital, passionate, [and] imaginative"
(*Development* 176). In 1981, Larzer Ziff described Hester Prynne as
"Hawthorne's greatest creation—a splendid, free individual who coura-
geously allows into her field of comprehension all the complexities that
life presents to her" (120). In 1982, Eric Mottram called Hester "a new
social power in a tired and hesitant community" (197). In 1983, David
Leverenz argued for Hester's "radical feminism" ("Mrs. Hawthorne"
557). In 1985, Donald Griener wondered "if Hester's adultery is not an
act of affirmation in an atmosphere of sterility. She creates while her accusers negate, and the result is that the first great adulteress in American
literature is also the first great artist figure" (60). In 1986, Nina Baym
called Hester "the first true heroine of American fiction" (*TSL: A Reading* 62). In 1988, David Reynolds described Hester Prynne as the "quintessential American heroine, reflecting virtually every facet of the antebellum woman's experience" (373). In 1990, Sam Girgus argued that
the "world [Hester] represents . . . offers an alternative to patriarchal
power" (*Desire* 67). In 1990, Harold Bloom called Hester Prynne "the
most representative fictive portrait of an American woman" (*Hester
Prynne* 2). In 1991, Charles Swann reacted to Hester Prynne as "gen-
uinely subversive in that she desires and prophesies a radical subversion
of the patriarchal structures of the society and, most significantly, of
the religion that legitimates that patriarchy" (90–91). For earlier views
on Hester, see, for example, Munger, Sherman, Carpenter, Abel, Van

Doren, Stein, Bewley—all collected in Gross's *Handbook;* see also Howells, Michaud, Rahv, Howe.

2. For example, Larzer Ziff claims (1981) that Hester Prynne and Hawthorne "conceive of a freedom beyond political rights" (121), and Brodhead describes Hawthorne's radicalism (1986) as "recognition of the inextricableness (imaged in [Hester's] letter) of subversion from the authority that calls forth subversion, of freedom from the law whose breaking creates freedom's possibility, of imaginative creation from the restricting conventions that allow such creation to be" (*School* 44). Zelda Bronstein argues (1987) for recognizing the "political motives" of *The Scarlet Letter* (194) and Robert Shulman for seeing Hawthorne in "crucial ways at odds with . . . American market society . . . [with] an intense intuition of the individualistic sources from which a new kinds of social union might develop" (176, 194). Robert Levine says (1989) that "[r]evolution so unnerved Hawthorne because he was imaginatively responsive to it" (161). Robert K. Martin claims (1990) that it "is in Hester's voice . . . that Hawthorne speaks as a revolutionary" (128). And, Emily Miller Budick has recently claimed (1992) that "Hawthorne's words place him, as the letter does Hester, in a richly aversive relation with America" ("Sacvan" 89).

3. Shumway notes, "The New Americanists do include some feminists, and the term does not necessarily exclude African Americanists or students of other countertraditions, but those most clearly identified with the 'movement' have focused on the established tradition" (*Creating* 387, 13n).

4. Sacvan Bercovitch, however, has recognized the problems of a radicalism based on such notions of individualism; see especially *The Office of the Scarlet Letter* 31, 120–21.

5. In a 1993 issue of *Academe,* Maureen Ryan, a dean of an honors college and an associate professor of English, explains the relationship of the academy to feminist scholarship and narratives, and argues that feminist criticism continues to be dismissed as critics continue, as in the past, to assume feminist scholarship is

> trendy or political. Some years before the publication of my book on American novelist and short story writer Jean Stafford, one of the most distinguished scholarly journals in the field of American literature rejected an article I wrote on Stafford with the assessment that she was not an important writer. Tenure committees have been known to dismiss a scholar's published work with a snide comment: "Sure, she published a lot, but it's on women's stuff." (23)

I am arguing that women's scholarship, whether feminist or not, *contin-ues* to be disregarded.

6. Many women have argued that Hester Prynne's return to Boston at the end of the text, her resumption of the wearing of the scarlet A, and her recognition that she is not "fit" to be the spokeswoman of change for women is evidence of Hawthorne's nonradical relationship to his character and to feminist issues of his time. Many have more gener-ally critiqued Prynne as a female representation, taking her creator to task for his male fantasizing about a strong woman whom he will later subdue completely. See chapter 4.

7. Against Miller Budick's reading of power in Hester Prynne's si-lence ("Sacvan Bercovitch" 86–88) I would argue that, if the silence of the oppressed is the response desired by the social order—and by its com-plicit constituency, then silence cannot function as a subversive, disrup-tive means to the ends of social justice and change. Silence is the logic of Hester Prynne. As Marjorie Pryse explains, "Hester has been given the power to tell her accusers who they are" (26); then, Hawthorne denies it to her. The previously ignored, silenced and marginalized "others" who are "noisily" disrupting the academy and the culture, foregrounding the sites and instances of oppression, have (fortunately) created discomfort, like Anita Hill, who said, "I could not keep silent." This noise has forced some academic and cultural self-reflexivity, though it is more often fol-lowed by defensive entrenchment than by change; Clarence Thomas *is* a Supreme Court justice, Lani Guinier *was* not allowed to speak before a Senate committee, and Joycelyn Elders *was* fired.

8. Michael Dunne reports in his essay "*The Scarlet Letter* on Film: Ninety Years of Revisioning" that Julian Smith says "there were at least five silent screen adaptations of *The Scarlet Letter* 'stretching back to 1904' (108). Little documentation exists about the first three adapta-tions" (31).

9. Although the academy in the United States has made claims that hirings of minorities have resulted in numbers great enough to be threat-ening, the statistics show that quite the opposite is true; especially inac-curate is the mythical claims that there have been "disproportionate gains [made] by minority women" (Chamberlain 50). As Marie Bun-combe argues in the *CLA Journal,* "in the past ten years, gains . . . in the populations of black college students and faculty on all campuses have steadily eroded" (5). From 1975 to 1983, minority women made slight gains in numbers of hirings, moving from 11 percent to 11.5 percent in eight years. As minimal as their gains were, however, they were "much smaller than those of minority males. . . . [Moreover,] [a]ll of the gains

made by minority women were made by nonblack majorities" (Chamberlain 54). In fact, the numbers of African-American women on faculties declined from 1979 to 1989—from 2.0 percent to 1.9 percent (*Black Issues in Higher Education* 36). Statistics from 1991 show that only 2.5 percent of all faculty positions in all fields at all institutions in the United States are held by black women, up from 2.1 percent in 1989, but almost the same as the 1979 rate of 2.0 percent. At doctoral granting institutions, only 1.6 percent of full-time faculty positions were held by black women in 1991. The percentage of African-American women with full-time administrative positions in institutions of higher education was 4.2 percent in 1989. Moreover, of all the U.S. doctorates award from 1958 through 1990, only 1.95 percent were awarded to black men and women. In the specific discipline of English and American languages and literature, African-Americans received 1.6 percent of all doctorates in 1989. "Minority women . . . made little progress at the graduate level. The fact that they are collecting a larger share of the graduate degrees going to minorities merely indicates that the share going to minorities must be declining" (*BIHE* 36–37; Chamberlain 47, 55–57; "American College Teacher"; "Investment in Human Potential"). Yolanda Moses reports that "[b]etween 1977 and 1986, the number of Blacks earning doctorates declined by 27 percent. Experts foresee severe shortages of minority faculty members for years to come" (13). She also notes that "Blacks in general have the lowest faculty progression, retention, and tenure rates in academe, with Black women most concentrated in the lower academic ranks. Black women faculty members are also concentrated in two- and four-year college and universities (including historically Black schools) rather than in research universities" (13).

10. Nellie McKay argues that "[t]oday, I and many of the black women . . . have scaled several resisting walls, and we have lasting scars to prove our efforts. Racism, sexism, and classism are unrelenting adversaries. No skirmish is minor. Each is a major confrontation with powerful forces of tradition, and there is always a price to pay for having been there" ("Troubled Peace" 29). Getting tenure, even recognition outside the walls of any single institution, does not change the problematic lived experience of black women. As McKay explains,

> By virtue of our new standing, some of us thought (and such thoughts were very unsettling) we had become a part of "them," that having fulfilled the requirements of the game as they defined it we now shared their legitimacy. Our discomfiture, however, was hardly warranted. We soon realized that although our status vis-a-vis such things as job security had altered appreciably, we were still

excluded from the centers of power vested in the premises of white maleness. . . . Student counseling, academic as well as on psychologically crisis-oriented issues, even for white students, continually appear on the doorstep of the black mother, the great bosom of the world. . . . In addition to work expectations of them, black women faculty often find themselves bearing the brunt of jokes and other over ethnic and gender insensitivities of their colleagues, which does little to enhance their comfort levels among their peers. (29, 35)

bell hooks describes an even more debilitating response to her tenure process; she says that prior to the tenure vote, she "was haunted by dreams of running away—of disappearing—yes, even of dying. These dreams were not a response to fear that I would not be granted tenure. They were a response to the reality that I would be granted tenure. I was afraid that I would be trapped in the academy forever" (*Teaching to Transgress* 1). Yolanda Moses has also articulated concerns about black women in the academy:

Black women not only experience the effects of racism but also those of sexism. . . . Black women may be ignored, isolated, or passed over in favor of less qualified people for promotions. . . . In high education . . . [t]he small number of people from other ethnic or racial groups are often seen by the dominant group to be "tokens" and are thus treated as representatives of their group or as symbols rather than individuals. . . . Black women are often asked to sit on committees as experts on Blacks, and they are asked to solve problems or handle situations having to do with racial difficulties that should be dealt with by others. There is often no reward for this extra work; in fact, Black women may be at a disadvantage when they are eligible for promotion or tenure because so much of their time has been taken up with administrative assignments. (14–15)

11. My description of Hester-Prynne-ism and some of its consequences is not a claim for an essential, shared women's experience; instead, I am trying to show that the culture and the academy often *impose* such totalizing judgments and attitudes *onto* women, which then affects their lived experience. How it specifically affects individual women's experience is not totalized or even predictable. In other words, it can affect different women in different ways and appear more consequential, threatening, limiting, and oppressive to some women than to others. Such differences in response, however, do not negate or eliminate the cultural phenomenon.

12. For example, in the past few years, many anthologies of American women writers, previously unknown or profoundly miscontextualized, have been published. Yet courses that focus on women are often viewed as special, one-time courses or strictly as part of a women's studies curriculum, not part of the mainstream departmental requirements. Courses on black women authors, such as Toni Morrison, are even more apt to be categorized as "special" courses, and her texts, such as *Beloved*, are certainly not part of most American literary survey courses. Kate Chopin's *The Awakening*, for example, remains only the thirty-seventh most-often taught text in American literary courses. When restructuring of the curriculum has occurred in order to include the perspectives of the Other,

> [n]owhere have these modifications been undertaken without significant opposition. The Ford Foundation estimates that in almost 40 percent of the universities that have initiated such revisions, faculty and/or administrators have resisted efforts to balance the curriculum. The recent debate at Stanford University over whether and how to expose students to the experiences and perspectives of women, African-Americans, and other minorities was so controversial and so protracted that it became national news. . . . [A] 1991 Modern Language Association study affirms that "English professors still rely heavily on traditional texts." (Ryan 24–25; see also Lauter)

Perhaps, women writers, particularly black women writers, are not consistently taught or integrated into curricular requirements, despite mythical claims to the contrary, because they challenge the fundamental ways that academics have thought about history and culture, as well as about literary conventions and literary history. The historical and cultural self-narrative of the United States and of the academy cannot admit the version of history articulated in, for example, *Beloved*, without calling into question—actually, without significantly undermining—their own self-definitions and self-narratives. I say this because history, as we know it, has always privileged the intentions of the victimizers (even our laws privilege their intentions and rights)—or in the case of literary studies, has privileged the intentions of canonical authors and mainstream scholars and critics. As Karla Holloway argues about *Beloved*, it

> proposes a paradigm for history that privileges the vision of its victims. . . . This is a critical posture for this novel to assume because slavery placed black women outside of the universe governed by the measure of history. Instead, the aspect of their being—the

quality, nature, and presence of their state of being—becomes the
appropriate measure of their reality. (169)

13. This claim has seemed easily repeatable, often not examined or
analyzed—see note 1. The consequence of this relentless claim and
focus (and set of unacknowledged assumptions) is that women's expressions of their experiences and their metaphorical representations of that
experience—their female fictional characters—are still not widely accepted or examined, despite such analyses as Louise DeSalvo's when she
says that "[r]eading Hawthorne's work within the context of a woman's
tradition, which reached the peak of its success by the end of the 1850s,
and which included within its ranks women novelists like Catherine
Maria Sedgwick and Caroline Lee Hinz, provides the feminist critic with
an opportunity to explore the impact of the women's tradition upon a
male writer, an influence that is customarily ignored" (14)—and despite
such work as Judith Fetterley's and Marjorie Pryse's *American Women
Regionalists, 1850–1910* (1992), Betsy Erkkila's *The Wicked Sisters*
(1992), Elizabeth Ammons's *Conflicting Stories: American Women Writers
at the Turn Into the Twentieth Century* (1991), Elaine Showalter's *Sister's
Choice* (1991), *Women on Women: An Anthology of American Lesbian
Short Fiction* (1990), Cathy Davidson's *Revolution and the Word* (1986),
Ellen Moers's *Literary Women* (1976), and Nina Baym's *Women's Fiction:
A Guide to Novels By and About Women in America, 1820–1870* (1978),
followed by essays reflecting Baym's "enlarged understanding of Ameri-
can women's literary discourse before the Civil War" (see *Feminism and
American Literary History,* Part II), and despite compelling arguments
made by critics like Baym in *Novels, Readers, and Reviewers* (1984) and
Jane Tompkins in *Sensational Designs* (1985). (See also *Women's Work,
Nine Short Novels by American Women, Home Girls: A Black Feminist
Anthology.*) When women's writing has been extensively surveyed—for
example, in David Reynolds's text, *Beneath the American Renaissance*
(1988)—that writing has been relegated (again) to secondary status
because the examination of it occurs inside the context of previously
agreed upon standards that in their genesis and practice already devalue
the women's texts under consideration. As Estelle Dansereau describes
such problems in *Gender Bias in Scholarship:* "Critics especially have
contributed towards silencing women by failing to recognize that [crit-
ics] generally criticize with sex-biased literary standards" (46). Reynolds
argues that the "classic" American authors were fully aware of theses
"popular" women writers and, in fact, incorporated their issues, concerns, genre conventions, and characterizations into their own novels.

Predictably, though, his conclusions is that these classic authors just did it better. (See Douglas, Earnest; see also Katharine Bates, *American Literature* [1897], for an early extensive survey of women writers.)

14. To refute this mythical received belief, even a sampling of seventy of the essays by women shows that they were published by respectable, even prominent journals in literary studies and in Hawthorne studies. Prominent university presses and major publishing houses have also published the books of the majority of the women who authored or coauthored texts that include work on *The Scarlet Letter* (see the listing of women's scholarship on *The Scarlet Letter*, a section in the bibliography). Using patriarchal logic, the question becomes: If these women deserved to be ignored, trivialized, appropriated, and marginalized, then why did these "good," even "best" journals and presses publish their essays and books? Using one kind of feminist logic, the answer to the questions seems more likely to be that after these women were published, mainstream scholarship paid them little or no attention—either failed or refused to engage with their arguments and ideas, or even to quote, note, or cite them.

3. The Scarlet Snub

1. In this same collection Michael Davitt Bell includes only Baym and Q. D. Leavis. In Colacurcio's own essay in the collection, he quotes no women's scholarship but notes Marion Kesselring, Judith Armstrong, and Ann Douglas. His collection does offer one essay by a woman, Carol Bensick, and the bibliography for the collection includes, in addition to Baym, Millicent Bell, Elaine Hansen, and Anne Marie McNamara.

2. According to *Lingua Franca*'s "Jobtracks 1990" (Feb. 1991), 193 men and 168 women were hired for jobs in English, reflecting an upswing in the number of hirings of women (38–41), but Susan Faludi reported in 1991 that only 10 percent of the tenured faculty at "all four year institutions" in this country are women, and only 3–4 percent of all tenured faculty at Ivy League colleges are women, "a rise of only 6 percent from the 1960s. Five times more women with Ph.D.'s are employed than men . . . only twelve women's studies chairs exist nationwide." Moreover, a

> census taken of the roughly fifteen hundred articles published annually in journals of history, literature, education, philosophy, and anthropology found that only 7.4 percent of them dealt with women or women's issues, a tiny 5 percent increase from the 1960s. . . . [I]n . . . philosophy, the proportion of women's issues

articles was the tiniest of all, 2.7 percent—... actually declin[ing]
from a 1974 "peak" of 5.4 percent. (293)

The rates for tenuring are almost the same for white and black women:
slightly more than half of those women who are hired on tenure-track
lines are actually tenured. Less than a percentage point separates the
tenuring rates of white and black women. To give this more of a context
for analysis, almost three-fourths of white men on tenure-track lines receive tenure. The rates for tenuring black and white women have barely
changed since 1979, when slightly more than half were receiving tenure;
in fact, for white women the rate of tenuring has remained stable (and
low) since 1983 (*BIHE* 36–37). Nellie McKay confirms the problematic consequences of such tenuring statistics when she says, "there can
be little question that in the present-day academy tenure is the hardest
test that everyone faces in the pursuit of an academic career" ("Troubled
Peace" 25). And, of course, she recognizes the test is greater for African-
American women, saying, in fact, that "in the white academy our loca-
tion is always contested spaces even though it is as rightfully our space
as that of others there" (28). The Modern Language Association reports
that

> 63% of the total growth in faculty numbers between 1970 and
> 1985 was due to increases in the number of part-time employees
> ... figures suggest that these employees are disproportionately
> likely to be women. ... By 1987, women accounted for almost
> half of the assistant professors in English. ... Women's gains were
> less dramatic at the full-professor level. ... [W]omen at this rank
> appear to be as disadvantaged vis-a-vis men in 1987 as they were
> in 1977. ... [T]hroughout the 1980s [women] were disadvan-
> taged at every post-PhD career stage. ... In 1979 women with
> PhDs in all humanities fields, as well as in the modern languages,
> were less likely than men to be employed by academic institu-
> tions. This difference persisted ... even though the percentage of
> women with academic employment increased. ... The percent-
> age of academically employed with tenure-track appointments
> decreased somewhat for both men and women between 1979 and
> 1987, but it decreased more for women than for men. As a result,
> men's percentage of tenure-track appointees exceeded women's by
> more in 1987 than it had in 1979. ... [In] 1987 ... approxi-
> mately 1 in 5 women PhDs served in a non-tenure-track posi-
> tion, compared with less than 1 in 14 men. ... [Moreover,] the
> percentage of tenure-track appointees with tenure is higher for
> men than for women. (Huber 60–66).

Martha West confirms this discouraging picture for all women faculty in all fields, arguing, in *Academe* (1995), that the "situation is getting worse":

> [I]t should be no surprise that an increasing percentage of women are found in the . . . less secure ranks of instructor and lecturer. In fact, the percentage of women among those classified as full-time instructors keeps increasing, from 52 percent in 1983 to 59 percent in 1994–95. . . . [O]nce women are successful in obtaining faculty positions, they continue to be paid lower salaries than men at the same ranks. These discrepant salary figures also seem frozen in time. From 1982 to 1995 there has been virtually *no improvement* in the relationship between men's and women's salaries. . . . This gap [between the percentage of women earning PhDs and the percentage of women faculty] has almost doubled over a ten-year period . . . from an 8 percent difference to a 16 percent difference. . . . Where are all the women recently earning PhD's going? Not into the tenured ranks. One of the most shocking set of statistics are on the percentage of women full-time faculty who have tenure. In 1975, 46 percent of women in full-time teaching in higher education had tenure. In 1992, this number was *exactly* the same: 46 percent. In the late 1970s this percentage had increased, reaching 48 percent in 1982, but it declined again from 1983 to 1992. . . . In contrast to women, men have consistently improved their tenure rates over the same time period: 64 percent of faculty men had tenure in 1975, 70 percent in 1982, and now 72 percent in 1994–95. While women's tenure rates show a net increased of only 1.5 percent over twenty years, men's rates have increased 8 percent. (27)

Overall hiring statistics show that "only 34% of those receiving English PhD's in 1996–97 found tenure-track positions within the year they received their degrees" (Laurence and Welles 6).

4. The Scarlet Woman and the Mob of Scribbling Scholars

1. Nina Auerbach, however, reads this scene as Hester Prynne's "majestic presence . . . [which] diminishes the gaping spectators that include the reader of the story" ("Woman" 165), and Rita Gollin argues that the scaffold "becomes neutral territory" as Hester's reveries are foregrounded: "The reader approaching Hester through her inner consciousness necessarily sympathizes with her" (*NH and the Truth of Dreams* 142–43). Carolyn Heilbrun claims that "no American literary character (if we exclude the characters of Henry James . . .) has so much

as touched the hem of [Hester's] gown, or drawn any inspiration from
her" (66–67), and Constance Rourke says that "In *The Scarlet Letter* a
woman was drawn as a full and living figure for the first time in American
literature" (189). Gloria Erlich sees Hester as fusing all of Hawthorne's
"early female images" (*Family Themes* 98) and "sharing her wisdom with
the coming generation" as a justification of "her life and sufferings" (32).
Jane Lundblad says that Hester "becomes, in spite of the red letter, a
generally esteemed woman . . . the reader may possibly feel tempted to
discern a faint halo around her saint-like head" (*Nathaniel Hawthorne
and the Tradition of Gothic Romance* 57). Carol Pearson and Katherine
Pope also celebrate Hester Prynne, seeing Hawthorne's *The Scarlet Letter*
as "document[ing] women's revolutionary courage to risk change, and
thus provid[ing] us with a positive alternative to social norms, similar
to those we find in the diaries and autobiographies and real lives of
women" (7)—as does Lois Cuddy who argues that "Hawthorne was
able to transcend his personal limitations in this novel" (114); she also
says that "[i]t is a delightful irony that an author like Nathaniel Hawthorne,
who has come under attack for his attitudes toward women, should
have created in Hester Prynne one of the richest female characters in
American fiction" (101). Myra Jehlen is even more emphatic in her
praise of Hawthorne; focusing on Hester Prynne as manifestation of
Hawthorne's subversiveness, Jehlen argues that the "author is more radical than the character: she rejects certain of Boston's moral tenets but he
challenges its moral authority as such" (135), and Elizabeth Aycock
Hoffman adds that Hawthorne "had intended to be more subversive
than Jehlen perhaps gives him credit for" (202). Emily Miller Budick,
too, calls for our recognition of Hawthorne's representation of Hester's
subversiveness, in fact, making her "the voice of the text itself" ("Sacvan"
86)—and Barbara Rogers says that "[i]n the rich promise of women like
Hester Prynne, Hawthorne acknowledges the threat of disorder" (229).
Mona Scheuermann studies *The Scarlet Letter* in terms of its generic relationship to novels of adultery, saying that

> [f]ar from going into the expected decline, [Hester] toughens and
> grows intellectually until Hawthorne himself seems scarcely to
> wish to draw her limits. . . . Unlike her sisters in novels of seduc-
> tion, she refuses to see her act as a sin. . . . Hawthorne, for the first
> time in the novel in English, has moved the sex act out of its usual
> context as social item. (113–15)

2. Susan Swarzlander explains that Hawthorne's text and his representation of Hester are steeped in ideas about witchcraft, particularly those of Charles Wentworth Upham's *Lectures on Witchcraft*, delivered at the Salem Lyceum in 1831 (227–28).

3. See also Patricia Marks for information about Hawthorne's knowledge of actual sightings of comets, phenomena that inform this chapter of Hawthorne's text. Peggy Kamuf sees Dimmesdale's readings of "natural phenomena" to consider his own "symptom" as the "particularization, the individualization of the shared belief in the transcendent meaning of the commonwealth" (78), and Paula White sees the "sign" and Dimmesdale's reading of it as consistent with atemporal, providential history ("Puritan Theories of History" 143–45).

5. Demi's Hester and Hester's Demi(se): *The* (New) *Scarlet Letter* and Its Spectators

1. The 1911 silent version starred King Baggot as Arthur Dimmesdale and Gene Gauntier as Hester Prynne. This film was produced by Kalem Studios (the name a combination of the initials of George Kleine, Samuel Long, and Frank J. Marion) and directed by Sidney Olcott, whom Gauntier "credited . . . with psychic powers and a virtually hypnotic control over his actors" (Wagenknecht *Movies* 53). During Gauntier's reign as "leading lady" of Kalem, she made over five hundred films, some finished in a day. In addition to acting in these films, she

> herself had written all except half a dozen. When you are sometimes required to turn out three scenarios during a single day, it is a great help to have standard literature to draw on. Miss Gauntier began by drawing on *Tom Sawyer*. She adapted *As You Like It, Evangeline, Hiawatha,* and *The Scarlet Letter.* (Wagenknecht, *Movies* 53–54)

Gauntier, like Demi Moore, had her own production company (Seger 9). The silent 1913 version of *The Scarlet Letter* starred D. W. Griffith's first wife, Linda Arvidson, as Hester Prynne. In addition to *The Scarlet Letter,* Arvidson acted in 118 films between 1908 and 1916. The 1917 film, produced by Fox Film Corporation and directed by Carl Harbaugh, starred Mary Martin as Hester Prynne and Stuart Holmes as Arthur Dimmesdale. Mary Martin's other films include *The Tiger Woman* (also 1917), *Eternal Sappho* (1916), *The Vixen* (1916), *Devil's*

Daughter (1915), and *Great Love Hath No Man* (1915) (Internet Movie Database). The next film adaptation of *The Scarlet Letter* was another silent version in 1926, produced by MGM and directed by Victor Sjöström, followed by a 1934 sound film, produced by Majestic Film Studios and directed by Robert G. Vignola (both are discussed in the text of the chapter). A German version in 1972 known as *Der Scharlachrote Buchstabe* (also released in Spanish and English) was directed by Wim Wenders and starred Senta Berger as Hester Prynne, Lou Castel as Arthur Dimmesdale, and Hans Christian Blech as Roger Chillingworth (see Gollin, "Wim Wenders's *Scarlet Letter*"). A PBS four-hour miniseries appeared in 1979—produced and directed by Rick Hauser, filmed in Salem, Massachusetts, and starring Meg Foster as Hester Prynne, John Heard as Arthur Dimmesdale, and Kevin Conway as Roger Chillingworth. The version was adapted for television by Allan Knee and Alvin Sapinsley. Hawthorne's *The House of Seven Gables* was also translated to film in 1940 by Universal Pictures and directed by Joe May. The cast included George Sanders as Jaffrey Pyncheon, Margaret Lindsay as Hepzibah, Vincent Price as Clifford, Nan Gray as Phoebe, and Dick Foran as Holgrave. Lester Cole and Harold Greene collaborated on the screenplay. Several of Hawthorne's stories/tales have also been made as films, including "Feathertop" (1912), "Rappaccini's Daughter" (1980), and "Young Goodman Brown" (1993); the latter two have been shown on television. In 1963 Admiral Pictures produced (under the genre of "Horror") one of Hawthorne's short-story collections, *Twice-Told Tales,* which was directed by Sidney Salkow. Vincent Price played Alex Medbourne, Rappaccini, and Gerald Pyncheon, Brett Halsey played Giovanni Guasconti, and Joyce Taylor played Beatrice Rappaccini. The cast also included Sebastian Cabot, Beverly Garland, Richard Denning, Mari Blanchard, and Jacqueline DeWit. The screenplay was written by Robert E. Kent (Internet Movie Database).

2. The 1926 film also received some negative reviews, particularly from *Photoplay.* "Their reviews of *La Boheme* (May, 1926) and *The Scarlet Letter* (Oct., 1926) were disgraceful" (Wagenknecht, *Movies* 237 n10). According to actor Louise Brooks, James Quirk of *Photoplay* waged a "war against Lillian Gish" (Wagenknecht, *Movies* 237 n10).

3. Mary Martin also played Hester Prynne as her last role—in the 1917 film version of *The Scarlet Letter.*

4. Gish left Griffith's production company after the completion of *Orphans of the Storm;* as Affron tells us

One of Gish's major accomplishments is the amount of personality and individuality she brings to the caricature [of the woman in peril], along with frightening dedication. *Orphans of the Storm* is the final step, where the pattern is pushed to its limit. Gish is introduced as the familiar wide-eyes ingenue . . . separated from her blind sister (Dorothy Gish), and Griffith fabricates for her the recognition/reunion scene par excellence. . . . Griffith spares no detail; photographing her in all possible positions, he fairly chortles over the scope of [the] final predicament. The logical conclusion of Gish's career with Griffith is the image of her head jutting out of that [guillotine] brace . . . she is offered up, as it were, to camera and posterity. If the blade doesn't drop in *Orphans of the Storm*, it does in the Griffith-Gish collaboration. There is little more to ask of an actress, but one shudders with apprehension over the outcome if it had. "Yes, Mr. Griffith, whatever you say."
In their first film, *An Unseen Enemy* (1912), Lillian and Dorothy Gish were locked in a room and menaced by a gun that appeared through a hole in the wall. The dangers became more sophisticated and elaborate in the intervening eleven years, and they were punctuated with scenes of tenderness and reflection. Yet Lillian Gish had to leave Griffith to get out of that locked room, to get her neck out of the guillotine. She had to grow up. Her subsequent films in the twenties prove that a fascinating and challenging woman was lurking all the time in those pinafores and beneath those funny hats. The dedication, force, sense of the camera, and above all, the belief in form developed with Griffith were to be channeled by Gish into some of the most remarkable films of the late silent era. No other actress ever passed through a more grueling initiation to earn her stardom. (52–58)

5. Affron argues that in "projecting the [Hester Prynne] role's sexuality, [Gish] is abetted by Seastrom's invention and fervor. After the avowal of her previous marriage, Seastrom sends [Gish's Hester] out into the snow hysterical, and then caps the sequence with a strategically projected shadow upon her apron," evoking the film's "symbolic sexuality" (80). Another film critic, Raymond Durgnat, views the sexuality in this film similarly, as he discusses Gish's Prynne:

> Every evening she sits, very much alone, in her cottage, spinning, the starched white collar of her Puritan dress covers her breasts and the fire flings the whirling shadows of her spinning wheel across her apron. The contrast between her rich femininity and

her loneliness; between the stiff dress and the tremulous delicacy of Lillian Gish; her placidity and industriousness; has . . . superb erotic solidity. (qtd. in Affron, 80 n1)

Like the critics of the other films of *The Scarlet Letter,* these critics may be saying more about themselves as spectators of Gish, caught in their own desire, than about the representation of Prynne by Gish.

6. Perhaps more than any of the other film translations of *The Scarlet Letter,* Rick Hauser's 1979 PBS production is guided by Hawthorne's text. As Hauser has said,

> Hawthorne's original keeps my feet on the ground. I repeatedly go back to his masterwork to check impressions, to gauge our collective success at creating his people and their world. His story, remains—a wry marvel, continually fascinating. What television viewers will see, of course, is one of innumerable *possible* "Scarlet Letters," this one filtered through the imaginative perception of the people who caused the thing to take the form it will have on the television screen. . . . Authentic we were not and could not be; faithful I dare to believe we were. ("Viewer's Guide")

7. Rick Hauser's 1979 PBS version of *The Scarlet Letter* imagined the Puritans' relationship to the wilderness differently—holding, one could say, the same historically romantic view as Hawthorne. As the "Viewer's Guide" to the film states:

> Nothing in [the Puritans'] experience had prepared them for the sight of a forest so thick and dark it threatened to extend endlessly and to harbor endless menace. Colonial diarists from Massachusetts to Carolina insisted on a single word—"howling"—to describe this wilderness at their backs. They seemed to mean by it something more than the cries of wolves and bears or the "outrageous roaring and whooping" of angry Indians: some profound subjective fear howled inwardly long after the range of objective dangers had been identified. And yet, despite such fears, New England's Puritans were uniquely prepared for this "vast and empty chaos."

This description, although mirroring canonical American literature's romanticized representation of life in the wilderness, is hardly more than another attempt at containment, failing to account, again, for the Native Americans' generous saving of the colonists from death and complete destruction. Also, the Puritans' inner turmoil and fears—which were immense, I agree—were considered more significant to discuss than their tendency to project these fears onto the external landscape, rather than, as this account does, assume their ability to separate themselves from and identify "the range of objective dangers." Moreover, this "range of objective dangers"—primarily caused by the Puritans' insensitivity to the land and to the human beings who inhabited it, consistently refusing to see the Native populations as anything more than howling, whooping, roaring, angry savages—is ignored in Hauser's film version, as it is in the novel.

8. See Louise Barnett's *Ignoble Savage* for her careful analysis of the narratives in which Hawthorne includes Native American characters or references to Indian life.

9. Rick Hauser's 1979 film maintained its focus on what was interpreted as Hawthorne's ability to recognize the "connections between the enforced uniformity of his ancestors' lives and the bland conformism of his contemporaries." The "Viewer's Guide" for the film thus suggests about the Puritans' relationship to nonconformists the following:

> not everybody in the colony qualified as a brother [or sister?]. Those who did not conform—Quakers or atheists or deviant Puritans like Anne Hutchinson—were considered subversives. Having barely escaped the persecuting English Church, the authorities of the Massachusetts Bay proceeded to persecute every dissenter stubborn enough to speak out. They set Catholic sympathizers in the stocks, lashed Quakers through the streets before banishing them from the territory and executed heretics in formal public hangings. From our vantage point the men and women who established Massachusetts in the name of "holy liberty" can seem arrogant fanatics, pure and simple. It takes a great deal of effort of the imagination to see them as they saw themselves: engaged in a sacred experiment to live and worship perfectly and to make their Commonwealth the saving model for a Christian universe.

It is this kind of demand for continuous focus on the intentions of the persecutors and oppressors that I have been discussing throughout this book, because, in so doing, the focus on those who have been oppressed has been so minimal as to be distorted when presented. While I am not arguing that we forget or lose this dominant historical heritage, I propose that we *also* listen to and tell the stories and histories of those who were oppressed, erased, dominated, even destroyed, by patriarchal groups like the Puritans of New England. Instead, the "Viewer's Guide," like almost every class I had in which *The Scarlet Letter* was taught—from high school through graduate school—encouraged me to "forget" my own perspective in relationship to this novel and its oppressed, explicit in Hester Prynne and implicit in the absence of other Others, and try my best to imagine how the Puritan patriarchs felt. I was encouraged to "understand" them and their intentions, not in addition to my own or those of Others, but in place of them. At best, my various fellow students and I were asked to think about how "we" were still influenced by the Puritans—although in no way connected with the oppressed. The "Viewer's Guide" for the 1979 film concurs with this *view* and *guides* its viewers as follows: "And, however different from us the Puritans at first appear, we might inquire in our time, as Hawthorne did in his, how the Puritan legacy still colors America's idea of itself." While a worthwhile goal, it is *how* we inquire, *how* we define "America's idea of itself," and *who* we focus on in such an inquiry which I have been trying to question in this book. Put more simply, it is what assumptions we find when we conduct such inquiries that I have been encouraging. If we continue to come to the same answer, generation after generation, yet claim progress and change, then there is no real inquiry, other than the kind always already guided by a GUIDE, always already steeped in the assumptions which have guided and shaped us. Roland Joffé's film of *The Scarlet Letter* functions in terms of the consequences of inquiries made by the production staff, writers, and actors—guided by expert Others, including Native American consultants to the film—into the histories and intentions of those oppressed by Puritan hegemony and focuses our gaze on the *consequences,* rather than the intentions, of their legacy.

10. In June 1996, at the conference of the American Literature Association in San Diego, California, I was on a panel with Roland Joffé at a session sponsored by the Hawthorne society, and chaired by T. Walter Herbert, which focused on Joffé's film. During Joffé's extemporaneous talk, he mentioned that part of his deal with the studio was that he had final say over each day's script and rewrites, as well as over the dailies of the film. He did not, however, have control over the film's final cuts. During his presentation he mentioned that the director's cut of the film includes many scenes, helpful to the progression of his narrative, which did not make it through the studio's final cutting sessions.

6. Conclusion: Implications of Hester-Prynne-ism and ReReading Women

1. Randal Johnson explains further:

> In any given field, agents occupying the diverse available positions (or in some cases creating new positions) engage in competition for control of the interests or resources which are specific to the

field in question. . . . In the cultural [e.g. literary] field, competition often concerns the authority inherent in recognition, consecration and prestige . . . *symbolic power* based on diverse forms of capital which are not reducible to economic capital. Academic capital, for example, derives from formal education and can be measured by degrees or diplomas held. (7)

Bibliography

Twentieth-Century Women's Scholarship
on *The Scarlet Letter*

Adkins, Lois. "Psychological Symbolism of Guilt and Isolation in Hawthorne." *American Imago* 11 (1954): 417–25.

Allen, Mary. "Smiles and Laughter in Hawthorne." *Philological Quarterly* 52 (1973): 119–28.

Armstrong, Judith. *The Novel of Adultery*. London: Macmillan, 1976. 100–105.

Auerbach, Nina. "The Rise of the Fallen Woman." *Nineteenth-Century Fiction* 35.1 (1980): 29–52.

———. *Woman and the Demon: The Life of a Victorian Myth*. Cambridge: Harvard UP, 1982. 165–77.

Balakian, Anna. "'. . . and the pursuit of happiness': *The Scarlet Letter* and *A Spy in the House of Love*." *Mosaic* 11.2 (1978): 163–70.

Banting, Pamela. "Miss A and Mrs. B: The Letter of Pleasure in *The Scarlet Letter* and *As for Me and My House*." *North Dakota Quarterly* 54.2 (1986): 30–40.

Bardes, Barbara, and Suzanne Gossett. *Declarations of Independence: Women and Political Power in Nineteenth-Century American Fiction*. New Brunswick: Rutgers UP, 1990.

Baris, Sharon Deykin. "The American Daniel as Seen in Hawthorne's *The Scarlet Letter*." *Biblical Patterns in Modern Literature*. Eds. David H. Hirsch and Nehama Aschkenasy. Chico: Scholars, 1984.

Barlowe, Jamie. "Rereading Women: Hester Prynne-ism and the Scarlet Mob of Scribblers." *American Literary History* 9.2 (1997): 197–225.

Barnett, Louise K. *Authority and Speech: Language, Society and Self in the American Novel*. Athens: U of Georgia P, 1993. 43–58.

———. *Ignoble Savage: American Literary Racism, 1790–1890*. Westport: Greenwood, 1975. 149–65.

———. "Speech and Society in *The Scarlet Letter*." *Emerson Society Quarterly* 29.1 (1983): 16–24.

Barrett, Phyllis. "More American Adams: Women Heroes in American Fiction." *Markham Review* 10 (1981): 39–41.

Bartsch-Parker, Elizabeth. "Further Hardy Debts to Hawthorne." *Notes and Queries* 40.4 (1993): 493.

Bates, Katharine. Introduction. *The Scarlet Letter*. By Nathaniel Hawthorne. Vol. 7–8. New York: Thomas Y. Crowell, 1902. v–xvi.

Baym, Nina. "George Sand in American Reviews: A Context for Hester." *Nathaniel Hawthorne Newsletter* 10.2 (1984): 12–15.

———. "Hawthorne's *Scarlet Letter*: Producing and Maintaining an American Literary Classic." *The Journal of Aesthetic Education* 30.2 (1996): 61–76.

———. "Hawthorne's Women: The Tyranny of Social Myths." *Centennial Review* 15 (1971): 250–72.

———. "Melodramas of Beset Manhood: How Theories of American Fiction Exclude Women Writers." *American Quarterly* 33 (1981): 123–39.

———. "Nathaniel Hawthorne and His Mother: A Biographical Speculation." *American Literature* 54 (1982): 1–27.

———. *Novels, Readers, and Reviewers: Responses to Fiction in Antebellum America*. Ithaca: Cornell UP, 1984.

———. "Passion and Authority in *The Scarlet Letter*." *New England Quarterly* 43 (1970): 209–30.

———. "Portrayal of Women in American Literature 1790–1870." *What Manner of Woman: Essays on English and American Life and Literature*. Ed. Marlene Springer. New York: New York UP, 1977. 211–34.

———. "The Romantic *Malgre Lui*: Hawthorne in the Custom House." *Emerson Society Quarterly* 70 (1975): 14–25.

———. *"The Scarlet Letter": A Reading*. Boston: Twayne, 1986.

———. *The Shape of Hawthorne's Career*. Ithaca: Cornell UP, 1976. 123–51. Expt. as "Hester's Defiance." *Readings on "The Scarlet Letter."* Ed. Eileen Morey. San Diego: Greenhaven, 1998. 88–98.

———. "Thwarted Nature: Nathaniel Hawthorne as Feminist." *American Novelists Revisited: Essays in Feminist Criticism*. Ed. Fritz Fleishmann. Boston: G.K. Hall, 1982. 58–77.

Bell, Millicent. *Hawthorne's View of the Artist*. Albany: State U of New York P, 1962.

———. "The Obliquity of Signs: *The Scarlet Letter*." *Massachusetts Review* 23 (1982): 9–26.

Ben-Bassat, Hedda. "Marginal Existence and Communal Consensus in *The Scarlet Letter* and *A Fringe of Leaves*." *The Comparatist: Journal of the Southern Comparative Literature Association* (1994): 52–70.

Bensick, Carol. "Dimmesdale and His Bachelorhood: Priestly Celibacy in *The Scarlet Letter*." *Studies in American Fiction* 21.1 (1993): 103–10.

————. "His Folly, Her Weakness: Demystified Adultery in *The Scarlet Letter*." *New Essays on "The Scarlet Letter*." Ed. M.J. Colacurcio. Cambridge: Cambridge UP, 1985. 137–59. Rpt. as "Demystified Adultery in *The Scarlet Letter*" in *Hester Prynne*. Ed. Harold Bloom. New York: Chelsea House, 1990. 146–61.

Benstock, Shari. "*The Scarlet Letter* (a)doree, or the Female Body Embroidered." *Nathaniel Hawthorne: "Scarlet Letter," Case Studies in Contemporary Criticism*. Ed. Ross C. Murfin. New York: St. Martin's, 1991. 288–303.

Bergmann, Harriet F. "Henry Adams' Esther: No Faith in the Patriarchy." *Markham Review* 10 (1981): 63–67.

Berlant, Lauren. *The Anatomy of a National Fantasy: Hawthorne, Utopia, and Everyday Life*. Chicago: U of Chicago P, 1991.

Bernstein, Cynthia. "Reading *The Scarlet Letter*: Against Hawthorne's Interpretive Community." *Language and Literature* 18 (1993): 1–20.

Bethurum, Dorothy, and Randall Stewart. "History, Art, and Wisdom in *The Scarlet Letter*." *Classic American Fiction*. Eds. Dorothy Bethurum and Randall Stewart. New York: Scott, Foresman and Company, 1954. Rpt. in *Readings on Nathaniel Hawthorne*. Ed. Clarice Swisher. San Diego: Greenhaven, 1996, 168–77.

Birdsall, Virginia. "Hawthorne's Fair-Haired Maidens: The Fading Light." *PMLA* 75 (1960): 250–56.

Bogan, Louise. Foreword. *The Scarlet Letter*. New York: Libra, 1960. ix–xvi.

Bonham, Sister M. Hilda. "Hawthorne's Symbols *Sotto Voce*." *College English* 20 (1959): 184–86.

Brady, Kristen. "Hawthorne's Editor/Narrator: The Voice of Indeterminacy." *CEA Critic* 47 (1985): 27–38.

Bronstein, Zelda. "The Parabolic Ploys of *The Scarlet Letter*." *American Quarterly* 39 (1987): 193–210.

Brooke-Rose, Christine. "A-for-But: The Custom-House in Hawthorne's *The Scarlet Letter*." *Word and Image* 3.2 (1987): 143–55.

Brown, Gillian. "Hawthorne, Inheritance, and Women's Property." *Studies in the Novel* 23.1 (1991): 107–18.

————. "Hawthorne's Endangered Daughters." *Western Humanities Review* 51.1 (1997): 327.

Browne, Nina, comp. *A Bibliography of Nathaniel Hawthorne*. Boston: Houghton, 1905.

Browner, Stephanie P. "Authorizing the Body: Scientific Medicine and *The Scarlet Letter*." *Literature and Medicine* 12.2 (1993): 139–60.

Brumm, Ursula. *American Thought and Religious Typology*. New Brunswick: Rutgers UP, 1970.

———. "Hawthorne's 'The Custom-House' and the Problem of Point of View in Historical Fiction." *Anglia* 93 (1975): 391–412.

———. "Motif of the Pastor." *Amerikastudien* 31.1 (1986): 61–70.

———. "Passions and Depressions in Early American Puritanism." *Le Passion dans le Monde Anglo-Américain aux XVIIe et XVIIIe Siècles*. 85–96.

Budick, Emily Miller. *Engendering Romance: Women Writers and the Hawthorne Tradition 1850–1990*. New Haven: Yale UP, 1994. 13–39.

———. *Fiction and Historical Consciousness: The American Romance Tradition*. New Haven: Yale UP, 1989.

———. "Hester's Skepticism, Hawthorne's Faith; or, What Does a Woman Doubt?: Instituting the American Romance Tradition." *New Literary History* 22 (1991): 199–211.

———. "Sacvan Bercovitch, Stanley Cavell, and the Romance Theory of American Fiction." *PMLA* 107 (1992): 78–91.

———. "We Damned-If-You-Do, Damned-If-You-Don't Mob of Scribbling Scholars." *American Literary History* 9.2 (1997): 233–37.

Burbick, Joan. *Healing the Republic: The Language of Health and the Culture of Nationalism in Nineteenth-Century America*. New York: Cambridge UP, 1994. 210–22, 235–39, 295–99.

Burton, Dolores. "Intonation Patterns of Sermons in Seven Novels." *Language Sciences* 3 (1975): 205–18.

Canfield, Dorothy. Introduction. *The Scarlet Letter*. Ed. Henry Varnum Poor. New York: Limited Editions Club, 1941.

Carlson, Patricia Ann. *Hawthorne's Functional Settings: A Study of Artistic Method*. Amsterdam: Editions Rodopi, 1977.

Cather, Willa. "The Novel *Demeuble*." *On Writing: Critical Studies on Writing as an Art*. New York: Knopf, 1949. 35–43.

Chandler, Elizabeth Lathrop. *A Study of the Sources of the Tales and Romances Written by Nathaniel Hawthorne Before 1853*. 1926. Rpt. Darby: Arden, 1978.

Clarke, Helen Archibald. *Hawthorne's Country*. New York: Baker, 1910.

Clasby, Nancy Tenfelde. "Being True: Logos in *The Scarlet Letter*." *Renascence* 45.4 (1993): 247–56.

Cocalis, Jane. "The 'Dark and Abiding Presence' in Nathaniel Hawthorne's *The Scarlet Letter* and Toni Morrison's *Beloved*." *Calvinist Roots of the Modern Era*. Eds. Aliki Barnstone, Michael Thomasek, and Carol J. Singley. Hanover: UP of New England, 1997: 250–62.

Cuddy, Lois. "Mother-Daughter Identification in *The Scarlet Letter.*" *Mosaic* 19.2 (1986): 101–15.

Dalke, Anne French. "The Sensational Fiction of Hawthorne and Melville." *Studies in American Fiction* 16.2 (1988): 195–207.

Daniel, Janice B. "'Apples of the Thoughts and Fancies': Nature as Narrator in *The Scarlet Letter.*" *American Transcendental Quarterly*, ns 7.4 (1993): 307–19.

Davis, Sarah. "Another View of Hester and the Antinomians." *Studies in American Fiction* 12.1 (1984): 189–98.

————. "Self in the Marketplace, or, A For Alienation." *South Atlantic Review* 54.2 (1989): 75–92.

De Jong, Mary Grosselink. "The Making of a 'Gentle Reader': Narrator and Reader in Hawthorne's Romances." *Studies in The Novel* 16.4 (1984): 359–77.

DeSalvo, Louise. *Nathaniel Hawthorne.* Atlantic Highlands: Humanities P International, 1987.

Diehl, Joanne Feit. "Re-Reading The Letter: Hawthorne and Fetish, and the (Family) Romance." *New Literary History* 19.3 (1988): 655–73.

Donaldson, Susan. "'Let That Anvil Ring': Robert Penn Warren's *The Cave* and Hawthorne's Legacy." *Southern Literary Journal* 15.2 (1983): 59–75.

Donohue, Agnes McNeill. *Hawthorne: Calvin's Ironic Stepchild.* Kent: Kent State UP, 1985. 35–67.

Dove-Rume, Janine. "Hawthorne, l'alchimiste, et son Grand-O'euve, *The Scarlet Letter.*" *Social Science Information* 30.1 (1991): 157–78.

Dreyer, Eileen. "Confession in *The Scarlet Letter.*" *Journal of American Studies* 25.1 (1991): 78–81.

Duffey, Carolyn. "Tituba and Hester in the Intertextual Jail Cell: New World Feminisms in Maryse Conde's *Moi, Tituba, sorciere . . . noire de Salem.*" *Women in French Studies* 4 (1996): 100–10.

Dukats, Mara. "The Hybrid Terrain of Literary Imagination: Maryse Conde's Black Witch of Salem, Nathaniel Hawthorne's Hester Prynne, and Aime Cesaire's Heroic Poetic Voice." *Order and Partialities: Theory, Pedagogy, and the "Postcolonial."* Eds. Kostas Myrsiades and Jerry McGuire. Albany: State U of New York P, 1995. 325–40.

Dwight, Sheila. "Hawthorne and the Unpardonable Sin." *Studies in the Novel* 2.4 (1970): 449–58.

Easton, Alison. *The Making of the Hawthorne Subject.* Columbia: U of Missouri P, 1996. Expt. as "Critique of Puritan Society." *Readings on "The Scarlet Letter."* Ed. Eileen Morey. San Diego: Greenhaven, 1998. 114–26.

Eberwein, Jane Donahue. "'The Scribbler of Bygone Days': Perceptions of Time in Hawthorne's 'Custom-House.'" *Nathaniel Hawthorne Journal* (1977): 239–47.

Elbert, Monika. *Encoding the Letter "A": Gender and Authority in Hawthorne's Early Fiction.* Frankfurt am Main, Germany: Haag und Herchen, 1990. 188–244.

———. "Hawthorne's Reconceptualization or Transcendental Charity." *American Transcendental Quarterly* 11.3 (1997): 213–32.

———. "Hester on the Scaffold, Dimmesdale in the Closet: Hawthorne's Seven-Year Itch." *Essays in Literature* 16.2 (1989): 234–55.

———. "Hester's Maternity: Stigma or Weapon." *Emerson Society Quarterly* 36.3 (1990): 175–207.

———. Introduction. *The Scarlet Letter.* New York: Washington Square, 1994.

———. "No (Wo)man's Land: Hawthorne's 'Neutral Territory' and Hester 'Magic Circle' as Home." *Mid-Hudson Language Studies* 12.2 (1989): 27–39.

Elder, Marjorie. *Nathaniel Hawthorne: Transcendental Symbolist.* Athens: Ohio UP, 1969. 121–41.

Ensor, Allison. "'Whispers of the Bad Angel': A *Scarlet Letter* Passage as a Commentary on Hawthorne's 'Young Goodman Brown.'" *Studies in Short Fiction* 7 (1970): 467–69.

Erlich, Gloria. "Deadly Innocent: Hawthorne's Dark Women." *New England Quarterly* 41 (1968): 163–79.

———. *Family Themes and Hawthorne's Fiction: The Tenacious Web.* New Brunswick: Rutgers UP, 1984.

Faust, Bertha. *Hawthorne's Contemporaneous Reputation: A Study of Literary Opinion in American and England, 1828–1864.* New York: Octagon, 1968. 67–146.

Flanders, Jane. "The Fallen Woman in Fiction." *Feminist Visions: Toward a Transformation of the Liberal Arts Curriculum.* Eds. Diane Fowlkes and Charlotte S. McClure. University: U of Alabama P, 1984. 97–109.

Fleischner, Jennifer. "Female Eroticism, Confession, and Interpretation in Nathaniel Hawthorne." *Nineteenth-Century Literature* 44.4 (1990): 514–33.

———. "Hawthorne and the Politics of Slavery." *Studies in the Novel* 23.1 (1991): 96–106.

Fowler, Lois Josephs, ed. *Insight: American Literature.* New York: Noble and Noble, 1968.

Franchot, Jenny. *Roads to Rome: The Antebellum Protestant Encounter with Catholicism*. Berkeley: U of California P, 1994. 260–69, 350ff.

Franklin, Rosemary F. "The Cabin by the Lake: Pastoral Landscapes of Poe, Cooper, Hawthorne, Thoreau." *Emerson Society Quarterly* 22.2 (1976): 59–70.

Fryer, Judith. *The Faces of Eve: Women in the Nineteenth-Century American Novel*. New York: Oxford UP, 1976. 72–84.

Gabler-Hover, Janet. *Truth in American Fiction: The Legacy of Rhetorical Idealism*. Athens: U of Georgia P, 1990. 85–120.

Garlitz, Barbara. "Pearl: 1850–1955." *PMLA* 72 (1957): 689–99.

Gilligan, Carol. "Joining the Resistance: Psychology, Politics, Girls and Women." *Michigan Quarterly Review* 29 (1990): 501–36.

Gitenstein, Barbara. "The Seventh Commandment: Adultery as Barometer of Communal Disintegration." *Comparatist* 1 (1977): 16–22.

Gollin, Rita. "Again a Literary Man: Vocation and *The Scarlet Letter*." *Critical Essays on Hawthorne's "The Scarlet Letter."* Ed. David Kesterson. Boston: G.K. Hall, 1988. 171–82.

————. "Hawthorne and the Anxiety of Aesthetic Response." *Centennial Review* 29.1 (1985): 94–104.

————. "Hester, Hetty, and the Two Arthurs." *Nathaniel Hawthorne Journal* 1977: 319–22.

————. *Nathaniel Hawthorne and the Truth of Dreams*. Baton Rouge: Louisiana State UP, 1979. 140–51.

————. "Nathaniel Hawthorne: The Flesh and the Spirit; or, Gratifying Your Coarsest Animal Needs." *Studies in the Novel* 23.1 (1991): 82–95.

————. "Wim Wenders' *Scarlet Letter*." *Nathaniel Hawthorne Review* 17.1 (1991): 21–22.

Gollin, Rita, and John Idol. *Prophetic Pictures: Nathaniel Hawthorne and the Uses of the Visual Arts*. New York: Greenwood, 1991.

Gottschalk, Jane. "The Continuity of American Letters in *The Scarlet Letter* and 'The Beast in the Jungle.'" *Wisconsin Studies in Literature* 4 (1967): 39–45.

Green, Carlanda. "The Custom-House: Hawthorne's Dark Wood of Error." *New England Quarterly* 53.2 (1980): 184–95.

Greene, Maxine. "Man Without God in American Fiction." *Humanist* 25 (1965): 125–8.

Greenwald, Elissa. *Realism and the Romance: Nathaniel Hawthorne, Henry James, and American Fiction*. Ann Arbor: UMI Research, 1989. 57–77.

Gussman, Deborah. "Inalienable Rights: Fiction of Political Identity in *Hobomok* and *The Scarlet Letter.*" *College Literature* 22.2 (1995): 58–80.

Hamblen, Abigail. "Protestantism in Three American Novels." *Forum* (Houston) 3 (1960): 40–43.

Hanscom, Elizabeth Deering. Introduction. *The Scarlet Letter.* By Nathaniel Hawthorne. Ed. Hanscom. New York: Macmillan, 1927. vii–xxii.

Hansen, Elaine Tuttle. "Ambiguity and the Narrator in *The Scarlet Letter.*" *Journal of Narrative Technique* 5 (1975): 147–63.

Hardwick, Elizabeth. *Seduction and Betrayal: Women and Literature.* New York: Random House, 1974. 177–208.

Hazard, Lucy Lockwood. *The Frontier in American Literature.* New York: Thomas Y. Crowell, 1927. 27–39.

Heilbrun, Carolyn. *Toward a Recognition of Androgyny.* New York: Knopf, 1964. 63–67.

Herzog, Kristen. *Women, Ethnics, and Exotics: Images of Power in Mid-Nineteenth-Century American Fiction.* Knoxville: U of Tennessee P, 1983. 7–16.

Hodges, Elizabeth Perry. "The Letter of the Law: Reading Hawthorne and the Law of Adultery." *Law and Literature Perspectives.* Eds. Bruce L. Rockwood and Robert Kevelson. New York: Peter Lang, 1996. 133–68.

Hoffman, Elizabeth Aycock. "Political Power in *The Scarlet Letter.*" *American Transcendental Quarterly* ns 4.1 (1990): 13–29.

Horton, Tonia L. "The Born Outcast: Nathaniel Hawthorne's Pearl and Symbolic Action in *The Scarlet Letter.*" *Ritual in the United States: Acts and Representations.* Ed. Don Harkness. Tampa: American Studies P, 1985: 10–14.

Hurst, Mary Jane. *The Voice of the Child in American Literature: Linguistic Approaches to Fictional Child Language.* Lexington: UP of Kentucky, 1990. 66–67.

Jehlen, Myra. *American Incarnation: The Individual, the Nation, and the Continent.* Cambridge: Harvard UP, 1986.

Johnson, Claudia D. "Hawthorne and Nineteenth-Century Perfectionism." *American Literature* 44 (1973): 585–95.

———. "Impotence and Omnipotence in *The Scarlet Letter.*" *New England Quarterly* 66.4 (1993): 594–612.

———. *The Productive Tension in Hawthorne's Art.* University: U of Alabama P, 1981.

———. *Understanding "The Scarlet Letter": A Student Casebook to Issues, Sources, and Historical Documents.* Westport: Greenwood, 1995. Expt.

as "The Meaning of the Scarlet A." *Readings on "The Scarlet Letter."*
Ed. Eileen Morey. San Diego: Greenhaven, 1998. 127–37.

Jones, Betty H., and Alberta Arthurs. "The American Eve: A New Look
at American Heroines and Their Critics." *International Journal of
Women's Studies* 1.1 (1978): 1–12.

Jones, Grace. "Literary Kinship, Nathaniel Hawthorne, John Fowles, and
Their Scarlet Women." *South Atlantic Quarterly* 86.1 (1987): 69–78.

Jones, Phyllis. "Hawthorne's Mythic Use of Puritan History." *Cithara*
12 (1972): 59–73.

Jordan, Cynthia. *Second Stories: The Politics of Language, Form, and Gender in Early American Fiction.* Chapel Hill: U of North Carolina P,
1989. 152–72.

Jordan, Gretchen Graf. "Adultery and Its Fruit in *The Scarlet Letter* and
The Power and the Glory." *Yale Review* 71.1 (1981): 72–87.

Josephs, Lois. "One Approach to the Puritans." *English Journal* 50
(1961): 183–87.

Kalfopoulou, Adrianne. "Gendered Silences and the Problem of Desire in
Nathaniel Hawthorne's *The Scarlet Letter,* Gertrude Stein's 'Melanctha,'
and Gayl Jones's *Correigidora.*" *Nationalism and Sexuality: Crisis of Identity.* Eds. Yiorgos Kalogeras and Domna Pastourmatzi. Thessaloniki,
Greece: Hellenic Association of American Studies, 1996. 115–23.

———. "Hester's Ungathered Hair: Hawthorne and 19th Century
Women's Fiction." *Gamma* 1 (1993): 40–61.

Kamuf, Peggy. "Hawthorne's Genres: The Letter of the Law *Appliquee.*"
After Strange Texts: The Role of Theory in the Study of Literature. Eds.
Gregory Jay and David Miller. University: U of Alabama P, 1985.
69–84.

Kane, Patricia. "The Fallen Woman as Free-Thinker in *The French Lieutenant's Woman* and *The Scarlet Letter.*" *Notes on Contemporary Literature* 2 (1972): 8–10.

Keane, Ellen Marie, Judith P. Saunder, and Ellen S. Silber. "Female Out-
laws: Exploring Ethical Choice Through Literature." *Women's Voices.*
Eds. Lorna Duphiney, Judith P. Saunders, Ellen S. Silber. Littleton:
Copley, 1987. 13–29.

Kearns, Francis E. "Margaret Fuller as a Model for Hester Prynne."
Jahrbuch für Amerikastudien 10 (1965): 191–97.

Kehler, Dorothea. "Hawthorne and Shakespeare." *American Transcendental Quarterly* 22 (1974): 104–105.

Kesselring, Marion L. *Hawthorne's Reading 1828–1850.* 1949; Folcroft:
Folcroft Library Editions, 1969.

Kilcup, Karen L. "'Ourself Behind Ourself, Concealed—': The Homo-
erotics of Reading in *The Scarlet Letter*." *Emerson Society Quarterly*
42.1 (1996): 1–28.

Korobkin, Laura Hanft. "The Scarlet Letter of the Law: Hawthorne and
Criminal Justice." *Novel* 30.2 (1997): 193–217.

Koskenlinna, Hazel. "Setting, Image, and Symbol in Scott and Hawthorne."
Emerson Society Quarterly 19.1 (1973): 50–59.

Kurjiaka, Susan K. H. "Rage Turned Inward: Woman Against Herself in
Hawthorne's Fiction." *Mount Olive Review* 7 (1993–94): 33–40.

Kushens, Betty. "Love's Martyrs: *The Scarlet Letter* as Secular Cross."
Literature and Psychology 22.3 (1972): 108–20.

Lander, Dawn. "Women and Wilderness: Tabus in American Literature." *University of Michigan Papers in Women's Studies* 2.3 (1977):
62–83.

Lang, Amy Schrager. *Prophetic Woman: Anne Hutchinson and the Problem of Dissent in the Literature of New England*. Berkeley: U of California P, 1987. 161–92.

Lathrop, Rose Hawthorne. *Memories of Hawthorne*. 1897; New York:
AMS, 1969.

Leavis, Q. D. "Hawthorne as Poet." *Sewanee Review* 59 (1951): 179–205.

LePore, Jill. "*The Scarlet Letter/Pocahantas.*" *American Historical Review*
101.4 (1996): 1166–68.

Letteny, Alice. "Hawthorne's Heroines and Popular Magazine Fiction."
DAI 41.8 (1981): 3582A.

Li, Haipeng. "Hester Prynne and the Folk Art of Embroidery." *University of Mississippi Studies in English* 10 (1992): 80–85.

Lucke, Jessie. "Hawthorne's Madonna Image in *The Scarlet Letter*." *New
England Quarterly* 38 (1965): 391–92.

Luecke, Sister Jane Marie. "Villains and Non-Villains in Hawthorne's
Fiction." *PMLA* 78 (1963): 551–58.

Lundblad, Jane. *Nathaniel Hawthorne and the European Literary Tradition*. 1947; New York: Russell, 1965.

———. *Nathaniel Hawthorne and the Tradition of Gothic Romance*.
1947; New York: Haskell House, 1964. 55–61.

Maddox, Lucy. *Removals: Nineteenth-Century American Literature and
the Politics of Indian Affairs*. New York: Oxford UP, 1991. 89–130.

Madsen, Deborah L. "'A for Abolition': Hawthorne's Bond-servant and
the Shadow of Slavery." *Journal of American Studies* 25.2 (1991):
255–59.

Maes-Jelinek, Hena. "Roger Chillingworth: An Example of the Creative
Process in *The Scarlet Letter*." *English Studies* 49.4 (1975): 341–48.

Marble, Annie. "Gloom and Cheer in Hawthorne." *Critic* 45 (1904): 28–36.

Marion, Frances. "The Scarlet Letter." *Motion Picture Continuities: A Kiss for Cinderella, "The Scarlet Letter," The Last Command.* Ed. Frances Taylor Patterson. 1929. New York: Garland, 1977. 91–156.

Marks, Patricia. "'Red Letters' and 'Showers of Blood': Hawthorne's Debt to Increase Mather." *American Notes and Queries* 15 (1977): 100–105.

Marston, Jane. "Howells' *A Modern Instance*." *Explicator* 40.3 (1982): 41.

Martin, Wendy. "Seduced and Abandoned in the New World: The Fallen Woman in American Fiction." *The American Sisterhood: Writings of the Feminist Movement from Colonial Times to the Present.* Ed. Wendy Martin. New York: Harper & Row, 1972. 257–72.

Mathe, Sylvie. "The Reader May Not Choose: Oxymoron as Central Figure in Hawthorne's Strategy of Immunity from Choice in *The Scarlet Letter*." *Style* 26.4 (1994): 604–33.

McClure, Charlotte S. "Expanding the Canon of American Renaissance Frontier Writers: Emily Dickinson's 'Glimmering' Frontier." *The Frontier Experience and the American Dream: Essays on American Literature.* Eds. David Mogen, Mark Busby, and Paul Bryant. College Station: Texas A & M UP, 1989. 67–86.

McMaster-Harrison, June. "'What Hast Thou Done with Her?': Analogical Clues to the Lost Feminine." *Canadian Woman Studies/Les Cahiers de la Femme* 11.3 (1991): 83–86.

McNamara, Anne Marie. "The Character of Flame: The Function of Pearl in *The Scarlet Letter*." *American Literature* 27 (1965): 537–53. Expt. as "The Role of Pearl." *Readings on "The Scarlet Letter."* Ed. Eileen Morey. San Diego: Greenhaven, 1998. 79–87.

Miller, Elsie. "The Feminization of American Realist Theory." *American Literary Realism* 23.1 (1990): 20–41.

Moers, Ellen. "*The Scarlet Letter:* A Political Reading." *Prospects: The Annual of American Cultural Studies* 9 (1984): 48–70.

Moore, Benita A. "Hawthorne, Heidegger, and the Holy: The Uses of Fiction." *Soundings* 64.2 (1981): 170–96.

Morey (-Gaines), Ann-Janine. "Blaming Women for the Sexually Abusive Male Pastor." *Christian Century* 105.28 (1988): 866–69.

———. *Religion and Sexuality in American Literature.* Cambridge: Cambridge UP, 1992. 58–63.

Morey, Eileen. "Foreword; Introduction; Nathaniel Hawthorne: Haunted by the Guilt of his Ancestors." *Readings on "The Scarlet Letter."* Ed. Eileen Morey. San Diego: Greenhaven, 1998. 8–21.

Nagy, Phyllis. *"The Scarlet Letter." American Theatre* (1995): 21–38.

Newman, Joan. "Autobiography: The Limitations of the Quest." *Journal of Narrative Technique* 21.1 (1991): 83–97.

Nudelman, Franny. "'Emblem and Product of Sin': The Poisoned Child in *The Scarlet Letter* and Domestic Advice Literature." *Yale Journal of Criticism* 10.1 (1997): 193–214.

O'Connor, Evangelina Maria Johnson. *An Analytical Index to the Works of Nathaniel Hawthorne.* Boston: Houghton Mifflin, 1882; Detroit: Gale, 1967.

Parsons, Melinda B., and William Ramsey. *"The Scarlet Letter* and the Herbal Tradition." *Emerson Society Quarterly* 29.4 (1983): 197–207.

Parulis, Cheryl. "Hawthorne's Genre of Romance: The Seduction of Betrayal in *The Scarlet Letter.*" *Collages and Bricolages: The Journal of International Writing* 5 (1991): 108–16.

Pearson, Carol, and Katherine Pope. *The Female Hero in American and British Literature.* New York: Bowker, 1981.

Peck, Elizabeth Weller. *Nathaniel Hawthorne's "Scarlet Letter" Dramatized.* Boston: Franklin, Rand, Avery, 1876.

Poe, Elizabeth Ann. "Alienation from Society in *The Scarlet Letter* and *The Chocolate War.*" *American Literature as a Complement to the Classics.* Norwood: Christopher-Gordon, 1993. 185–94.

Price, Barbara. "Substance and Shadow: Mirror Imagery in *The Scarlet Letter.*" *Publications of the Missouri Philological Association* 6 (1981): 35–38.

Pryse, Marjorie. *The Mark and the Knowledge: Social Stigma in Classic American Fiction.* Columbus: Ohio State UP, 1979. 15–48.

Przemecka, Irena. "Hester Prynne, Her Critics and Her Author." *Litterae et Lingua: In Honorem Premislavi Mroczkowski.* Ed. Jan Nowakowski. Wroclaw: Zaklad Narodowy im. Ossolinskich, 1984. 137–40.

Rajec, Elizabeth Molnar. "Onomastics in *The Scarlet Letter.*" *University of Mississippi Studies in English* 11–12 (1993–95): 455–59.

Reed, Amy. "Self-Portraiture in the Works of Nathaniel Hawthorne." *Studies in Philology* 23 (1926): 40–54.

Reid, Margaret. "From Revolutionary Legends to *The Scarlet Letter:* Casting Characters for Early American Romanticism." *Comparative Romances: Power Gender, Subjectivity.* Ed. Larry H. Peer. Columbia: Camden House, 1998. 59–80.

Roberts, Nancy. *"The Scarlet Letter* and 'The Spectacle of the Scaffold.'" *Schools of Sympathy: Gender and Identification Through the Novel.* Montreal: McGill-Queen's UP, 1997: 46–69.

Rogers, Barbara J. "Entropy and Organization in Hawthorne's America." *Southern Quarterly* 16 (1978): 223–39.

Rourke, Constance. *American Humor: A Study of the National Character.* New York: Harcourt, Brace, 1931.

Rowe, Joyce. *Equivocal Endings in Classic American Novels.* Cambridge: Cambridge UP, 1988. 27–45.

Rozakis, Laurie. "Another Possible Source of Hawthorne's Hester Prynne." *American Transcendental Quarterly* 59 (1986): 63–71.

Ruderman, Judith. "The New Adam and Eve." *Southern Humanities Review* 17.3 (1983): 225–36.

Sachs, Viola. "The Breaking Down of Gender Boundaries in American Renaissance Mythical Texts." *Social Science Information* 27.1 (1988): 139–51.

———. "The Gnosis of Hawthorne and Melville: An Interpretation of *The Scarlet Letter* and *Moby Dick.*" *American Quarterly* 32 (1980): 123–44.

———. *The Myth of America: Essays in the Structures of Literary Imagination.* The Hague: Mouton, 1973. 13–45.

———. "The Myth of America in Hawthorne's *The Scarlet Letter.*" *Kwartalnik Neofilologiczny* 14 (1967): 245–67.

———. "*The Scarlet Letter:* An Initiatory Reading." *Linguistique, Civilization, Littérature.* Paris: Didier-Erudition, 1980. 105–15.

Schauber, Ellen, and Ellen Spolsky. "How to Know a Hypocrite When You Meet One." *Rhetoric 78: Proceedings of Theory of Rhetoric.* Eds. Robert L. Brown and Martin Steinmann, Jr. Minneapolis: U of Minnesota Center for Advanced Studies, 1979. 297–309.

Scheuermann, Mona. "The American Novel of Seduction: An Explanation of the Omission of the Sex Act in *The Scarlet Letter.*" *Nathaniel Hawthorne Journal* (1978): 105–18.

———. "Outside the Human Circle: Views from Hawthorne and Godwin." *Nathaniel Hawthorne Journal* (1975): 182–91.

Schriber, Mary Suzanne. *Gender and the Writer's Imagination: From Cooper to Wharton.* Lexington: UP of Kentucky, 1987. 45–60.

Schwab, Gabriele. "Seduced by Witches: Nathaniel Hawthorne's *The Scarlet Letter* in the Context of New England Witchcraft Fictions." *Seduction and Theory: Reading of Gender, Representation and Rhetoric.* Ed. Dianne Hunter. Champaign: U of Illinois P, 1989. 170–91. Rpt. in *The Mirror and The Killer-Queen: Otherness in Literary Language.* Bloomington: Indiana UP, 1996: 103–23.

Segal, Naomi. *The Adulteress's Child: Authorship and Desire in the Nineteenth-Century Novel.* Cambridge: Polity, 1992. 146–66.

———. "The Adulteress's Children." *Scarlet Letters: Fictions of Adultery from Antiquity to the 1990s.* Eds. Segal and Nicholas White. Houndsmills, Great Britain: Macmillan; New York: St. Martin's, 1997. 109–22.

Sheldon, Sara. *Nathaniel Hawthorne's "The Scarlet Letter."* Woodbury: Barron's, 1984.

Shinn, Thelma. *Radiant Daughters: Fictional American Women.* New York: Greenwood, 1986.

Shipman, Carolyn. "Illustrated Editions of *The Scarlet Letter.*" *The Critic* 45 (1904): 46–51.

Sims, Diana Mae. "Chillingworth's Clue in *The Scarlet Letter.*" *Nathaniel Hawthorne Journal* (1976): 292–93.

Skey, Miriam. "The Letter A." *Kyushu American Literature* 11 (1968): 1–10.

Smith, Lisa Herb. "'Some Perilous Stuff': What the Religious Reviewers Really Said about *The Scarlet Letter.*" *American Periodicals: A Journal of History, Criticism, and Bibliography* 6 (1996): 135–43.

Spears-Burton, Linda A. "Welcome to My House." *Journal of Negro Education* 59.4 (1990): 566–76.

Stephens, Rosemary. "A Is for Art in *The Scarlet Letter.*" *American Transcendental Quarterly* (1969): 23–27.

Stephenson, Mimosa, and Will Stephenson. "Adam Blair and *The Scarlet Letter.*" *Nathaniel Hawthorne Review* 19.2 (1993): 1–10.

Sterling, Laurie. "Paternal Gold: Translating Inheritance in *The Scarlet Letter.*" *American Transcendental Quarterly* ns 6.1 (1992): 15–30.

Stone, Deborah A. "Sex, Lies, and *The Scarlet Letter.*" *American Prospect* 21 (1995): 105–9.

Stout, Janis P. "The Fallen Woman and the Conflicted Author: Hawthorne and Hardy." *American Transcendental Quarterly* ns 1.3 (1987): 233–46.

———. *Sodoms in Eden: The City in American Fiction Before 1860.* Westport: Greenwood, 1976. 96–101.

Stryz, Jan. "The Other Ghost in *Beloved:* The Spectre of *The Scarlet Letter.*" *Genre* 24.4 (1991): 417–34.

Swartzlander, Susan. "'Amid Sunshine and Shadow': Charles Wentworth Upham and Nathaniel Hawthorne." *Studies in American Fiction* 15.2 (1987): 227–33.

Sweeney, Susan Elizabeth. "The Madonna, The Women's Room, and *The Scarlet Letter.*" *College English* 57.4 (1995): 410–25.

Swisher, Clarice. "Foreword and Biography of Nathaniel Hawthorne." *Readings on Nathaniel Hawthorne.* Ed. Clarice Swisher. San Diego: Greenhaven, 1996. 11–27.

Thickstun, Margaret Olofson. *Fictions of the Feminine: Puritan Doctrine and the Representation of Women*. Ithaca: Cornell UP, 1988. 132–56.

Tomc, Sandra. "'The Sanctity of the Priesthood': Hawthorne's 'Custom-House.'" *Emerson Society Quarterly* 39 (1993): 161–84.

Tompkins, Jane. *Sensational Designs: The Cultural Work of American Fiction, 1790–1860*. New York: Oxford UP, 1985.

Torgovnick, Marianna. *Closure in the Novel*. Princeton: Princeton UP, 1981. 80–100.

Vivan, Itala. "The Scar in the Letter: An Eye on the Occult in Hawthorne's Text." *Social Science Information* 23.1 (1984): 155–79.

Wagner, Linda. "Embryonic Characterizations in 'The Custom-House.'" *English Record* 16 (1966): 32–35.

Warren, Joyce W. *The American Narcissus: Individualism and Women in Nineteenth-Century American Fiction*. New Brunswick: Rutgers UP, 1984. 189–230.

Webb, Jane Carter. "The Implications of Control for the Human Personality: Hawthorne's Point of View." *Tulane Studies in English* 21 (1974): 57–66.

Weldon, Roberta. "From 'The Old Manse' to 'The Custom-House': The Growth of the Artist's Mind." *Texas Studies in Literature and Language* 20 (1978): 36–47.

————. "*The Rose Tattoo*: A Modern Version of *The Scarlet Letter*." *Interpretations: A Journal of Ideas, Analysis, and Criticism* 15.1 (1983): 70–77.

Wellborn, Grace Pleasant. "The Golden Thread in *The Scarlet Letter*." *Southern Folklore Quarterly* 29 (1965): 169–78.

————. "The Mystic Seven in *The Scarlet Letter*." *South Central MLA Studies* (1961): 23–31.

————. "Plant Lore and *The Scarlet Letter*." *Southern Folklore Quarterly* 27 (1963): 160–67.

————. "The Symbolic Three in *The Scarlet Letter*." *South-Central Bulletin* 23 (1963): 10–17.

Wershoven, Carol. *Child Brides and Intruders*. Bowling Green: Bowling Green State U Popular P, 1993. 161–76.

White, Paula Kopacz. "'Original Signification': Post-structuralism and *The Scarlet Letter*." *Kentucky Philological Association Bulletin* (1982): 41–54.

————. "Puritan Theories of History in Hawthorne's Fiction." *Canadian Review of American Studies* 9 (1978): 135–53.

Whitford, Kathryn. "'On a Field Sable, the Letter 'A' Gules.'" *Lock Haven Review* 10 (1968): 33–38.

Willett, Maurita. "'The Letter A, Gules,' and the Black Bubble." *Melville and Hawthorne in the Berkshires.* Ed. Howard Vincent. Kent: Kent State UP, 1968. 70–78.

Wilton, Marilyn Mueller. "Paradigm and Paramour: Role Reversal in *The Scarlet Letter.*" *The Critical Response to Nathaniel Hawthorne's "The Scarlet Letter.*" Ed. Gary Scharnhorst. New York: Greenwood, 1992. 220–32.

Woidat, Caroline M. "Talking Back to Schoolteacher: Morrison's Confrontation with Hawthorne in *Beloved.*" *Modern Fiction Studies* 39.3–4 (1993): 527–46.

Wolff, Cynthia Griffin. "Play It as It Lays: Didion and the Diver Heroine." *Contemporary Literature* 24.4 (1983): 480–95.

Wright, Dorena Allen. "The Meeting at the Brook-side: Beatrice, the Pearl-Maiden and Pearl Prynne." *Emerson Society Quarterly* 28.2 (1982): 112–20.

Yellin, Jean Fagan. *Women and Sisters: The Antislavery Feminists in American Culture.* New Haven: Yale UP, 1989.

Young, Virginia Hudson. "D. H. Lawrence and Hester Prynne." *Publications of the Arkansas Philological Association* 13.1 (1987): 67–78.

Additional Works

Abel, Darrel. *The Moral Picturesque: Studies in Hawthorne's Fiction.* West Lafayette: Purdue UP, 1988.

Acker, Kathy. *Blood and Guts in High School.* New York: Grove Weidenfeld, 1978.

Adinah, June. "Norplant: The 'Scarlet Letter' of Birth Control." *Misdiagnosis: Woman as a Disease.* Ed. Karen M. Hicks. Allentown: People's Medical Society, 1994.

Adler, Jerry. "Hester Prynncesse." *Newsweek* 4 April 1994: 58.

Affron, Charles. *Star Acting: Gish, Garbo, Davis.* New York: E. P. Dutton, 1977.

"American College Teacher, 1989–90." *Higher Education Research Institute*, UCLA, 1990.

Ammons, Elizabeth. *Conflicting Stories: American Women Writers at the Turn Into the Twentieth Century.* New York: Oxford UP, 1991.

Amore, Adelaide P. "Mary Rowlandson." *The Oxford Companion to Women's Writing in the United States.* Eds. Cathy Davidson and Linda Wagner-Martin. New York: Oxford UP, 1995. 770–71.

Anderson, Quentin. *The Imperial Self: An Essay in American Literary and Cultural History.* New York: Knopf, 1971.

Angell, Roger. "Sins Like Flinn's." *New Yorker* June 1, 1997: 4–5.

Arac, Jonathan. "The Politics of *The Scarlet Letter*." *Ideology and Classic American Literature*. Eds. Sacvan Bercovitch and Myra Jehlen. Cambridge: Cambridge UP, 1986. 247–66.

Auerbach, Jonathan. *The Romance of Failure: First-Person Fictions of Poe, Hawthorne, and James*. New York: Oxford UP, 1989.

Bakhtin, Mikhail. "Discourse in the Novel." Expt. in *The Critical Tradition*. Ed. David Richter. New York: St. Martin's, 1989.

Balio, Tino. *Grand Design: Hollywood as a Modern Business Enterprise*. New York: Scribner's, 1993.

Barker-Benfield, G. J. "Anne Hutchinson and the Puritan Attitude Toward Women." *Feminist Studies* 1 (1972): 65–96.

———. *The Horrors of the Half-Known Life: Male Attitudes Toward Women and Sexuality in Nineteenth-Century America*. New York: Harper and Row, 1976.

Barlowe, Jamie. "Reading Against the Grain: Feminist Criticism of American Narratives." *Journal of Narrative Technique* 19.1 (1989): 130–40.

———. "Response to the Responses." *American Literary History* 9.2 (1997): 238–43.

Barlowe, Jamie, and Molly Abel Travis. "Dialogue of the Imaginary." *Women and Language* 18.1 (1995): 37–40.

Barto, William T. "*The Scarlet Letter* and the Military Justice System." *The Army Lawyer* 297 (1997): 3.

Basic Instinct. Director, Paul Verhoeven. TriStar Pictures, 1992.

Bauer, Dale. *Feminist Dialogics: A Theory of Failed Community*. Albany: State U of New York P, 1988.

Baym, Nina. "The Madwoman and Her Languages: Why I Don't Do Feminist Literary Theory." *Feminist Issues in Literary Scholarship*. Ed. Shari Benstock. Bloomington: Indiana UP, 1984. Rpt. in *Feminisms: An Anthology of Literary Theory and Criticism*. Eds. Robyn R. Warhol and Diane Price Herndl. New Brunswick: Rutgers UP, 1991. 154–67.

Bell, Michael Davitt. "Arts of Deception: Hawthorne, 'Romance,' and *The Scarlet Letter*." *New Essays on "The Scarlet Letter."* Ed. M. J. Colacurcio. Cambridge: Cambridge UP, 1985. 29–56.

———. *The Development of the American Romance*. Chicago: U of Chicago P, 1980.

———. *Hawthorne and the Historical Romance of New England*. Princeton: Princeton UP, 1971.

———. "Old and New Worlds in *The Scarlet Letter*." *Readings on Nathaniel Hawthorne*. Ed. Clarice Swisher. San Diego: Greenhaven, 1996. 153–58.

Bercovitch, Sacvan. "The A-Politics of Ambiguity in *The Scarlet Letter.*" *New Literary History* 19.3 (1988): 629–54.

———. "Hawthorne's A-Morality of Compromise." *Representations* 24 (1988): 1–27.

———. *The Office of "The Scarlet Letter."* Baltimore: Johns Hopkins UP, 1991.

———. *The Rites of Assent: Transformations in the Symbolic Construction of America.* New York: Routledge, 1993.

Bigsby, C. W. E. *Hester: A Romance.* London: Weidenfeld and Nicolson, 1994.

Black Issues in Higher Education 9 (27 Aug. 1992): 32–36.

Blair, Walter. "Hawthorne." *Eight American Authors: A Review of Research and Criticism.* Ed. Floyd Stovall. New York: Norton, 1963. 100–152.

Bloom, Harold, ed. *Hester Prynne.* New York: Chelsea House, 1990.

———. *Modern Critical Interpretations of Nathaniel Hawthorne's "The Scarlet Letter."* New York: Chelsea House, 1986.

Body of Evidence. Director, Ulrich Edel. De Laurentiis, 1993.

Boehm, Volker. Description of 1917 *The Scarlet Letter* film. Internet Movie Database Ltd. <http://us.imdb.com/Plot?Scarlet+Letter,+The +(1917)>.

Bona, Damien. "Starring Demi Moore as Hester Prynne." *Hollywood's All-Time Worse Casting Blunders.* Secaucus: Carol Publishers, 1996.

Boswell, Jeanetta. *The American Renaissance and the Critics: The Best of a Century in Criticism.* Wakefield: Longwood Academic P, 1990.

Bourdieu, Pierre. *The Field of Cultural Production: Essays on Art and Literature.* Ed. Randal Johnson. New York: Columbia UP, 1993.

Brodhead, Richard. *Cultures of Letters: Scenes of Reading and Writing in Nineteenth-Century America.* Chicago: U of Chicago P, 1993.

———. *Hawthorne, Melville, and the Novel.* Chicago: U of Chicago P, 1973.

———. *The School of Hawthorne.* New York: Oxford UP, 1986.

Brown, Dee. *Bury My Heart at Wounded Knee: An Indian History of the American West.* New York: Henry Holt, 1970.

Buncombe, Marie H. "CLA's Second Half-Century: Language and Literature in the Black Diaspora." *CLA Journal* 32 (1988): 1–8.

Cady, Edwin H., and Louis J. Budd, eds. *On Hawthorne: The Best from American Literature.* Durham: Duke UP, 1990.

Cameron, Sharon. *The Corporeal Self: Allegories of the Body in Melville and Hawthorne.* Baltimore: Johns Hopkins UP, 1981.

Carpenter, Frederic. "Scarlet A Minus." *College English* 5 (1944): 173–80.

Carroll-Segun, Rita, and James Geschwender. "Exploding the Myth of African-American Progress." *Signs* 15 (1990): 285–99.

Carton, Evan. *The Rhetoric of American Romance: Dialectic and Identity in Emerson, Dickinson, Poe, and Hawthorne.* Baltimore: Johns Hopkins UP, 1985.

Cerio, Gregory, and Carolyn Ramsey, Jeff Schnaufer, Liz McNeil, and Greg Aunapu. "Cover Story of Demi Moore." Internet Movie Database Ltd. <http://www.imdb.com>.

Chamberlain, Mariam K., ed. *Women in Academe: Progress and Prospects.* New York: Russell Sage Foundation, 1988.

Chase, Richard. "The Ambiguity of *The Scarlet Letter.*" *Readings on Nathaniel Hawthorne.* Ed. Clarice Swisher. San Diego: Greenhaven, 1996. 145–52.

Chase, Susan. "The Woman Who Fell to Earth." *Elle* 13.5 (1998): 74.

Coale, Samuel Chase. *In Hawthorne's Shadow: American Romance from Melville to Mailer.* Lexington: UP of Kentucky, 1985.

Code, Lorraine. *What Can She Know?: Feminist Theory and the Construction of Knowledge.* Ithaca: Cornell UP, 1991.

Cohen, Bernard. *The Recognition of Nathaniel Hawthorne: Selected Criticism Since 1828.* Ann Arbor: U of Michigan P, 1969.

Colacurcio, Michael. "Introduction: The Spirit and the Sign" and "'The Woman's Own Choice': Sex, Metaphor, and the Puritan Sources of *The Scarlet Letter.*" *New Essays on "The Scarlet Letter."* Ed. M. J. Colacurcio. Cambridge: Cambridge UP, 1985. 1–28.

Consenting Adults. Director, Alan J. Pakula. Hollywood Pictures, 1992.

Crews, Frederick. *The Sins of the Fathers: Hawthorne's Psychological Themes.* New York: Oxford UP, 1966.

Cronin, M. "Hawthorne on Romantic Love and the Status of Women." *PMLA* 49 (1954): 89–98.

Crowley, J. Donald, ed. *Nathaniel Hawthorne: A Collection of Criticism.* New York: McGraw-Hill, 1975.

Daly, Brenda. *Authoring a Life: A Woman's Survival In and Through Literary Studies.* Albany: State U of New York P, 1998.

Dansereau, Estelle. "Reassessing Interpretive Strategies in Literary Criticism." *Gender Bias in Scholarship: The Pervasive Prejudice.* Eds. Winifred Tomm and Gordon Hamilton. Waterloo: Wilfrid Laurier UP, 1988.

Davidson, Cathy. *Revolution and the Word: The Rise of the Novel in America.* New York: Oxford UP, 1986.

Davidson, Cathy, and Linda Wagner-Martin, eds. *The Oxford Companion to Women's Writing in the United States.* New York: Oxford UP, 1995.

"Demi Has a Red-Letter Day as a Pious Hoochie-Koochie Girl." *Toledo Blade* 10 Nov. 1995: C1.

"Demi Is No Hester Prim." *Toledo Blade* 29 Oct. 1995: H1.

Derrick, Scott. "'A Curious Subject of Observation and Inquiry': Homoeroticism, the Body, and Authorship in Hawthorne's *The Scarlet Letter.*" *Novel* 18 (1995): 308–26.

Diehl, William. *Primal Fear.* New York: Villard Books, 1993.

Doane, Mary Ann. "*Caught* and *Rebecca*: The Inscription of Femininity as Absence." *Feminism and Film Theory.* Ed. Constance Penley. New York: Routledge, 1988. 196–215.

———. *Femmes Fatales: Feminism, Film Theory, Psychoanalysis.* New York: Routledge, 1991.

Dolis, John. *The Style of Hawthorne's Gaze: Regarding Subjectivity.* Tuscaloosa: U of Alabama P, 1993.

Doubleday, Neal F. "Hawthorne's Hester and Feminism." *PMLA* 54 (1939): 825–28.

Douglas, Ann. *The Feminization of American Culture.* New York: Knopf, 1977.

Dryden, Edgar. *Nathaniel Hawthorne: The Poetics of Enchantment.* Ithaca: Cornell UP, 1977.

Dunne, Michael. "*The Scarlet Letter* on Film: Ninety Years of Revisioning." *Literature/Film Quarterly* 25.1 (1997): 30–39.

Dyer, Richard. "The Colour of Virtue: Lillian Gish, Whiteness, and Femininity." *Women and Film: A Sight and Sound Reader.* Eds. Pam Cook and Philip Dodd. Philadelphia: Temple UP, 1993. 1–9.

Eakin, Paul John. *The New England Girl: Cultural Ideals in Hawthorne, Stowe, Howells, and James.* Athens: U of Georgia P, 1976.

Earl-Hubbard, Michele L. "The Child Sex Offender Registration Laws." *Northwestern University Law Review* 90 (1997): 788–862.

Earnest, Ernest. *The American Eve in Fact and Fiction, 1775–1914.* Urbana: U of Illinois P, 1974.

Easton, Susan. "Review of *Equal to the Task.*" By Joan M. Mills and Diane Kramer Winokur. *Choice* 20 (1983): 740.

Ebert, Roger. "Review of *The Scarlet Letter.*" *Chicago Sun Times* 13 Oct. 1995; rpt. Internet Movie Database, Ltd. <http://www.suntimes.com/ebert/ebert_reviews/1995/10/1001618.html>.

Edmunds, R. David. "Indian-White Relations in the United States, 1776–1900." *Encyclopedia of North American Indians.* Ed. Frederick E. Hoxie. Boston: Houghton Mifflin, 1996.

Egan, Ken, Jr. "The Adulteress in the Market-Place: Hawthorne and *The Scarlet Letter.*" *Studies in the Novel* 27 (1995): 26–41.

"Embattled Female Pilot Gets a General Discharge." *Toledo Blade* 23 May 1997: 1.

Erkkila, Betsy. *Wicked Sisters: Women Poets, Literary History, and Discord.* New York: Oxford UP, 1992.

Etter-Lewis, Gwendolyn. "Breaking the Ice: African-American Women in Higher Education." *Women's Studies Quarterly* 19 (1991): 154–64.

Faludi, Susan. *Backlash: The Undeclared War Against American Women.* New York: Crown, 1991.

Fatal Attraction. Director, Adrian Lyne. Paramount Pictures Corporation, 1987.

Feldman, Daniel L. "The 'Scarlet Letter Laws' of the 1990s: A Response to Critics." *Albany Law Review* 60.4 (1997): 1081–125.

Ferraiuolo, Perucci. "Women on the Affront Lines." *Religious Broadcasting* 27.1 (1995): 22–25.

Fetterley, Judith. *The Resisting Reader: A Feminist Approach to American Literature.* Bloomington: Indiana UP, 1978.

Fetterley, Judith, and Marjorie Pryse. *American Women Regionalists: 1850–1910.* New York: Norton, 1992.

Fiedler, Leslie. *Love and Death in the American Novel.* Cleveland: Meridian, 1960.

Final Analysis. Director, Phil Joanou. Warner Bros., 1992.

Flint, Joe. "Violence Code Could Be Economic Scarlet Letter." *Broadcasting and Cable* 123.25 (1993): 33–34.

Flitterman-Lewis, Sandy. *To Desire Differently: Feminism and the French Cinema.* Urbana: U of Illinois P, 1990.

Fogle, Richard Harter. *Hawthorne's Fiction: The Light and the Dark.* Norman: U of Oklahoma P, 1952.

———. *Hawthorne's Imagery: The "Proper Light and Shadow" in the Major Romances.* Norman: U of Oklahoma P, 1969.

———. "The Poetics of Concealment: *The Scarlet Letter*." *Nathaniel Hawthorne: A Collection of Criticism.* Ed. J. Donald Crowley. 63–74.

Fontana, Tony. "Biographical Information for Lillian Gish." Internet Movie Database. <http://us.imdb.com/Bio?Gish+Lillian>.

Fowles, John. *The French Lieutenant's Woman.* Boston: Little, Brown, 1969.

Francke, Lizzie. "Men, Women, Children and the Baby Boom Movies." *Women and Film: A Sight and Sound Reader.* Ed. Pam Cook and Philip Dodd. Philadelphia: Temple UP, 1993. 148–55.

French, Peter. "The Hester-Prynne Sanction." *Business Ethics: A Philosophical Reader.* Ed. Thomas I. White. New York: Macmillan, 1993. 276–86.

Gates, Henry Louis. *Loose Canons: Notes on the Culture Wars.* New York: Oxford UP, 1992.

Gilmore, Michael. "Hawthorne and the Making of the Middle Class." *Discovering Difference.* Ed. Christoph Lohmann. Bloomington: Indiana UP, 1993. 88–104.

Girgus, Sam B. *Desire and the Political Unconscious in American Literature.* New York: St. Martin's, 1990.

———. *The Law of the Heart: Individualism and the Modern Self in American Literature.* Austin: U of Texas P, 1979.

Glenn, Cheryl. *Rhetoric Retold: Regendering the Tradition from Antiquity Through the Renaissance.* Carbondale: Southern Illinois UP, 1997.

Goodrich, Norma Lorre. *Heroines: Demigoddess, Prima Donna, Movie Star.* New York: HarperCollins, 1993: 103–5.

Gordon, John Steele. *The Scarlet Woman of Wall Street.* New York: Weidenfeld and Nicolson, 1988.

Griener, Donald J. *Adultery in the American Novel: Updike, James and Hawthorne.* Columbia: U of South Carolina P, 1985.

Gross, Seymour, ed. *"A Scarlet Letter" Handbook.* Belmont: Wadsworth, 1960.

Grossberg, Lawrence, Cary Nelson, and Paula Treichler. *Cultural Studies.* New York: Routledge, 1992.

Hadd, Harry E. "The Scarlet Letter: Reichstein's Substance S." *Steroids* 60.9 (1995): 650–55.

Hand That Rocks the Cradle, The. Director, Curtis Hanson. Hollywood Pictures, 1992.

Harris, Kenneth Marc. *Hypocrisy and Self-Deception in Hawthorne's Fiction.* Charlottesville: UP of Virginia, 1988.

Haskell, Molly. *From Reverence to Rape: The Treatment of Women in the Movies.* New York: Holt, Rinehart, and Winston, 1973.

Hatton, Joseph. *The Scarlet Letter, or, Hester Prynne: A Drama in Three Acts.* London: Lindley, 187?.

Hawthorne, Nathaniel. *The Blithedale Romance* and *Fanshawe.* Vol. 3. Columbus: Ohio State UP, 1964.

———. *The Letters.* Vols. 15–18. Columbus: Ohio State UP, 1984–87.

———. *The Marble Faun.* Vol. 4. Columbus: Ohio State UP, 1968.

———. *Mosses From An Old Manse.* Vol. 10. Columbus: Ohio State UP, 1974.

———. "Mrs. Hutchinson." *Nathaniel Hawthorne: Tales and Sketches.* New York: Library of America, 1982. 18–24.

———. *The Scarlet Letter.* Norton Critical Edition. Eds. Bradley, Beatty, and Long. New York: Norton, 1961.

———. *The Scarlet Letter.* Vol 1. Columbus: Ohio State UP, 1962.

———. *The Scarlet Letter (Casebook Edition).* Ed. Ross Murfin. New York: St. Martin's, 1993.

Herbert, T. Walter. *Dearest Beloved: The Hawthornes and the Making of the Middle-Class Family.* Berkeley: U of California P, 1993.

————. "Nathaniel Hawthorne, Una Hawthorne, and *The Scarlet Letter:* Interactive Selfhoods and the Cultural Construction of Gender." *PMLA* 103.3 (1988): 285–97.

————. "Response to Jamie Barlowe, 'Rereading Women . . .'" *American Literary History* 9.2 (1997): 230–32.

Hill, Anita. Senate Hearings for Clarence Thomas, televised Friday, October 11, 1991.

Holloway, Karla F. C. *Moorings and Metaphors: Figures of Culture and Gender in Black Women's Literature.* New Brunswick: Rutgers UP, 1992.

hooks, bell. *Teaching to Transgress: Education as the Practice of Freedom.* New York: Routledge, 1994.

Houston, Beverle. "Missing in Action: Notes on Dorothy Arzner." *Multiple Voices in Feminist Criticism.* Eds. Diane Carson, Linda Dittmar, and Janice Welsch. Minneapolis: U of Minnesota P, 1994: 271–79.

Howe, Irving. "Hawthorne and American Fiction." *American Mercury* 68 (1949): 367–74.

Howells, William Dean. "Hawthorne's Hester Prynne." *Heroines of Fiction.* New York, 1901.

Hoxie, Frederick E. *Encyclopedia of North American Indians.* Ed. Frederick E. Hoxie. Boston: Houghton Mifflin, 1996.

Huber, Bettina. "Women in the Modern Languages, 1970–90." *Profession* 90 (1990): 58–73.

Hurst, Blake. "A Farmer's Scarlet Letter: Four Generations of Middle-Class Welfare Is Enough." *Policy Review* 72 (1995): 8–11.

Hutner, Gordon. *Secrets and Sympathy: Forms of Disclosure in Hawthorne's Novels.* Athens: U of Georgia P, 1988.

Internet Movie Database, Ltd. <http://www.imdb.com>.

"Investment in Human Potential." American Association for the Advancement of Sciences, 1991.

Jackson, Rosemary. *Fantasy: The Literature of Subversion.* London: Methuen, 1981.

"Jobtracks 1990–91." *Lingua Franca: The Review of Academic Life* 1.3 (Feb. 1991): 34–43.

Johnson, Barbara. *The Critical Difference.* Baltimore: Johns Hopkins UP, 1980.

Johnson, Randal, ed. Editor's Introduction. *The Field of Cultural Production: Essays on Art and Literature.* By Pierre Bourdieu. New York: Columbia UP, 1993.

Jones, E. Michael. *The Angel and the Machine: The Rational Psychology of Nathaniel Hawthorne.* Peru: Sherwood Sugden, 1991.

Kabat, Alan R. "Scarlet Letter Sex Offender Databases and Community Notification: Sacrificing Personal Privacy for a Symbol's Sake." *The American Criminal Law Review* 35 (1998): 333–70.

Kaplan, E. Ann. "The Case of the Missing Mother: Maternal Issues in Vidor's *Stella Dallas*." *Heresies* 16 (1983): 81–85.

————. "Reply to Linda Williams." *Cinema Journal* 24.2 (1985): 40–43.

Kempley, Rita. "Review of *The Scarlet Letter*." *Washington Post* 13 Oct. 1995; rpt. on Internet Movie Database Ltd. <http://www.washingtonpost.com/wp-srv/style/longterm/movies/videos/thescarletletterrkempley_c0320b.htm>.

Kesterson, David B. *Critical Essays on Hawthorne's "The Scarlet Letter."* Boston: G. K. Hall, 1988.

Kibbey, Ann. "Ann Hutchinson." *The Oxford Companion to Women's Writing in the United States*. Eds. Cathy Davidson and Linda Wagner-Martin. New York: Oxford UP, 1995. 410.

Kimball, Claire M. "A Modern Day Arthur Dimmesdale: Public Notification When Sex Offenders Are Released into the Community." *Georgia State University Law Review* 12.4 (1996): 1187–221.

Kinkead-Weekes, Mark. "The Letter, the Picture, and the Mirror: Hawthorne's Framing of *The Scarlet Letter*." *Nathaniel Hawthorne: New Critical Essays*. Ed. A. Robert Lee. New York: Barnes and Noble, 1982. 68–87.

Kolodny, Annette. *The Lay of the Land: Metaphor as Experience and History in American Life and Letters*. Chapel Hill: U of North Carolina P, 1981.

Kramer, Michael. *Imagining Language in America*. Princeton: Princeton UP, 1992.

Lane, Anthony. "Scarlet Women." *New Yorker* November, 1995: 112–14.

Larson, Charles R. *Arthur Dimmesdale*. New York: A and W Publishers, 1983.

Lathrop, George Parsons (libretto), and Walter Damrosch (music). *The Scarlet Letter: A Dramatic Composition* (opera). New York: Transatlantic Publishing, 1896.

Laurence, David, and Elizabeth Welles. "New Job Information List Statistics." *MLA Newsletter* 31.1 (1999): 6–7.

Lauter, Paul. "Race and Gender in the Shaping of the American Literary Canon." *Feminist Studies* 9.3 (1983): 435–63.

Layden, Tim. "Scarlet Letter." *Sports Illustrated* 87.16 (1997): 30–35.

Lee, A. Robert. "'Like a Dream Behind Me: Hawthorne's 'The Custom-House' and *The Scarlet Letter*." *Nathaniel Hawthorne: New Critical Essays*. Ed. A. Robert Lee. New York: Barnes and Noble, 1982. 48–67.

Leverenz, David. *Manhood and the American Renaissance.* Ithaca: Cornell UP, 1989.

———. "Mrs. Hawthorne's Headache: Reading *The Scarlet Letter.*" *Nineteenth-Century Fiction* 37.4 (1983): 552–75.

Levine, Robert S. *Conspiracy and Romance: Studies in Brockden Brown, Cooper, Hawthorne, and Melville.* Cambridge: Cambridge UP, 1989.

Lewis, R. W. B. *The American Adam: Innocence, Tragedy, and Tradition in the Nineteenth Century.* Chicago: U of Chicago P, 1955.

Ling, Amy. "I'm Here: An Asian American Woman's Response." *New Literary History* 19 (1987): 151–60.

Lloyd-Smith, Allan. *Eve Tempted: Writing and Sexuality in Hawthorne's Fiction.* New York: Barnes and Noble, 1984.

Lorde, Audre. "Transformation of Silence into Language and Action." *Zami: Sister Outsider, Undersong.* New York: Quality Paperback, 1993. 41.

Lucas, Blake. "Acting Style in Silent Films." *The Stars Appear.* Ed. Richard Dyer MacCann. Metuchen: Scarecrow, 1992. 33–43.

Luedtke, Luther. *Nathaniel Hawthorne and the Romance of the Orient.* Bloomington: Indiana UP, 1989.

Lynd, Helen. *On Shame and the Search for Identity.* New York: Harcourt, Brace, 1958.

MacCann, Richard Dyer, ed. *The Stars Appear.* Metuchen: Scarecrow, 1992.

Male, Roy. *Hawthorne's Tragic Vision.* Austin: U of Texas P, 1957.

Malice. Director, Harold Becker. Castle Rock Entertainment in association with New Line Cinema, 1994.

Mandell, Daniel R. "Metacom (King Philip)." *Encyclopedia of North American Indians.* Ed. Frederick E. Hoxie. Boston: Houghton Mifflin, 1996. 373–75.

Manzi, Warren. *Perfect Crime.* New York: S. French, 1990.

Maron, Margaret. *Up Jumps the Devil.* New York: Mysterious P, 1996.

Martin, Robert K. "Hester Prynne, C'est Moi: Nathaniel Hawthorne and the Anxieties of Gender." *Engendering Men: The Question of Male Feminist Criticism.* Eds. Joseph Boone and Michael Cadden. New York: Routledge, 1990. 122–39.

Martin, Terence. *Nathaniel Hawthorne.* Rev. ed. Boston: Twayne, 1983.

Mathews, Chesley. "Bibliographic Supplement." *Eight American Authors: A Review of Research and Criticism.* Ed. Floyd Stovall. New York: Norton, 1963. 419–66.

May, Thornton. "Electronic Commerce." *Computerworld* 30.20 (1996): 37–57.

Mayne, Judith. *The Woman at the Keyhole: Feminism and Women's Cinema.* Bloomington: Indiana UP, 1990.

McCormack, Lisa. "The Scarlet Letter." *Campaigns & Elections* 11.2 (1990): 26–33.

McDowell, Deborah E. "'The Self and the Other': Reading Toni Morrison's *Sula* and the Black Female Text." *Critical Essays on Toni Morrison.* Ed. Nellie McKay. Boston: G. K. Hall, 1988. 77–90.

McKay, Nellie Y. "A Troubled Peace: Black Women in the Halls of the White Academy." *Bucknell Review* 36.2 (1992): 21–37.

McMahan, Elizabeth, Susan Day, Robert Funk, eds. *Nine Short Novels by American Women.* New York: St. Martin's, 1993.

McWilliams, John. *Hawthorne, Melville, and the American Character: A Looking-Glass Business.* Cambridge: Cambridge UP, 1984.

Meese, Elizabeth. *Crossing the Double-Cross: The Practice of Feminist Criticism.* Chapel Hill: U of North Carolina P, 1986.

Michie, Helena. *Sororophobia: Differences among Women in Literature and Culture.* New York: Oxford University Press, 1992.

Milburn, Michael A., and Sheree D. Conrad. *The Politics of Denial.* Cambridge.: MIT P, 1996.

Millington, Richard. *Practicing Romance: Narrative Form and Cultural Engagement in Hawthorne's Fiction.* Princeton: Princeton UP, 1992.

Mizruchi, Susan L. *The Power of Historical Knowledge: Narrating the Past in Hawthorne, James, and Dreiser.* Princeton: Princeton UP, 1988.

Modleski, Tania. *Feminism Without Women: Culture and Criticism in a "Postfeminist" Age.* New York: Routledge, 1991.

Moers, Ellen. *Literary Women.* Garden City: Doubleday, 1976.

Montgomery-Fate, Tom. "Beyond the Multi-Culture." *The Other Side* 33.2 (1997): 16–51.

Moore, Colleen. "Up From the Extra Ranks." *The Stars Appear.* Ed. Richard Dyer MacCann. Metuchen: Scarecrow, 1992. 247–50.

Moore, Thomas. *A Thick and Darksome Veil: The Rhetoric of Hawthorne's Sketches, Prefaces, and Essays.* Boston: Northeastern UP, 1994.

Morris, Pam. *Literature and Feminism.* Oxford: Blackwell, 1993.

Morrison, Toni. *Beloved.* New York: Knopf, 1987.

———. *Playing in the Dark: Whiteness and the Literary Imagination.* New York: Vintage Books, 1991.

———. "Unspeakable Things Unspoken: The Afro-American Presence in American Literature." *Criticism and the Color Line: Desegregating American Literary Studies.* Ed. Henry B. Wonham. New Brunswick: Rutgers UP, 1996.

Moses, Yolanda T. "Black Women in Academe: Issues and Strategies." Washington, D.C.: Project on the Status and Education of Women, Association of American College, 1989. 12–40.

Mottram, Eric. "Power and Law in Hawthorne's Fictions." *Nathaniel Hawthorne: New Critical Essays.* Ed. A. Robert Lee. New York: Barnes & Noble, 1982. 187–228.

Mukherjee, Bharati. *The Holder of the World.* New York: Knopf, 1993.

Mulvey, Laura. "Visual Pleasure and Narrative Cinema." *Feminism and Film Theory.* Ed. Constance Penley. New York: Routledge, 1988. 57–67.

Najac, Emile de, Count, and Jean M. Lander. *The Scarlet Letter: Founded on Hawthorne's Story of the Early Settlers: An American Tragedy in 5 Acts.* 1876? (193 leaves in various foliations; copyrighted by Jean M. Lander).

Naremore, James. "*True Heart Susie* and the Art of Lillian Gish." *The Stars Appear.* Ed. Richard Dyer MacCann. Metuchen: Scarecrow, 1992. 76–83.

Nathaniel Hawthorne Review 14.1 (1988).

Nathaniel Hawthorne Review 17.2 (1991).

Nathaniel Hawthorne Society Newsletter 8.2 (1982).

Nelson, Cary. "Superstars." *Academe* 83.1 (1997): 38–43.

Newberry, Frederick. *Hawthorne's Divided Loyalties: England and America in His Works.* London: Associated UP, 1987.

Newfield, Christopher. "The Politics of Male Suffering and Hegemony in the American Renaissance." *differences* 1.3 (1989): 55–87.

Oates, Joyce Carol. "Rewriting *The Scarlet Letter*: Hawthorne's Heroine Goes Hollywood." *New York Times* 15 Oct. 1995: op-ed page.

Osborne, N. G. "Genital Herpes Simplex Virus Infection: The Forgotten Scarlet Letter." *Journal of Gynecologic Surgery* 14.1 (1998): 47.

Pearce, Roy Harvey, ed. *Hawthorne Centenary Essays.* Columbus: Ohio State UP, 1964.

Pease, Donald. "Leslie Fiedler, the Rosenberg Trial, and the Formulation of an American Canon." *boundary 2* 17.2 (1990): 155–98.

———. "New Americanists: Revisionist Interventions Into the Canon." *boundary 2* 17.1 (1990): 1–37.

———. *Visionary Compacts: American Renaissance Writings in Cultural Context.* Madison: U of Wisconsin P, 1987.

Penley, Constance. *The Future of an Illusion: Film, Feminism, and Psychoanalysis.* Minneapolis: U of Minnesota P, 1989.

Perkins, Barbara, Robyn Warhol, and George Perkins, eds. *Women's Work: An Anthology of American Literature.* New York: McGraw-Hill, 1994.

Person, Leland. *Aesthetic Headaches: Women and a Masculine Poetics in Poe, Melville, and Hawthorne.* Athens: UP of Georgia, 1988.

Peterson, Karen S. "*Scarlet Letter* Has 'A' Position on Reading Lists." *USA Today* 27 Dec. 1994: d1.15.

Pfister, Joel. *The Production of Personal Life: Class, Gender, and the Psychological in Hawthorne's Fiction.* Stanford: Stanford UP, 1992.

Ponder, Melinda M. "Katharine Lee Bates: Hawthorne Critic and Scholar." *Nathaniel Hawthorne Review* 21.1 (1990): 6–11.

Presumed Innocent. Director, Alan J. Pakula. Warner Bros. 1990.

Primal Fear. Director, Gregory Hoblit. Paramount Pictures, 1996.

Queen, Ellery. *The Scarlet Letters.* Boston: Little, Brown, 1953.

Railton, Stephen. "The Address of *The Scarlet Letter.*" *Readers in History.* Ed. James Machor. Baltimore: Johns Hopkins UP, 1993. 138–63.

Reising, Russell. *The Unusable Past: Theory and the Study of American Literature.* New York: Methuen, 1986.

Reske, Henry J. "Scarlet Letter Sentences." *ABA Journal* 82 (1996): 16–17.

Reynolds, David S. *Beneath the American Renaissance: The Subversive Imagination in the Age of Emerson and Melville.* New York: Knopf, 1988.

Robertson, Dale. "Scarlet Letters for Red Sox." *Houston Post* 24 Feb. 1989: C1.1.

Rosen, Marjorie. "Style." *New York Times Magazine* 1 Sept. 1996: 37.

Ryan, Maureen, "Women's Challenge to Higher Education." *Academe* 79.3 (1993): 22–27.

Sachs, Andrea. "Handing Out Scarlet Letters." *Time* 136.14 (1990): 98.

Scarlet Letter, The. Director, Sidney Olcott. Kalem Studios, 1911.

Scarlet Letter, The. Director not known. Studio not known, 1913.

Scarlet Letter, The. Director, Carl Harbaugh. Fox Film Corporation, 1917.

Scarlet Letter, The. Director, Victor Sjöström. Metro-Goldwyn-Mayer, 1926.

Scarlet Letter, The. Director, Robert G. Vignola. Majestic Films, 1934.

Scarlet Letter, The. Director, Rick Hauser. WGBH, 1979.

Scarlet Letter, The. Director, Roland Joffé. Cinergi, 1995.

"Scarlet Letters in Illinois." *Toledo Blade* 29 Apr. 1997.

Scharlachrote Buchstabe, Der. Director, Wim Wenders. 1972.

Scharnhorst, Gary, ed. *The Critical Response to Nathaniel Hawthorne's "The Scarlet Letter."* New York: Greenwood, 1992.

Schell, Jessica. "Three-Time Loser DUIs Get a Scarlet Letter 'Z'." *Governing* 4.12 (1991): 17–18.

Scott, Joyce Hope. "Slavery." *The Oxford Companion to Women's Writing in the United States.* Eds. Cathy Davidson and Linda Wagner-Martin. New York: Oxford UP, 1995. 814–17.

Sedgwick, Eve Kosofky. *Between Men: English Literature and Male Homosocial Desire.* New York: Columbia UP, 1985.

Seger, Linda. *When Women Call the Shots: The Developing Power and Influence of Women in Television and Film.* New York: Henry Holt, 1996.

Shattered. Director, Wolfgang Petersen. Davis Entertainment Company, Palace Pictures, 1991.

Shaw, Peter. *Rediscovering American Literature.* Chicago: Ivan R. Dee, 1994.

Showalter, Elaine. *Sister's Choice: Tradition and Change in American Women's Writing.* Oxford: Clarendon, 1991.

Shulman, Robert. *Social Criticism and Nineteenth-Century American Fictions.* Columbia: U of Missouri P, 1987.

Shumway, David R. *Creating American Civilization: A Genealogy of American Literature as an Academic Discipline.* Minneapolis: U of Minnesota P, 1994.

————. "The Star System in Literary Studies." *PMLA* 112.1 (1997): 85–100.

Silver, Joseph. "Low Number of African American Faculty at White Colleges Tied to the Character of the Society." *Black Issues in Higher Education* (30 Jan. 1992): 84.

Simonson, Harold P. *Radical Discontinuities: American Romanticism and Christian Consciousness.* Rutherford: Fairleigh Dickinson UP, 1983.

Smith, Barbara, ed. *Home Girls: A Black Feminist Anthology.* New York: Kitchen Table/Women of Color P, 1983.

Smith, James Edgar. *The Scarlet Stigma: A Drama in Four Acts.* (Founded upon Nathaniel Hawthorne's novel.) Washington, D.C.: James J. Chapman, 1899.

Smith, Julie. *The Axeman's Jazz.* New York: Ballantine Books, 1992.

Sochen, June. "The New Woman and Twenties America: *Way Down East* (1920)." *American History/American Film: Interpreting the Hollywood Image.* Eds. John E. O'Connor and Martin Jackson. New York: Frederick Ungar, 1979. 1–15.

Sosnoski, James. "A Mindless, Mind-Driven Theory Machine: Intellectuality, Sexuality, and the Institution of Criticism." *Feminism and Institutions: Dialogues on Feminist Theory.* Ed. Linda Kauffmann. Oxford: Basil Blackwell, 1989. Rpt. in *Feminisms: An Anthology of Literary Theory and Criticism.* Eds. Robyn R. Warhol and Diane Price Herndl. New Brunswick: Rutgers UP, 1991. 40–57.

Steinberg, Sybil. "Scarlet Letters: Tales of Adultery from Ellery Queen's Mystery Magazine." Ed. Eleanor Sullivan. *Publishers Weekly* 238.29 (5 July 1991): 59.

Stephan, Ed. "Biographical Information for Colleen Moore." Internet Movie Database Ltd. <http://us.imdb.com/Bio?Moore,+Colleen+(I)>.

Stern, Milton. *Contexts for Hawthorne: "The Marble Faun" and the Politics of Openness and Closure in American Literature.* Urbana: U of Illinois P, 1991.

Suffolk University Law School. "Constitutional Law—An Ex Post Facto Analysis of Sex Offender Registration Statutes: Branding Criminals with a Scarlet Letter." *Suffolk University Law Review* 29.4 (1995): 1199–1208.

Sultzman, Lee. "Wampanoag History." <http://dickshovel.netgate.net/wampa.html>.

Sundquist, Eric. *Home As Found: Authority and Genealogy in Nineteenth-Century American Literature.* Baltimore: Johns Hopkins UP, 1979.

Swade's Tribal Voice: Lesbian History. <http://www.swade.net/swade pages/lez_hist.htm>.

Swann, Charles. *Nathaniel Hawthorne: Tradition and Revolution.* Cambridge: Cambridge UP, 1991.

Tanner, Laura. "Rape." *The Oxford Companion to Women's Writing in the United States.* Eds. Cathy Davidson and Linda Wagner-Martin. New York: Oxford UP, 1995. 741–43.

Tanner, Tony. *Scenes of Nature, Signs of Men.* Cambridge: Cambridge UP, 1987.

Tharp, Louisa Hall. *The Peabody Sisters of Salem.* Boston: Little, Brown, 1950.

Thompson, G. R., and Virgil Lokke, eds. *Ruined Eden of the Present: Hawthorne, Melville, and Poe.* West Lafayette: Purdue UP, 1981.

Turner, Arlin. *Studies in "The Scarlet Letter."* Columbus: Charles Merrill, 1970.

Turow, Scott. *Presumed Innocent.* New York: Warner Books, 1987.

Updike, John. *Roger's Version.* New York: Knopf, 1986.

———. *S.* New York: Knopf, 1988.

Uricchio, Marylynn. "Demi Is No Hester 'Prim.'" *Toledo Blade* 29 Oct. 1995: H.1–2.

van Dam, M. Nicole. "The Scarlet Letter 'A': AIDS in a Computer Society." *Computer/Law Journal* 10.2 (1990): 233–64.

VanDeusen, Marshall. "Narrative Tone in 'The Custom-House' and *The Scarlet Letter.*" *Nathaniel Hawthorne: A Collection of Criticism.* Ed. J. Donald Crowley. New York: McGraw-Hill, 1975. 53–62.

Van Leer, David. "Hester's Labyrinth: Transcendental Rhetoric in Puritan Boston." *New Essays on "The Scarlet Letter."* Ed. M. J. Colacurcio. Cambridge: Cambridge UP, 1985. 57–100.

Vertigo. Director, Alfred J. Hitchcock. Alfred J. Hitchcock Productions, Inc., Paramount Pictures, 1958.

"Viewer's Guide to *The Scarlet Letter,* A four-part television drama produced by WGBH Boston." National Endowment for the Humanities and Exxon. Boston: Clark-Franklin-Kingston Press, 1979.

Wagenknecht, Edward. *The Movies in the Age of Innocence.* Norman: U of Oklahoma P, 1962.

———. *Nathaniel Hawthorne: The Man, His Tales, and Romances.* New York: Continuum, 1989.

Waggoner, Hyatt. *Hawthorne: A Critical Study.* Cambridge: Cambridge UP, 1955.

———. "History, Art, and Wisdom in *The Scarlet Letter.*" *Readings on Nathaniel Hawthorne.* Ed. Clarice Swisher. San Diego: Greenhaven P, 1996. 159–67.

———. *The Presence of Hawthorne.* Baton Rouge: Louisiana State UP, 1979.

Walker, Alice. *Possessing the Secret of Joy.* New York: Harcourt Brace Jovanovich, 1992.

Walton, Priscilla, and Manina Jones. *Detective Agency: Women Re-writing the Hard-Boiled Tradition.* Berkeley: U of California P, 1999.

Waxner, Jennifer. "If You Ask Me." *Premiere* 9.5 (1996): 50.

Wear, Delese. "Birth." *The Oxford Companion to Women's Writing in the United States.* Eds. Cathy Davidson and Linda Wagner-Martin. New York: Oxford UP, 1995. 110–14.

Welch, Rosanne. "Does Changing 'Scarlet' Make for a Red-Letter Day?" *Los Angeles Times* 30 Oct. 1995: F3.

Welsh, Jim. "Classic Folly: *The Scarlet Letter.*" *Film/Literature Quarterly* 23 (1995): 299–300.

West, Martha S. "Women Faculty: Frozen in Time." *Academe* 81.4 (1995): 27–29.

Williams, Patricia J. "A Rare Case of Muleheadedness and Men." *Racing Justice, En-gendering Power.* Ed. Toni Morrison. New York: Pantheon, 1992. 159–71.

Willson, Meredith. *The Music Man: A Musical Comedy.* New York: Frank Music Corp. and Rinimer Corp., Bradley Publications, 1978. Sound Recording: Broadway Angel, 1992.

Wilson, Amy. "This Is Beverly LaHaye." *Detroit Free Press* 16 May 1993: J1–4.

Young, Philip. *Hawthorne's Secret: An Un-Told Tale.* Boston: David R. Godine, 1984.

Ziff, Larzer. *Literary Democracy: The Declaration of Cultural Independence in America.* New York: Penguin, 1981.

Zoerner, Tom. "Biographical Information for Demi Moore." Internet Movie Database, Ltd. <http://us.imdb.com/Bio?Moore+Demi>.

Index

Abbott, Anne, 33, 37
Abel, Darrel, 14
academic conditions for women, x,
   3–4, 6–7, 13–14, 25–31, 40–41,
   121–23, 129–37nn. 5, 9, 10, 11,
   12, 13, 2
Acker, Kathy, 17
Adams, Margo, 15
Adinah, June, 15
Adkins, Lois, 37
Adler, Jerry, 19, 81
adultery, 33, 48, 53, 56, 57, 69, 108,
   110, 114, 128n.1
Affron, Charles, 86, 87–88, 89, 141–
   42nn. 4, 5
African Americans, 1–2, 4, 6–7, 23–
   24, 102–7, 129n.. 3, 130–32nn.
   9, 10, 133n. 12, 136–37n. 2
Ahab, 30
AIDS, 15
Albright, Hardie, 83
Algonquin nations, 93, 94
American Literature, 34
Americanness, 1–2, 99, 103
Ammons, Elizabeth, 134n. 13
Amore, Adelaide, 112–13, 114
Anderson, Quentin, 35
Angell, Roger, 16
anthologies of women's writing, 133–
   34nn. 12, 13
Antinomians, 99, 112
Arac, Jonathan, 11, 41
Armstrong, Judith, 33, 56, 135n. 1
Arvidson, Linda, 139–40n. 1
Auerbach, Jonathan, 41
Auerbach, Nina, 137n. 1

Baggot, King, 139n. 1
Bakhtin, M. M., 7
Balakian, Anna, 57
Balio, Tino, 83
Banting, Pamela, 57
Bara, Theda, 85
Bardes, Barbara, 68
Barker-Benfield, G. J., 38
Barlowe, Jamie, ix, 13, 24
Barnett, Louise, 55, 68, 97, 98, 99,
   143n. 8
Barrett, Phyllis, 30
Barto, William, 16
Basic Instinct (film), 20
Bates, Katharine, 35, 135n. 13
Bauer, Dale, 124
Baym, Nina, 3, 11, 32, 33, 34, 35, 36,
   39–42, 65, 69, 128n. 1, 134n. 13,
   135n. 1
Beatty, Richard Croom, 37
Bell, Michael Davitt, 11, 35, 36, 128n.
   1, 135n. 1
Bell, Millicent, 18, 35, 36, 38, 39, 42,
   49, 58, 65, 70, 135n. 1
Bellingham, Governor, 60–61, 67, 94,
   117, 118
Bensick, Carol, 64, 74, 135n. 1
Benstock, Shari, 47, 48, 51, 54, 55,
   56
Bercovitch, Sacvan, 13, 18, 36, 102,
   104, 129n. 4, 130n. 7
Berger, Senta, 140n. 1
Berlant, Lauren, 36, 50
Bethurum, Dorothy, 36
Beverly Hills Cop (film), 20
Bible, 10, 24, 111, 115

Jamie Barlowe is an associate professor of English and Women's Studies, and chair of the Department of Women's and Gender Studies at the University of Toledo. Her essays on American writers and on feminist literary theory have appeared in such journals and collections as *American Literary History; Women and Language; Hemingway Review; Canadian Review of American Studies; Novel; Reclaiming Rhetorica: Women in the Rhetorical Tradition;* and *Common Ground: Feminist Collaboration in the Academy.*